New World,
New Ways,
New Management

New World, New Ways, New Management

PHILIP R. HARRIS

American Management Associations

*To two elegant professors of management
who helped open my mind to
new worlds, new ways, and new ideas:*

Dr. Dorothy Lipp Harris, *my wife and colleague,*
associate dean at the School of Business & Management,
United States International University, San Diego, California;
and

Dr. James J. Cribbin, *my mentor and friend,*
distinguished faculty member of the Graduate School of Business,
St. John's University, Jamaica, New York.

Library of Congress Cataloging in Publication Data

Harris, Philip, 1926–
  New world, new ways, new management.

  Bibliography: p.
  Includes index.
  1. Industrial management. 2. Organizational
change. I. Title.
HD38.H3484 1983   658.4′062   82-71325
ISBN 0-8144-5755-X

© 1983 AMACOM Book Division
American Management Associations, New York.
All rights reserved.
Printed in the United States of America.

This publication may not be reproduced,
stored in a retrieval system,
or transmitted in whole or in part,
in any form or by any means, electronic,
mechanical, photocopying, recording, or otherwise,
without the prior written permission of
AMACOM, 135 West 50th Street, New York, NY 10020.

First Printing

Foreword

Writing in 1968, Peter Drucker noted in his book *The Age of Discontinuity* that "the future is, of course, always 'guerrilla country' in which the unsuspected and apparently insignificant derail the massive and seemingly invincible trends of today." Drucker was trying to alert managers to some of the macroeconomic and social changes taking place around them. In *New World, New Ways, New Management*, Phil Harris takes on the challenge of sketching the "guerrilla country" of organizational management for the 1980s and 1990s. This is a formidable task, one that he accomplishes with intriguing results.

Harris has worked as a cartographer for the "metaindustrial manager"—the manager who must cope with trends emerging in corporate life that are in discontinuity with the norms by which organizations have functioned during the industrialization of the last fifty years. He examines the "corporate cultures" of the 1980s, which will provide the foundation for new norms governing management and leadership in companies of the future. His book explores the challenges to management in microelectronics, genetic engineering, and other areas, challenges that are at the same time global and personal, comprehensive yet specific, synergistic while competitive.

The knowledge workers of the new corporate cultures will be men and women of the highest caliber who not only understand products and services on a transnational level, but are also cognizant of the effects of social and human dynamics on corporate productivity and profitability.

Harris describes the emerging corporate values and norms that will affect every aspect of work, plan, and leadership for many years to come. The new managerial philosophy that he discovers is one that stresses innovation, candidness, feedback, collaboration, and competence.

While humanistic in its managerial style, the future organization will exist in an electronic information society that values knowledge as well as rapid, relevant, comprehensive interchange of data. The impact of this new information-based technology will be felt throughout corporations of the future. It will direct managers and workers to assess their self-concepts, their roles and responsibilities, and their organizational purpose and image. Added to the turbulence created by this electronic revolution will be a wave of mergers, acquisitions, and relocations that will alter the landscape of corporate life and continue to fuel vast, complex changes in every aspect of organizational behavior. Harris's journey through this maze focuses on three major factors: technology, change, and leadership. He finds technology, and particularly the microelectronic revolution, to be the driving force of the "new worlds and new ways" that will be the greatest challenge to managers in the 1980s and 1990s. He explores the emergence of robotics—"tin-collar workers"—and hints at what management will be like when we confront space industrialization.

The changes that this technology will force on our postindustrial society will be systemic, multinational, and ever-present. As we see daily speculation about the new base rate of inflation or unemployment, it will not be long before we will be talking about a "base rate of change." For it increasingly appears that all of us will need to learn to deal with an escalating level of change in our personal and corporate lives. Subtle acknowledgment of this fact is already emerging in the new services that have developed in recent years involving training to manage stress, prevent burnout, and develop "wellness" strategies.

Harris describes the kind of manager needed to meet these challenges. It is the "cosmopolitan and transformational" manager who understands new uses of power and authority for collaboration rather than subjugation, who can motivate diverse, multicultural, pluralistic workforces in a synergistic rather than adversarial manner. Following the path of William Ouchi's Theory Z management style, Harris predicts that future managers will need to be holistic in their approach to their colleagues and subordinates. The integrity of the individual will be a paramount concern as everyone in the metaindustrial society, workers and managers alike, will strive for recognition and rewards that go beyond financial benefits to concerns for the quality of life.

This book carries to the corporate level the transformational theme started by Drucker on a macroeconomic level in the 1950s and 1960s and continued astutely on a personal and social level by Marilyn Ferguson in her recent work, *The Acquarian Conspiracy.* Together, the writings of Drucker, Ferguson, and Harris are an attempt to provide an "early warning system" for today's managers. They outline the far-reaching changes taking place on a global, societal, corporate, and personal level which will affect not only the goods and services we will be producing during the next twenty years, but the way in which people will need to be managed in order to meet the new stresses and demands of an ever-changing and more complex world.

Ultimately, these writers are encouraging. They are optimistic about the future. All three believe that managers in their professional roles and individual lives will be able to identify, acknowledge, and manage the social, organizational, and cultural changes taking place today. Phil Harris's book can be of great help in better understanding the terrain we are approaching. It is our responsibility, as managers, colleagues, and human beings, to become better acquainted with the territory in order to contribute meaningfully to the peaceful emergence of the metaindustrial world.

>   Stephen H. Rhinesmith, Ph.D.
>   *Executive Vice President and*
>   *Chief Operating Officer*
>   *Moran, Stahl & Boyer, Inc.*

Preface

Contemporary organizations are in a state of profound transition, as is all of society. Since the early 1950s, there has been a move away from industrial-age institutional models and managerial styles. Human systems are shifting from bureaucratic organizational cultures, with their emphasis on a pyramidal structure that precisely places an employee in a hierarchy, as well as from authoritarian decision making. Human systems are moving toward more ad-hocracy, with fluid, temporary arrangements and with greater participation by personnel in total operations. Traditional managers who resist such changes find their organization suffering severe institutional crises, or "organization shock." The challenge of the superindustrial age is for existing organizations to go through a process of planned renewal, while innovators create new organizational forms and leadership approaches.

But this is only one dimension of the organizational transformation of the next two decades. A committee of the National Academy of Science put it best in *The Futurist,* February 1981:

> The modern era of electronics has ushered in a second industrial revolution. . . . its impact on society could even be greater than that of the original industrial revolution.

Research into outer space and rapid developments in computers and cybernation continually spawn new technologies and industries. The high-technology businesses that result are created around the innovative application of silicon chips, microprocessing, and miniaturization. Such breakthroughs have aided and abetted the production of robots for computerized assembly lines and other displacements of humans from the drudgery of mindless work. Accompanying the rapid advances of microelectronics have been swift developments in genetic engineering, leading to the formation of "gen tech" businesses. Such new commercial enterprises are *metaindustrial* organizations. They are the harbingers of the humans systems of the twenty-first century.

The field of cultural anthropology offers many insights to help contemporary executives, managers, and other leaders understand what is happening to their organizations. Dr. Robert Moran and I borrowed from this discipline and drew on other behavioral sciences for *Managing Cultural Differences* (1979) and *Managing Cultural Synergy* (1982).* Each text contained a chapter on the phenomenon of organizational culture. *New Worlds, New Ways, New Management* expands on these observations and applies an anthropological paradigm to permit a better understanding of the transformation under way in human systems. It is my hope that readers will use these observations to manage metaindustrial enterprises better and to renew industrial-age organizations.

I am especially indebted to Dr. Leonard Nadler, distinguished human resources development consultant and professor at The George Washington University in Washington, D.C. It was his seminal article "The Organization as a Micro-Culture"[†] that sparked my interest in this subject. My appetite was further whetted by Stephen H. Rhinesmith. His monograph on the interrelationship of value orientations and managerial behavior, *Cultural Organizational Analysis*,[‡] published over a decade ago, has contributed significantly to the current volume.

In compiling the information and insights of this text, many other writers, researchers, and fellow consultants contributed. Where feasible, the footnotes and references pay tribute to their help. I want to cite in particular Dr. Martin A. Apple, founder of the International Plant Research Institute, who made a special contribution to the last chapter. After a year of research into the new technologies, it was a pleasure to meet this "ag-tech" pioneer at a course of The Presidents Association. He confirmed the themes of this book and helped formulate its conclusions.

Finally, without family "support services," this undertaking would not have been possible. The partial dedication of *New World, New Ways, New Management* to my wife, Dr. Dorothy L. Harris, is my way of saying "thank you so much." As one who has survived and flourished after open-heart surgery, I owe an acknowledgment to my physician, who keeps me healthy—Dr. Herbert I. McCoy.

> Philip Robert Harris, Ph.D.
> La Jolla, California

---

*I wish to express my appreciation to Gulf Publishing, Houston, Texas, for permission to use that material as required.
† *Personnel Journal*, December 1969.
‡ Cambridge, Mass.: McBer, 1970.

Contents

1	Getting Ready Today for Tomorrow's Organizations	1
2	The Impact of Culture on Organizational Behavior	15
3	New Corporate Rationale and Identity	37
4	Changing Corporate Purposes and Standards	54
5	Transforming Corporate Look and Style	69
6	Revolutionizing Corporate Processes and Activities	91
7	Transforming Organizational Communications	117
8	Changing Career Development Patterns	146
9	Transforming Organizational Relationships	175
10	Transforming Organizational Recognition and Rewards	201
11	Technological Work Culture of the Future	227
12	Developing Organizational Potential	256

Appendix A	Organizational Culture Survey Instrument	286
Appendix B	Management Communications Inventory	295
Appendix C	Change Inventory for Leaders	297
Appendix D	Intercultural Relations Inventory	301
Appendix E	Leadership Motivation Inventory	305

Source Notes and References	307
Recommended Readings	313
Index	315

CHAPTER 1　Getting Ready Today for Tomorrow's Organizations

Consider this intriguing analogy between modern managers, products of the industrial culture, and today's Mongolian descendants of Genghis Khan and his Golden Horde. Reading a daily news feature on the latter in the *Los Angeles Times* (July 20, 1981), one is struck by the similarity of adjustments! The story contrasts Juderemly, a 57-year-old cattle breeder who lives on the Mongolian steppes in a conical "yurt," with his son, Gurragcha, a cosmonaut and lieutenant colonel in the Mongolian air force. The contrast in lifestyles between the father, who basically follows a way of life comparable to his nomadic forebears, and the son, who was copilot on the Soviet Union's Soyuz, is startling. Staff writer Michael Parks quotes from an interview on the phenomenon of a herdsman's son becoming an aeronautical engineer and cosmonaut. The local high school teacher in Ulan Bator observed:

> Had we read some 40 or 50 years ago about life today, it would seem science fiction. Mongols living in cities, working in factories, becoming scientists, changing a way of life we had for centuries. My father, who is still a horse-breeder, hunter, and semi-nomadic, would say it was all too fanciful to be believed.

So, too, many managers today find as fanciful the quantum leap they must now take from an industrial to a postindustrial world of work. They are as unprepared for the emerging organizational environments as Juderemly was for his son to be catapulted from the hunting and agricultural society into industrial and technological society.

Whether one sits in the executive suite today, or prepares for it tomorrow, "industrial-age" blinders should be removed. Traditional assumptions about the nature of work, the worker, and the workplace should be questioned. New images of management, personnel, and employment must be forged. Otherwise, managers, whether in a corporation, government agency, or nonprofit institution, will find worklife increasingly uncomfortable and supervisory practice increasingly obsolete. There is a profound worldwide shift under way in society from a manufacturing or industrialized way of life and work to a computerized, information-based society. Graham T. T. Molitor, president of Public Policy Forecasting, reminds us of the structural dislocations that will result as we focus more on the new major resource of knowledge. Writing in *The Futurist* (April 1981), he comments sagely:

> Intangibles have replaced tangible material goods as the dominant factor in commercial enterprise, the central assets, and the primary source of wealth and power. A new set of "knowledge industries" [is] on the rise.

Molitor, former research director for the White House Conference on the Industrial World Ahead, makes his point dramatically with the chart shown in Figure 1 on the distribution of American workers as our society evolves in the twentieth century from agricultural to postindustrial. The chart shows that 50 percent of the U.S. workforce has been in the information industries since the mid-seventies! In order to better comprehend the organizational cultures of the future, managers should analyze such industries *today.*

What is happening globally has been referred to as the new—or next, or second—industrial revolution. Primary forces behind this transition are microelectronics, information sciences, and genetic engineering. For managers, this means creating and operating in a *metaindustrial* organization*—one that is as different from our disappearing bureaucracies as a horse and buggy are to the space shuttle! The National Academy of Science maintains that modern microelectronics alone will have a greater impact on

---

* The term *metaindustrial* can be applied to the present age, contemporary organizations, or current work culture. It is synonymous with postindustrial and superindustrial, and means above or beyond the traditional industrial organization or way of life. Social institutions are in transition from the industrial mode of organizing and operating to the metaindustrial form. Today, corporations in the new technologies (high-tech, gen-tech, ag-tech, med-tech, computer fields) seem to be the forerunners of metaindustrial organizations.

FIGURE 1. Distribution of the workforce in the postindustrial society.

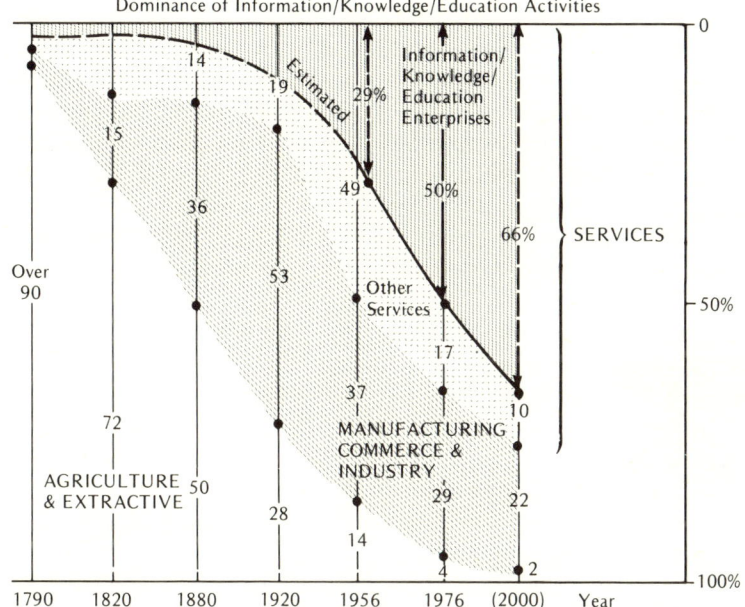

Source: *The Futurist*, April 1981. © Public Policy Forecasting, Inc.

society than the Industrial Revolution. Astute managers can become pioneers in the emerging metaindustrial organizations and societies.

Just as many Mongolian herders were unprepared for the recent changes in their way of life, many industrial leaders are unready for the alterations already under way in managerial and worker lifestyles. The signs of these organizational changes are evident to those who can read and understand them. They range from changes in project and team management to office automation and cybernation.* Many of the new technology firms may be

---

* The term cybernetics was coined by physicist Norbert Wiener. It comes from the Greek and means "steersman." It is the science of control and communication in humans and machines. Laypersons might refer to this as "advanced automation," but it implies a self-regulating system—that is, feedback control influencing the input and output process in a human or mechanical system (such as an oil refinery or an automatic heating system). From this have come related words, such as *cybernation*, which refers to the process. A *cybernated* factory requires fewer

the real harbingers of future organizational cultures. The last half of the twentieth century has seen the emergence of a series of new technologies, many of them offshoots of space technology, that can be distinguished from the mature manufacturing technologies of the industrial age and its organizations. The dominance of computers/communications/microelectronics has led to firms being organized in the field of high technology. They cluster also around genetic technology ("gen tech"), agricultural technology ("ag tech") and medical technology ("med tech"). The fusion of microelectronics with biological, genetic, and other engineering innovations not only brings into being new businesses but spawns different corporate cultures and management styles.

Clues to these new directions in commerce and work culture are available in articles in newspapers and periodicals about the pacesetters. Their names are becoming legion, and include such luminaries as Hewlett-Packard, Intel, Signetics, National Semiconductor, Zilog, and Texas Instruments. Intel, for example, has an employee training program worth studying because it carries out the new philosophy and culture of that company, a possible indicator of where many corporations will be headed. Such new-technology companies are not limited to California's West Coast from San Jose to San Diego, or even to the East Coast's New England corridor; they can be found in Ireland, India, Malaysia, and Third World countries.

Most of today's prototypes of future business are not even listed in *Standard & Poor's Register* for the last decade. Adam Osborne reminds us that there is a common element in these firms that produce everything from computer chips to electronic games; they usually represent products with no previous history. Osborne maintains that the space race established an environment of opportunism, a generation of chance-takers, and the possibility for success, which led to the spinoff of these new technological companies and their manner of operating. The emerging

---

workers to produce things, because computers now control the programmed machines. The term *cybercultural revolution* refers to the contemporary postindustrial work environment, which is undergoing a profound change in occupations and careers as a result of increasing automation. *Cyberculture* refers to the superindustrial society now emerging—namely, a world culture dominated by information processing, automation, and knowledge workers. Thus masses of individuals suffer "future shock," while social institutions experience "organization shock," as society rapidly changes from its traditional way of life into this new world culture.

microelectronics-based industrial revolution may eliminate not only traditional business, but also trade unions, which are products of the passing industrial age. Unprecedented developments in both microelectronics and information processing are revolutionizing not only our technologies, but the age in which we live. As a result, human systems and organizational cultures are being tranformed.

TRANSFORMING INFLUENCES

A number of corporations are currently studying emerging issues and the forces influencing society and business in these new directions. A report by AT&T summarizes the situation:

> Societies exist and endure through the communication of information. What separates our "information age" from those that preceded it is the unprecedented access to information and the speed of its transmission made possible by microminiaturization and semiconductor technology. What connects it with those that preceded it is the transformation of political, social, and economic institutions and traditions developed to serve in an era now by-gone.*

Unexpected inventiveness by technicians creates unanticipated markets. What is different about the closing decades of the twentieth century is the global scale on which the new technologies are automating jobs, while altering corporate structures and processes. Some futurists predict the elimination of half the existing jobs and radical alterations in organizational cultures by the turn of the century. Many influences propelling this industrial transformation underscore the fact that managers can no longer afford to do business as usual. Three such factors are described below:

1. *Technological innovations,* especially in telecommunications, change our response to satisfying human needs through manufacturing and marketing. The ability to imprint thousands of electronic components and complex circuits on silicon chips by miniaturization is but one example. The resulting microelectronic processes and products have a major influence on employment patterns, productivity, and trade. Although these innovations may cause severe temporary dislocations, they also lead to economic booms and new types of jobs. Two million people are already employed in the electronics industry in North America and West-

*See E. R. Coleman, ed., *Information and Society.*

ern Europe. Jean-Jacques Servan-Schreiber proposes that the "computerized society" can work a miracle through microcomputers for the development of Third World countries. The point is that these technological advances will affect not only the macrocultures of such societies but the microcultures as well.*

2. *Technology transfer* among nations is accelerating on a scale never before experienced in human history. In unprecedented numbers, these transcultural exchanges are going from west to east and from north to south as a result of advances in communication and transportation. What the immediate future holds almost staggers the imagination. Besides exchanges of raw materials, products, and information, the international scientific and business communities share technical know-how across national and ideological boundaries. Currently, the principal mechanism is the multinational corporation or transnational enterprise. It may be formed in industrially developed or developing countries. It fosters a global subculture of managers and technicians who are comfortable anywhere on the planet and with each other, regardless of nationality or professional discipline. It requires personnel who are culturally sensitive and skilled and more cosmopolitan in their management approach.

Typically, the defusion of technologies begins when an American, Western European, or Japanese multinational corporation introduces its process-related technology and organizational culture through a subsidiary in a less industrially developed nation. After the manufacturing technology and management skill have been absorbed and adapted, the Third World company may export a more appropriate technology to its counterparts in less industrialized countries. The Republic of Ireland is an interesting case in point. With its entry into the European Common Market, Ireland sought and obtained investments for plant facilities and

---

*The *macroculture* is the majority or mainstream culture in a country, or the main organizational culture in a multinational corporation or conglomerate. In human systems, it refers to the principal social system that dominates group behavior. The concept of culture refers to the customs, traditions, communication, and thought patterns of a distinct group of people. In a nation, there is usually one dominant or macroculture and many subcultures.

Within a macroculture, there are *microcultures,* or subcultures (such as a department, subsidiary, youth, Hispanic Americans). A microculture can influence not only the behavior of its adherents but also that of the dominant culture. In a global corporation, for instance, the microcultures might be subsidiaries in various countries or groups of specialists within the enterprise (such as management information or financial specialists in a scientific organization).

technologies from North America, Western Europe, and Japan. Now the Irish Development Authority reports:

> We are looking to the future in areas like robotics and biotechnology. We will increasingly go after industries of high technology. We have accepted the challenge of change.*

This is an apt illustration of how international technology transfer may help a preindustrialized people leap forward into a postindustrialized society.

3. The *global marketplace* is a third example of the influences promoting organizational revolution. For centuries, trade and commerce sought to bypass or penetrate national borders and local ideologies that barred their business. Now, technological advances make a global information exchange possible, especially through telecommunications and satellites, despite efforts of local governments to restrict such an exchange. Another AT&T report emphasizes the new reality:

> Labor issues are becoming increasingly global in nature.... Examples can be cited in international labor activities, the problem of job security, the spread of industrial democracy, and even the growth of white-collar unions. Intertwined with, and propelled by national employment and labor concerns, is the issue of transborder data flow (TDF). There are growing concerns regarding electronic transmission of information across borders in terms of social impact, control, privacy.

The old attitudes, regulations, and mechanisms no longer work in the emerging information society. Furthermore, we are in an age of transnational products, processes, services, and consumerism. The spread of international franchising is but one demonstration of this new reality. Industrial-age economics and regulations become obsolete, forcing companies within an industry to collaborate in order to compete. State trading companies, international cartels, government-assisted multiple-industry combinations, and regional economic trading blocs are all indicators that large-scale economic organizations are necessary to meet the demands of this global marketplace. Someday we may even see the establishment of world corporations chartered by supranational agencies to meet the planetary needs of the world economy. Soon market and production efforts that span this planet will expand into outer space. As the market moves out into the universe, in the twenty-

* *Los Angeles Times,* May 21, 1981.

first century, we will need not only different organic structures and cultures to do business, but also more cosmopolitan managers.

TRENDS IN POSTINDUSTRIAL ORGANIZATIONS
Most contemporary organizations and their managements are undergoing profound change. Managers and workers in industrial-age organizations are aware of pressures for renewal caused by declining markets and profitability or by public disillusionment and reduced support. In the search to streamline operations and improve productivity, classical authoritarian organizational models are being abandoned, and more participative managerial styles are being adopted. Attempts to prop up industrial cripples are severely questioned. Traditional bureaucracies suffer "organization shock," and some disappear. The technologies of organization development (OD) and quality circles are introduced in desperate attempts to improve employee performance and productivity. Reindustrialization and deregulation of industry are advocated as temporary solutions to the crisis. But leaders with vision recognize that since the 1950s, we have been in a postindustrial situation. These leaders see the need to revitalize existing systems or to create new ones. They recognize that the new technology is bringing *fundamental* change to both the workplace and the very culture of organizations.

One corporate president referred to some large companies in mature industries as "arthritic freaking elephants." Barry Minkin, senior consultant at SRI International, maintains that the U.S. economy abounds with such entities, many of which are in mid-life crises: "These industries are over the hump. They have entered an era in which they will never again experience the growth of the past." Although these elephants may look healthy by short-term standards and still be good at turning work out, the business may have peaked. According to Minkin, they are characterized by (1) strategic unresponsiveness, or lack of vision and focus, (2) structural unresponsiveness, lacking in mechanisms to harvest and profit from new ideas and opportunities, and (3) lack of forward thinking and entrepreneurship, often constrained by ultratraditional executives who shun innovation, risk taking, and new ventures.

Some corporate planning groups are seeking to comprehend the transition under way and to propose a different style of executive and employee behavior. Emily Coleman, in an AT&T report (*Labor Issues of the '80s*), offered this conclusion to an interpretive essay on the new industrial revolution:

> The metaindustrial revolution proceeding apace around us is more profound in effect and affect than a discussion of microprocessors, an increasingly large service section, the rapidly growing sophistication of communications technology, and the "global village" concept.... It is the ultimate challenge of the metaindustrial age to create structures and strategies that conform to this new developing whole, without ignoring and dislocating any of its less obvious parts.

The designation *metaindustrial* seems especially appropriate to describe the ongoing social revolution, the culture that is evolving, and the organizations coming into being. Norbert Wiener, for example, suggested *cyberculture*, while Jonas Salk offered *Epoch B*. But metaindustrial seems to say it best—something above and beyond the previous industrial stage of human development.

The shape of the metaindustrial organization is somewhat evident. It has been compared with Rensis Likert's System ¾ organization, which required a style of management comparable to Douglas McGregor's Theory Y. Perhaps it would be helpful here to review and revise the description of tomorrow's organization, which is already observable in companies with matrix management and very evident in the microelectronics industry. This summary offers clues to managers seeking innovative directions:

○ *Organizational culture*—futuristic, fast-moving, information-rich, kinetic organization. A modern human system with transient units, mobile personnel, and continuous reorganization. Role assignments are more temporary and less rigid or precise. Expertise, talents, and professional disciplines converge in task accomplishment. Organizational arrangements are fluid and participative to accommodate changing roles, relationships, and structures. Characterized by task forces and project teams, disposable divisions and ad hoc units. Self-renewing and dynamic environment in a continually adapting enterprise.

○ *Power and authority*—horizontal disbursement with a shift of decisions sideways or to lower levels of responsibility. More emphasis on the authority of competence and a team approach. More sharing of decision-making and seeking diverse input, including workers and consumers. Organizational communication is more circular and lateral, demanding fast information flow by computerized systems. Requires complex problem-solving to meet increasingly non-routine, novel, and unexpected problems or challenges. Organizational focus on human resource development and people maintenance.

○ *Synergistic personnel*—associative persons skilled in collaboration and cooperation. Varied, competent people, including women and minorities with responsibilities, who are self-energizers and actualizers. Seeking primarily challenges for personal and professional development, these are mobile cosmopolitans. See executives and managers as coordinators and consultants, who often work on mixed, temporary work teams. Operate in complex settings within a responsibility matrix requiring flexibility and functional skills. Skilled in human relations and group dynamics, these knowledge workers and technicians are capable of quick, intense work relationships and disengagements. Agents of planned change, they find transience can be liberating. Advocates of quality profitable service, and cooperation among labor-management-government-consumer. As part of entrepreneurial groupings, often within complex systems, metaindustrial personnel may have ownership in the activity and are not afraid to enter new fields of human endeavor. For them, interdependence is an operating norm.

This is not academic fantasy; such trends are becoming reality now in emerging metaindustrial corporations.

The September 1980 issue of the *Atlantic Monthly* offered a contemporary portrait of American industry in an ambitious survey by the magazine's Washington editor, James Fallows. His snapshot of the new corporate culture provides a description of a Silicon Valley firm which in many ways fits the summary just presented. Intel (Integrated Electronics) was founded only in 1968, but has averaged a 30 percent annual increase, almost a third of which comes from foreign markets. Its rapid growth can be seen in stock price increase over 12 years of 10,000 percent. Pretax profits run from 20 to 25 percent, and it doubled its workforce in two years to 14,000 in 1980. The fact that it puts 10 percent of its income back into research is typical of metaindustrial trends.

Fallows maintains that Intel has the classic ingredients of American business success: venture capital, initial risks, technical pioneering, and plowing profits back into the company for more business growth. Like many new metaindustrial enterprises, its creators are scientists who broke away from a larger organization, in this case Fairchild Semiconductor. Among Intel's innovations that push back the frontiers of size, cost, and complexity that delimit computer applications were memory chips, microprocessors, and microcomputers. Always seeking new markets, Intel now moves toward software production. Its founders, Robert Noyce and Gordon Moore, promote a company spirit in which profits are its lifeblood, and the corporate atmosphere is different from mature manufacturing industries. That is, Intel is more flexible, less concerned with the normal trappings of rank, and has an executive team that carries on the work of president.

This metaindustrial organization uses a multiple-executive approach: one outside person, one thinker, and one organizer and action person. These chief executives are informal and modest, with no traditional executive suites, just corners in open-floor layouts with shoulder-high partitions. The employees refer to the corporation as "we" and participate in a special stock-purchase plan. The industry is characterized by virtually no unions, an air of cooperation, and a sense of being on a "winning team." The emphasis is on people who are well motivated and well rewarded, on coping effectively with international competition, and on innovative application of research and development for the purpose of making a profit.

CAPSULE CONCLUSION: PROFILE OF METAINDUSTRIAL ORGANIZATIONAL CULTURE

The macroculture of society has an impact on the microculture of organizations. Accelerating social change becomes a driving force for organizational change. In advanced technological societies, a profound transition is thus under way in the worklife of corporations and other human systems. This can be called a *metaindustrial revolution*. The thesis here is that the information technologies are the catalyst for this transformation process. Managers who wish to maintain a leadership position must effectively employ these technologies, which utilize computing and telecommunications based on microelectronics. Furthermore, the developments within the new technological industries today provide insight into tomorrow's organizational culture. The information organization is a convenient designation for one such contemporary corporation. Its main business and tools center around information processing. Its personnel are referred to as knowledge workers.

As a conclusion, a profile is presented of these metaindustrial enterprises. The characteristics are typical of the management coping challenges that lie ahead.

1. The enterprise may start as a small venture capital technical division or company that rapidly expands into a large market-

oriented organization. Frequently, it experiences unprecedented, volatile growth. Often, it is a spinoff of a larger corporation. If it is a subsidiary of a larger entity, it must have a high degree of autonomy and flexibility.

2. The metaindustrial enterprise can be found throughout the world, even in less industrially developed nations. It usually operates in the international marketplace.

3. The enterprise makes principal use of microprocessors and microcomputers, and may be often in the business of producing them or components and microelectronic services.

4. The enterprise is less labor intensive and more automated. Although there are fewer employees, these knowledge workers are better educated, usually university graduates, and technically oriented. A younger generation of mixed ethnic and social origins, they are sometimes referred to as "Third Wave whiz kids," or mavericks, who question the usual way of doing things. They have a short company history and a skepticism of conventional wisdom, and they are concerned with the preservation of individualism at work.

5. The enterprise makes increasing use of robotics. Robot "thinking machines" with their own microprocessors are programmed to perform the most delicate and complex tasks with great speed and accuracy. Not only may these expensive, computer-controlled machines displace 90 percent of the traditional workforce, they are intended to free human beings from mindless job drudgery. Their widespread use will profoundly alter the workplace and open a new stage in human-machine relations.

6. The enterprise creates new organizational roles and alters old ones. Automated information processing, for example, changes both the functions of and relationship between manager and secretary. It can also improve both productivity and quality of service.

7. The metaindustrial enterprise usually provides a relaxed environment with informal dress, casual and friendly organizational relations, and reduced emphasis on rank and titles. Personnel tend to be more involved in the company and its future. They expect the job to offer challenge, responsibility, and flexibility.

8. The enterprise's managers are visionary and entrepreneurial and take risks. Although profit conscious, they have a "long-run success mentality" in contrast to a "short-term profits outlook."

9. The enterprise is seen as an energy exchange system; it

values the intelligent use of human energy, both psychic and physical. Therefore, there is time for thinking and analysis, and priority is given to research and development.

10. These enterprises now focus on production and services related to semiconductors, personal computers, video applications, telecommunications, and medical and genetic technology. Further exploration and commercialization of outer space will open up undreamed-of careers and industries. The microelectronics, or metaindustrial, revolution is now spreading to banking, construction, food and agriculture, textiles and manufacturing, and public and voluntary service.

Perhaps Jean-Jacques Servan-Schreiber said it most astutely:

> In the years immediately ahead computerization will spread more rapidly than electricity did at the beginning of this century. It will expand in the fields of creative activity as quickly as it will in daily work and leisure. Powerful, versatile, and inexpensive microcomputers will become as much a part of our lives as the air we breathe. Computerization is to an exhausted industrial society what the latter was to agricultural society—a fundamental transformation, not only in methods of production and consumption, but in ways of living, in the organization of the social fabric, in the definition of needs.

Managers with foresight should be in the forefront of this transformation process.

World society, and especially workers, are unprepared for this metaindustrial challenge, yet it can contribute to the management of contemporary crises, confusion, and conflict. Leaders can give their people hope and education regarding available opportunities in the metaindustrial work culture. For example, the Japanese author Yoneji Masuda envisions many ways in which social transformation will occur through information technology, including:

- A new time value, providing more leisure for self-fulfillment.
- A freedom of decision and equality of opportunity to pursue chosen goals in the use of this free time.
- An opportunity to form creative voluntary communities once the new technology frees us from subsistence labor.
- A chance to formulate synergistic societies since cooperative effort will replace industrial competition in the pursuit of shared goals.

Like Masuda, other managers can share realistic visions about the possibilities for establishing synergistic organizational cultures. The liberation offered by microelectronics and information technology makes this feasible, as the application of these new managerial tools improve organizational effectiveness.*

* Organizational effectiveness refers to the optimal relationship among production, efficiency, satisfaction, adaptiveness, and development for the achievement of organizational goals. While efficiency is concerned with such short-term factors as benefit/cost, cost/output, and cost/time, organizational effectiveness seeks long-term survival and development through innovation, planned change, forecasting, and human resources development. By improving communications, relationships, the management of change and conflict, productive behavior, and profitability or service, an organization is effective. To be effective, the organizational culture must provide work satisfaction, stimulation, and achievement that energizes people. Effectiveness has been described by Stanley M. Davis of Boston University as doing the right thing, while efficiency is doing that "thing" in the right way.

CHAPTER 2 The Impact of Culture on Organizational Behavior

If a manager wishes to get a better fix on what is happening in a company, government agency, or other such enterprise, an awareness of the entity's culture will be very helpful. The term *culture* is used in its broad sense as the unique lifestyle of a group of people, the coping strategies and skills developed and adapted for particular purposes. It represents a body of communicable knowledge and learned behavior that humans acquire and pass on for survival and success within an environment.

Its culture makes the group unique and gives its members a sense of identity. They manifest it in their artifacts as well as in their social institutions. A people's culture is seen in its customs and traditions, knowledge and morals, laws and regulations. In fact, it is exemplified in the entire way of life: language and communication systems, values and goals, ideas and attitudes. Some of this culture is obvious and the participants are conscious of it; some of the practices and beliefs are hidden in the group's unconscious. Cultural anthropologists describe this as overt versus covert culture. Although few managers have had formal study in cultural anthropology—the science of human similarities and divergences—insights from this discipline are increasingly important to leaders who wish to better understand organizational behavior, multinational business activity, and the reason for the culture gap between society and technology.

Executives, for example, have awakened to the significance of culture for their operations. The magazines of commerce have begun to offer articles on the issue. *Business Week* (October 27, 1980) had a cover feature on "Corporate Culture—The Hard-to-Change Values That Spell Success or Failure," which described how a CEO's strategy can be thwarted by a company's culture:

Culture implies values, such as aggressiveness, defensiveness, or nimbleness that set a pattern for a company's activities, opinions, and action. That pattern is instilled in employees by managers' example and passed down to succeeding generations of workers.... A corporation's culture can be its major strength when it is consistent with its strategies.... But a culture that prevents a company from meeting competitive threats, or from adapting to changing economic or social environments, can lead to the company's stagnation and demise, unless it makes a conscious effort to change.

This is why an understanding of culture is, or should be, integral to all management development and not just limited to managers involved in foreign deployment. In addition, today's leaders need to know not just how to manage cultural differences, but also how to promote cultural synergy in their organizations and in their representatives' global interfaces.

Another example of the popularization of this topic was a *Fortune* article (June 15, 1981) entitled "Westinghouse's Cultural Revolution." It described how the old electric company was converting to Japanese-style management or Theory Z in the hope of achieving dramatic increases in productivity. Severe need can produce cultural change, even in the world's nineteenth-largest corporation! The success of the Japanese model for worker involvement has finally forced American industrial giants toward participative management. For ten years prior to its momentous decision to change its organizational culture, the author conveyed the same message to Westinghouse managers. The dominant value in that company's culture is profits. Only when profitability was threatened were Westinghouse executives ready to listen and to plan change in their organizational structures and approaches. *Now* they are willing to alter the industrial culture and create an organizational environment in tune with postindustrial realities.

Culture conditions us; it provides a script for our behavior that is acted out according to organizational norms, values, and procedures. It is the subtle history of our nonbiological traits and actions. Along with genetics, it explains human behavior. It can be thought of in terms of majority cultures, or macrocultures, as in the American, Mexican, Chinese, and French cultures. It can be conceived of in terms of minority cultures or microcultures, such as groups of Mexican Americans, youth, or even managers across the world. Behavioral scientists are only now beginning to seriously study the impact of culture on organizations. Yet over a decade ago, Leonard Nadler wrote in *Personnel Journal* (December 1969) of "The Organization as a Microculture":

> Each organization has a culture of its own which is unique, and within a large organization it is possible to identify more than one culture as we move from one unit to another.... A definition this writer evolved in introducing this topic to managers is: culture can be viewed as the habits and customs that people develop to cope with changing conditions.... Our own cultural baggage can impose limitations on our creativity. Too strong an identification with a particular microculture may deny us the possibility of changes which new experiences in new cultures can demand. Cultural baggage of which we are not aware may produce tunnel vision, which prevents us from seeing the world except through a very narrow peephole.

If a manager is simply changing jobs and entering a different human system, cultural knowledge is useful. But if a manager is being assigned abroad, cultural sensitivity and skill are essential. As traditional bureaucracies disappear with the passing of the industrial age, and new metaindustrial enterprises emerge, cultural insights are valuable. But to operate *effectively* in organizations and to understand the influence of culture on personnel behavior, the analysis of culture and the application of the knowledge gained are, again, essential. As Warren Bennis recently reminded organization development specialists gathered for an Academy of Management meeting, "Studying and influencing organizational culture is a key trend."

Before proceeding with this inquiry, perhaps clarification of terms is in order so that we read from a common data base. What do we mean by *organization* and *organizational behavior?* One thoughtful student of organizational culture, Stephen H. Rhinesmith, has provided these useful definitions:

> A formal organization is a system of consciously coordinated activities or forces of two or more persons who interact for the attainment of personal and common objectives (a la Chester A. Barnard).... Management involves the abilities of designated persons in an organization to coordinate human and nonhuman resources available to accomplish organizational objectives (a la Herbert G. Hicks).

My own explanation is this:

> An organization is a collection of human objectives, expectations, and obligations which structure human roles. Reorganization involves

the severing of existing relationships; a dissolution of existing structures; a transformation through renewal. The management of change involves the stimulation of innovation and creativity in the achieving of organizational goals.

An organization involves goal-directed behavior by a group of people, establishment of meaningful structure and processes to accomplish purposes, and concerted action by individuals for the realization of said objectives.

Organizations are essential for human life and have an impact on every facet of our daily existence. But humans and their behavior are what make organizations work. Thus a manager needs to know something about human motivation, decision making, and communication. That is why the field of behavioral science management came into existence—so that leaders could manage people more effectively. Organizations provide people with a context in which to create and perform and with an opportunity through work relationships to confirm and express themselves. It is thus understandable that in contemporary schools of business, a whole new discipline has evolved around the theme *organizational behavior*. One university textbook defines it this way:

Organizational behavior is a field of study concerning the behavior of individuals and groups within organizational settings. The objective of organizational behavior knowledge is to increase employee satisfaction, productivity, and organizational effectiveness.*

Unfortunately, that text does not refer to the influence of culture, and several other volumes on the subject barely mention this significant aspect of human behavior. But back in 1973 Fred Luthans did comment:

The important role that culture plays in human behavior may be one of the most underrated concepts in the behavioral sciences. The culture dictates what a man learns and how he behaves.... The culture not only tells a person what fork to use when eating a salad; it also indicates what is right and good or wrong and evil.

Yes, employees and their organization have a culture that dictates what to value and what priorities to establish, whether to be creative or passive, whether to be competitive or cooperative, whether to be subservient or participative.

*See R. D. Middlemist and M. A. Hitt.

Many practicing managers have limited appreciation of the impact of culture on organizational behavior. The situation in schools is no better; the subject is largely bypassed or underplayed by professors. A review of textbooks on organizations and organization theory reveals few references to anthropology and anthropological research on culture. An exception is the classic volume *Organizations: Behavior, Structure, and Processes* (Gibson, Ivancevich, and Donnelly), which provides us with a workable, if incomplete, definition:

The organizational culture refers to the impact on the environment resulting from group norms, values, and informal activities. The impact of traditional behavior which is sanctioned by group norms, but not normally acknowledged, was first documented in the Hawthorne studies.

GLOBAL MANAGEMENT SIMILARITIES AND DIFFERENCES

Managers from all over the world have much in common. Despite differences of nationality, they probably would be more comfortable with one another than with some line workers in their own organizations. Global managers everywhere form a unique subculture. However, even though these international managers might agree on certain basic activities for the role of manager, the cultures of their respective societies would greatly influence their approach to these functions and their lists of managerial responsibilities would not be similar. Universities offer courses in comparative management so that students of business will understand such cultural differences. Then Western managers become more appreciative of the Asian manager's concern for the spiritual aspects of leadership, such as treating the employee with great dignity and respect. The society's culture affects our perception and practice of both leadership and management. So too, work culture at some point influences managerial style and organizational modes. Managers who are locked into the past industrial-age conception of their role can become obsolete in the emerging metaindustrial work culture.

Theodore Weinshall points out that culture also influences the roles of other human groups within the organization, such as workers, trade unions, customers, suppliers, shareholders, and so forth. In a quotation in Weinshall's book, Frederick Harbison and Charles Meyers note that management is an elite in both the enterprise and the industrial society. They remind us that culture—family, government, political party, education—often dictates who may enter management. In many Latin cultures, patrimonial management is common, while in Soviet-bloc culture, Communist party affiliation is paramount for admission. The metaindustrial culture will favor the technically proficient in management.

The management school of INSEAD in Fontainebleau, France, is a center of study and exchange for managers from all over Europe. There Professor André Laurent has been conducting an ongoing comparative study of management conceptions in ten national cultures (nine European cultures plus the United States). His study aims at identifying and assessing the impact of national cultures on managers' implicit models of management and organization. Viewing the organization as a symbolic system in the varied cultures, Laurent has analyzed the organization in terms of four dimensions or subsystems: the political arena, the levels of authority, role formalization, and hierarchical relationships. His findings point up interesting cultural similarities and differences with regard to management:

- The power orientation of French and Italian managers seems greater than that of Danish or British managers.
- Some cultures influence managers toward more political behavior than in those countries where the patterns of relationships are perceived as stable and well defined.
- Managers in Latin cultures, such as Italy, France, and Belgium, perceive hierarchical structure as necessary so that everyone knows who has authority over whom; American, Swiss, and German managers were at the lower end of the continuum in this regard.
- Similarly, it was the Italian, French, and Belgian managers who most thought there was an authority crisis in organization while the lowest perception of this was again registered by the Americans, Germans, and Swiss.
- Of the 817 managers surveyed in 1979, 43 percent agreed that the manager of tomorrow would be mainly a negotiator. The French, Belgians, and Dutch felt the most certain of this; the Germans, Americans, and Swiss were equally divided on this forecast.
- With regard to role formalization, there was a lower insistence on the need for this in Sweden, the United States, and The Netherlands than in the other seven cultures.
- Sharp differences in management attitudes toward organizational relationships appear as one moves from Northern Eu-

rope and America on one end of the spectrum to the Latin countries at the other end. For instance, one index indicated that matrix-type organizational arrangements might have a greater chance for success in the Swedith culture than in the Italian.

Transnational enterprises, which are of course cross-cultural, have considerable impact on local cultures. They also tend to homogenize world corporate culture somewhat, while globalizing management practice. At the same time, local culture influences multinational business operations, causing adaptations and hybrids in the national subsidiaries. Laurent's research at INSEAD does not thus far support the hypothesis that the multinational corporations cause managerial conceptions to become standardized across national cultures. His findings indicate that managers within a given country possess collective mental maps about organizations that resist the increasing professionalization of international management. Laurent concludes that neighboring Western cultures seem to be shaping fairly different visions of organizations and their management.

Obviously, it is wise to question assumptions about the universality of one's own culture's approach to management. This point is made in an amusing way in the executive epigram in Figure 2, in which organizational structure is looked at from a cross-cultural perspective. One might, of course, question how much cultural bias exists in the minds of the originators of this tongue-in-cheek illustration. Recent American representatives of various professions visiting China were surprised to find rather flat organizations in PRC plants and more participative or team management than they had expected.

According to William H. Newman of Columbia University, the cultural assumptions that underlie American management concepts fall into five categories, which are summarized here:

1. *The "master of destiny" viewpoint* is a belief that people can substantially influence the future. It is manifested in American confidence in self-determination, reliance on realistic cost-benefit analysis of objectives, faith in rewards for persistent hard work, obligation to fulfill commitments, belief in time as a critical factor, and belief that through planning managers can determine what will happen. Management practice based on this assumption favors decentralization for greater self-determination, supervision that is general and consultative, and control that is based

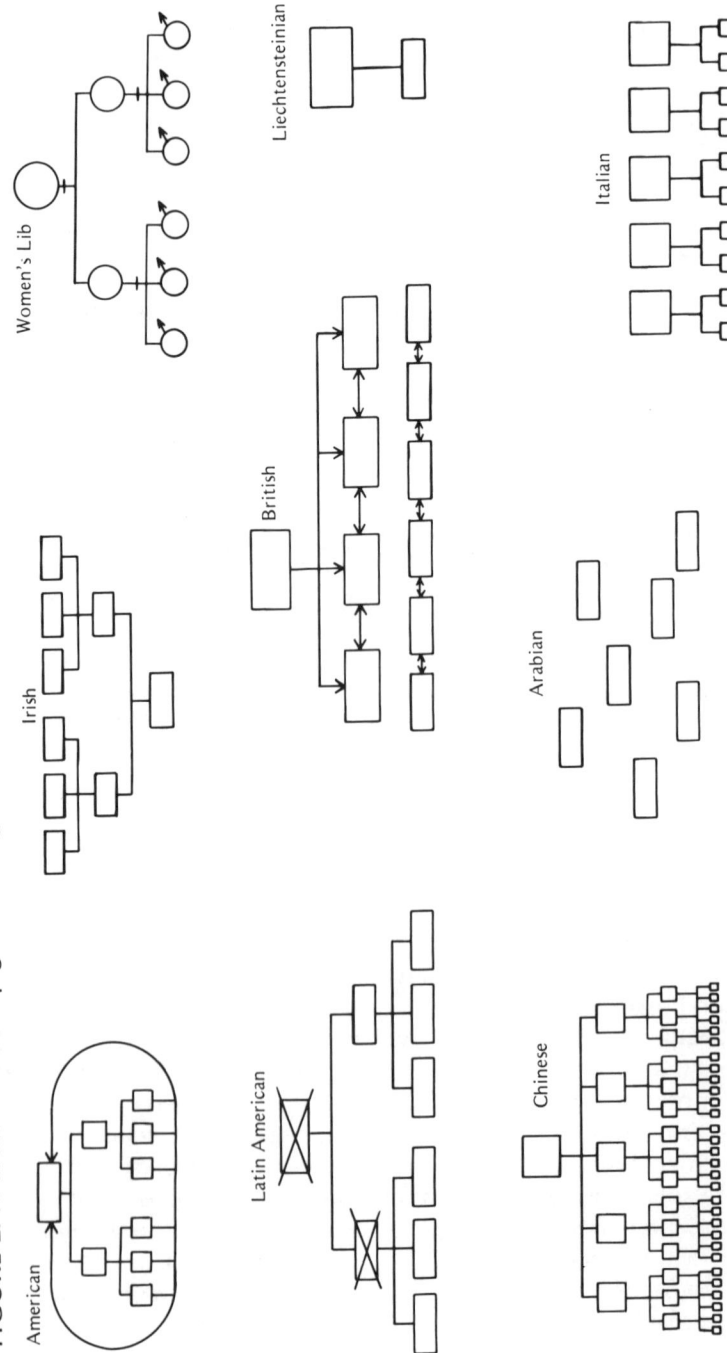

FIGURE 2. A cross-cultural epigram of organizational structures.

Reprinted with special permission from *International Management*, January 1981. © McGraw-Hill Publications Company. All rights reserved.

on constructive feedback. American multinational managers may find themselves in conflict abroad when the local culture does not espouse such assumptions and beliefs.

2. *Joint action through independent enterprise* is based on the strong conviction that enterprises, legal or otherwise, have the following characteristics for the conduct of business, American-style: The enterprise is a separate and vital social institution; employees are obligated and loyal to the enterprise; the employer-employee relationship can be dissolved by either; there is respect for the total management system with its own codes of behavior designed to help achieve its mission; conflict of interest or divided loyalties are avoided; helping family and friends will be subordinated to furthering corporate goals. Organizations operate in America with the idea that management coordinates efforts, duties are divided up and delegated, control is based on loyalty and undivided interest, and leadership is directed to mission accomplishment. Overseas one may discover that companies function on an entirely different set of premises.

3. *Personnel selection based on merit* stems from the belief that individuals should be placed in jobs solely because they are the best qualified persons available. From such a merit appointment assumption, these ideas follow: Remove second-raters or those who do not consistently perform well; provide opportunity for upward mobility or open career access; ensure freedom for horizontal mobility or lateral transfers; reconcile authority with egalitarian principles. Executive and other personnel selections should be based on merit, as well as all career development opportunities, for such practices are vital for employee motivation and control.

4. *Decisions based on objective analysis* is an assumption that reflects the American preference for managerial actions that are "scientific" or based on factual business information. Thus the following practices are required: Assemble relevant, factual data to support decisions; seek reliable, correct figures; maintain an open management information system that is available; encourage experts to present information and offer judgments. Americans value factual, rational support for decisions.

5. *Shared decision making,* both horizontally and vertically, is based on the cultural belief in the high potential of all employees at any level of the organization. This leads to the following ideas: Push down decision making to lower levels and encourage delegation; encourage the idea of "getting ahead" in one's career; foster the quest for improvement and the desirability of change; em-

phasize the importance of results achieved and constructive evaluation. Thus the U.S. manager is perceived as a change agent.* Planning and organization are for continued improvement.

This synthesis of the cultural premises in American management should alert U.S. managers abroad that foreign managers do not view management and organizations in the same manner as U.S. managers, and they should therefore avoid imposing their management systems on other cultures. U.S. managers should instead explore (relevant) valid management approaches and seek synergy with their organizational cultures. There is at the same time a need for domestic management readjustments as a result of increased investment and ownership of U.S. corporations by other nationals. In 1980, for example, foreign investments in U.S. business and property totaled $10 billion. Is it any wonder, then, that leading management thinkers call for more synergistic organizational cultures that match the realities of the world marketplace? Thus, William Ouchi of UCLA proposes a Theory Z corporate culture that fuses the best in both Japanese and American systems:

> A Theory Z culture has a distinct set of ... values, among them long-term employment, trust, and close personal relationships.... Of all its values, commitment of a Z culture to its people—its workers—is the most important.... Theory Z suggests that humanized working conditions not only increase productivity and profits for the company, but also self-esteem for employees.... Up to now American managers have assumed that technology makes for increased productivity. What Theory Z calls for instead is a redirection of attention to human relations in the corporate world.

A caution that all researchers in comparative management offer is worth repeating here: namely, that their descriptions are of common elements in each national culture, that is, of "typical"

---

* A *change agent* is a person who uses planned-change skills within a human or social system. The role of many people today requires them to be change agents. For example, managers and HRD specialists are expected to be innovators within their organizations and to promote organization renewal. The change agent uses a variety of strategies to move an individual or an institution beyond the status quo. This may range from instigating changes in attitude by education and training to fostering managerial decisions that cause changes in policy, procedures, and programs or products. A change agent mobilizes the driving forces of change in organizational space so as to overcome the resisting forces against necessary change. American managerial culture expects leaders to be change agents.

attitudes and values of "average" managers within a country. In nations with diverse cultural traditions, there will be many exceptions and deviations from the so-called norm. Many managers will move beyond their own national culture and become more cosmopolitan in their approach to management and organizational operations. Other findings indicate that managers of different nationalities can also be educated and trained to overcome their own cultural resistance to an approach that is quite different from their own. According to Geert Hofstede, director of human resources for Fasson Europe, cultural barriers to innovation can be overcome. The dilemma for the multinational corporations, he believes, is whether to adapt to the local culture or to try to change it. Hofstede cites the example of Third World countries that want technology transfer but that may need to go against local traditions to get it. He proposes:

In this case the local culture has to be changed; but this is a difficult task which should not be taken lightly, and which calls for a conscious strategy based on insight into the local culture, in which acculturated locals should be involved.

THE INFLUENCE OF CORPORATE CULTURE ON PERSONNEL

The organizational culture affects the behavior of the people with whom it interfaces. We can view this effect from the perspective of an organization's customers, suppliers, and subcontractors, but the greatest impact is obviously on the employees of the corporation. The Federal Aviation Agency, for instance, designs the role of air controller in such a way as to attract a unique personality type to that position. But research on such personnel indicates that the controllers' strike in 1981 could have been predicted, given the organizational culture within the agency. My professional dealings with the FAA allow me to confirm the findings of a massive study of that occupation by another psychologist, C. David Jenkins, who stated* that the FAA developed a strong, punitive attitude toward its controllers, which stimulates defiant behavior. Management's inadequate concern for people and poor communication patterns caused frustration in the controllers, who perceived management as unresponsive, bungling, inflexible, and irrational. Psychological tests indicated that the controllers as a group tended to be strong, dominant, aggressive, sociable, conscientious, and self-confident.

* *Los Angeles Times*, December 15, 1981.

Given to impulsive behavior, controllers find rigid authority and regulations obnoxious, are able to work under stress, and get things done in their own way, even if it means bending or breaking rules and regulations. Given these two sets of circumstances, it is no wonder that a calamitous strike of U.S. controllers occurred in 1981.

There is a great lesson to be learned here about the design of jobs and organizations, and the kind of culture to be maintained for productive employee behavior. Corporate culture does condition worker behavior, but the people within the organization can also bring about a change in company culture, and not just at the executive level. During organizational crises, middle management, line supervisors, or hourly workers and even their unions often force alterations in the work environment. Frequently, such changes have been spearheaded by a new hire type, such as college graduates, or by minorities, such as women and blacks, who organize for justice and opportunity on the job. Sometimes change results from mergers or acquisitions, especially when a management team from another country is brought into the organization through a corporate takeover. When a domestic company moves into international business, especially by forming a multinational corporation, the organizational culture and the traditional employee behavior are changed. In other words, people and circumstances can alter corporate traditions, organizational hierarchies, and institutionalized functions. The introduction of new technology can also produce change in organizational relations.

Speaking in San Diego, California, at the American Academy of Management on August 3, 1981, Roy H. Glen of Willamette University maintained that an organization can provide a coherent culture that its people can identify with and belong to, one that facilitates exchange relationships. Glen believes that an organization's culture bolsters the most important integrative device—authority, the voluntary acceptance of domination. Corporate ceremonies, rituals, taboos, and myths are cultural mechanisms for organizational integration and survival. But just as individuals may suffer culture shock, corporations and other social institutions can experience organization shock. Drastic drops in customers or membership, loss of markets and industrial leadership, obsolescence of products or services, social or personnel changes—all are manifestations of organizational crises that may produce alterations in corporate culture and employee behavior, that is, if the institution survives by effective management of change.

The very nature of new business may bring about a new organizational culture and employee behavior. This can be seen best through an analysis of the metaindustrial organizations now replacing classical industrial corporations. Let us go again to Intel, analyzed by Ouchi, where employees describe their *informal culture* along these lines:

○ *Technology/business*—to be and to be recognized as the best in their industry, to emphasize innovativeness and creativity in their technology, products, and approach, to have a high-technology orientation, which extends the concept of "excellence" even to support aspects of their business, to review all activity in terms of the "bottom line," and to be sensitive to projecting a credible image by meeting corporate commitments.

○ *Management style*—respect for individual differences while manifesting these general characteristics: self-criticism, open and constructive confrontation, consensus decision making, open and circular communication, organizational skill and discipline, ethical and creditable behavior, making difficult decisions versus evasions, placing the responsibility for subordinate development with direct line managers.

○ *Work ethic/environment*—integrate work assignments with career objectives; provide opportunity for rapid development, especially through training; be results-oriented, with emphasis on substance and quality; be proud of high productivity and performance; assume responsibility; make long-term career/company commitments; involve employees and be participative; and expect all employees to behave ethically.

○ *Team operations*—team performance is critical to meeting corporate objectives; teams and task forces may be formal or informal; team objectives take precedence over individual objectives; matrix management requires multiple interfaces.

Interestingly, when Ouchi created such organizational culture profiles of high-technology companies in his recent book, *Theory Z*, he did it in terms of categories for analysis—short- or long-term environmental focus, organizational communication, information sharing, individual orientation, and culture. Appendix A contains an "Organizational Culture Survey Instrument" that offers 99 questions for institutional self-analysis, covering these six categories: overall analysis, organizational communication, management team evaluation, work group assessment, managerial self-perception, organizational relations, and organizational changes. Such questionnaires, and other forms of human factor data gathering,* can provide a useful evaluation of organizational health, as well as powerful feedback to management.

Hay Associates, headquartered in Philadelphia, have developed an intriguing conceptual model for the management of human resources in multinational companies. They envision three types of organizational cultures that may be encountered in foreign subsidiaries. They propose that personnel policies reflect and fit the human resources requirements of such environments. These management consultants analyze the work cultures abroad in terms of these categories to facilitate understanding by expatriate managers. Figure 3 further illustrates this unique approach. The three organizational cultures are:

  o *The bureaucratic culture*—typical of protectionist and developing countries; most frequently found in companies operating within protected and stable markets. Characterized by impersonal style, absolute reliance on standards, norms, and rigid procedures. Best supported by pyramidal and centralized hierarchy with little internal competition and many "organization man" types.
  o *The technical culture*—typical of countries with a tradition of technical expertise; often found in companies operating in well-established and traditional industries. Characterized by paternalistic style, technical know-how, and a highly functionalized organization with fierce interdepartmental competition. Recognition and ultimate power at the top go to the technician. (*Note:* Contrast this description with the high-technology culture described earlier for Intel Corporation, which is more like the type described next.)
  o *The managerial culture*—typical of trading countries that were open early to free competition and enterprise; encountered in companies operating in highly competitive and innovative industries. Characterized by professional managerial style that is performance-oriented, and supported by a flexible and adaptive organization.

---

*Within human systems or organizations, data may be gathered from members or employees on their views, opinions, or reactions to the total situation or portions of it, to work and related activities, to policies and procedures. The information is gathered through interviews, oral or video or audio tapes; questionnaires, inventories, or checklists; or other forms of inquiry. Objective questions, capable of statistical analysis, are easier with large groups of people. The data are then analyzed for report purposes, and findings and conclusions are drawn from them. It is a feedback mechanism for management to engage in organizational diagnosis, so as to improve planning, effectiveness, and morale or productivity.

UNDERSTANDING GLOBAL ORGANIZATIONS

Anthropologists provide a variety of paradigms for understanding macrocultures. These conceptual models, with some adaptations, are equally applicable to microcultures, such as corporations or other human enterprises. One such model uses a *systems approach*. For example, one might examine the multidimensional facets of the entity in these terms:

- *Relationship system*—the network of social groupings, formal and informal, from departments and divisions to car pools and work teams.
- *Educational system*—the manner of recruiting, selecting, and training members of the society or organization, as well as informal opportunities for career development.
- *Economic system*—the manner in which the organization finances, produces, and markets its goods and services.
- *Political system*—the dominant means for governance for maintaining order and exercising authority or power.
- *Philosophical system*—the beliefs and ideals the organization uses in setting goals and objectives, and in providing meaning and motivation for its members.
- *Personnel system*—the policies and practices by which roles and relationships are defined, compensation plans and benefits are distributed, and special services from health to recreation or vacation are provided in the total company, agency, or association.

This model could be refined into additional categories for systems analysis of the culture, such as the technological or process system, the security system, and so forth.

For transnational enterprises, Vern Terpstra has offered a number of parameters that permit us to analyze, for example, how a multinational corporation adapts to the external environment or macroculture within which it functions. The parameters are:

1. *Cultural variability*—How does the organization react to change and make adjustment when it is in a stable versus a fluid environment?

2. *Cultural complexity*—How does the organization respond to a simple or low-context cultural environment versus a complex or high-context cultural environment?

3. *Cultural hostility*—How does the organization respond when the external situation is munificent or malevolent? (The latter, for example,

FIGURE 3. Managing human resources in different cultures.

		IN THE BUREAUCRATIC CULTURE
	• Structuring the Organization	• Establish rational and detailed organization chart to be communicated throughout the organization.
	• Designing Jobs	• Formalize and standardize job descriptions. • Put emphasis on tasks to be performed.
	• Delegating Decision-Making Authority	• Extremely limited delegation and freedom are required.
	• Controlling and Assessing Performance	• Need for a heavy system of administrative checks and balances to measure how tasks are performed. • Emphasis is on compliance with standards and norms.
• Designing Compensation Plans	• External Competitiveness	• Usually minimal.
	• Internal Equity	• Must be absolute and normative. • Must integrate seniority and diplomas.
	• Incentive Components	• None.
	• Benefits	• Highly formalized and common throughout the organization.
	• Providing Job Security	• Must be absolute.
	• Career Development	• Strict and objective rules and procedures must be established for promotions and career developments.

Source: Management Memo #316. Reprinted with permission of the Hay Group of Philadelphia, Pa.

IN THE TECHNICAL CULTURE	IN THE MANAGERIAL CULTURE
• Develop, organize and obtain consensus or interrelationships among functions.	• Keep organization minimal and adaptive to changes.
• Formalize relationships as accountabilities will be most often shared. • Put emphasis on processes to be adopted.	• Be flexible and formalize accountabilities. • Put emphasis on end results to be accomplished.
• Decision-making must be mostly controlled.	• High degree of delegation and freedom is supported.
• Effective cost accounting system is required to measure efficiency. • Emphasis is on qualitative criteria.	• Sophisticated control system is required to measure end results. • Emphasis is on quantitive criteria.
• Median.	• High.
• Limited. • Must reflect balance of power among functions. • Limited.	• Fair. • Must reflect job value and performance. • High.
• Formalized and personalized.	• Informal and personalized.
• Fair.	• Minimal.
• Develop bridges between functions to improve organizational integration.	• Reward high performers through rapid promotions.

might be when the economy is depressed or when local conditions threaten organizational goals, norms, values, profits, etc.)

5. *Cultural heterogeneity*—How does the organization cope with an external culture that is homogeneous versus one that is heterogeneous (or, it might be added, synergistic versus unsynergistic)? Organizational strategies and public relations will differ when the society is made up of people who are relatively similar in contrast to a society that is diverse and disparate.

6. *Cultural interdependence*—How sensitive is the organization to conditions and developments within the local culture? Is the organization independent, dependent, or interdependent with the surrounding culture and economy?

Global organizational cultures should seek synergy with the host culture when this is feasible, whether this be in terms of language and communications, laws and politics, values and belief, education and training, technology and resources, or local social organizations and practices. Many business strategists believe that transnational corporations should employ a variety of procedures to diagnose and influence the cultural environments in which they operate, and to adjust the organizational culture accordingly.

Figure 4 offers a model that should facilitate the reader's understanding of the varied dimensions of organizational culture. Although the facets of a culture are numerous, there are some essential characteristics to examine. They are at the same time useful as a guide to understanding the culture of an organization. For convenience, they have been combined under the following six related categories.

1. *Organizational rationale and identity.* What is the organization's sense of self and space? In other words, what is the corporate philosophy that makes this entity unique? What beliefs and attitudes prevail in this human system? Related to this aspect is its space, both psychological and physical. That is, what are the organization's boundaries that carve out its "territory" or set it apart from its competitors or others in its industry or field? Another way of putting this is to ask, How does it see itself? What is its image? How does it organize or structure itself to express this identity?

2. *Organizational purposes and standards.* First, what is the organization's perception of its goals, mission, or general objectives? Then, what are its values and norms? Thus we ask in another way about the organization's priorities and means for regulating behavior for meeting its goals. What is important to the

FIGURE 4. A conceptual illustration of some dimensions of culture in human systems.

(1) RATIONALE AND IDENTITY
- Philosophy, Beliefs, Attitudes, Boundaries, Images
- (2) PURPOSES AND STANDARDS: Goals, Missions, Objectives, Values, Norms
- (3) LOOK AND STYLE: Leadership Style, Dress, Appearance, Time Sense, Policies, Procedures
- (4) PROCESSES AND ACTIVITIES: Produces Goods, Provides Services, Personnel Activities
- (5) COMMUNICATION AND INFORMATION: Communication and Information Systems, Behavior, Technology
- (6) HUMAN RESOURCES AND RELATIONSHIPS: Personnel Images, Roles, Relationships, Expectations, Development, and Motivation

ORGANIZATIONAL CULTURE

organization gets translated into standards of performance, or rules and regulations in personnel manuals, or codes of ethics.

3. *Organizational look and style.* What is the system's ambiance (the mood, character, quality, tone, and atmosphere of this particular corporate environment)? This cultural dimension gets translated for practical purposes into company attitudes toward such matters as appearance and dress, or time and time consciousness. In other words, how does the organization project itself to its members and to outsiders? What are the corporate and leadership styles that capture its spirit and get manifested in policies and procedures?

4. *Organizational processes and activities.* What does the organization do, and how does it go about this? Whether it pro-

duces goods or provides services, there are processes that can be analyzed with regard to reasoning and human relations, information and marketing, manufacturing or technology. Such personnel and managerial activities continuously undergo change in response to external market and social forces and to internal alterations of people and practices.

5. *Organizational communication and information.* What are the organizational communication systems, both formal and informal, external and internal? More specifically, how does the management information system function, and what does it encompass? Are personnel communications open, circular, and authentic? What languages, signals, and special vocabularies are used? What new communications technology does it employ?

6. *Organizational human resources and relationships.* How does the organization view its personnel and determine their roles and relationships? What does it do to enforce or reinforce its expectations of workers? What is its human resources development program for recruitment, selection, training, and evaluation? How does it attempt to recognize, motivate, and reward its people through compensation and benefit plans, achievement incentives and performance controls, educational opportunities and learning processes? How does it prepare personnel for the impact of the microelectronics revolution, and how does it contribute to community retraining projects? What type of "human-machine" relations exist? What is the focus and quality of relationships externally with community institutions, and internally between and among its groups and subsidiaries? In all, what is the quality of life that this enterprise engenders for its various human constituencies? How wisely is power used within this human energy exchange system?

Culture is the medium by which the organization expresses itself to its employees or members, as well as to the outside world. Organizational culture is a human creation, subject to change and modification, for it touches every aspect of the institution's life—from corporate structure to corporate climate. Knowledge of the six general classifications, all aspects of a corporate culture, may help managers increase their awareness of the workings of the organization and their effectiveness as managers. The questions presented here are more useful when people apply them to the organizational culture to which they have their primary affiliation. In the next eight chapters, the above major six themes or categories will be developed. The context for this will be the emerging metaindustrial work culture.

CULTURE TIPS FOR MANAGERS

For leaders who would use cultural understanding and skills to improve personal and organizational effectiveness, these strategies may prove useful:

- Examine the influence of our own national and corporate cultures on our behavior as managers, as well as upon employee behavior.
- Develop action plans for influencing change in one's organizational culture so that it is more in harmony with the realities of postindustrial society and the needs of knowledge workers. This implies that a cultural dimension should be brought to such activities as strategic planning, controlling, organizing, staffing, marketing, procuring, and producing.
- Revitalize international business policies and procedures so that they reflect cross-cultural sensitivity with regard to both employees sent abroad and overseas customer relations. A foreign deployment *system* is essential for multinational operations.
- Reassess the cultural factors in domestic operations related to managing minority personnel, relocation of employees, and relations at home (or abroad) with customers, suppliers, contractors, and government officials.
- Consider the cultural factors involved in acquisitions, mergers, and joint ventures. By facilitating the integration of these various organizational cultures, productivity and profitability will be enhanced.
- Plan for new work cultures when moving or establishing new plants and facilities.
- Move beyond differences in people and situations, and create cultural synergy!*

CAPSULE CONCLUSIONS

Each organization creates a unique institutional culture, some aspects of which are explicit, others implicit. The more managers understand this cultural environment, the more effective they can be not only in functioning within it but in changing it as need dictates. In addition, when we change jobs, we tend to carry the

---

* *Synergy:* The concept of cooperative, collaborative, or combined actions by individuals and groups so as to produce results greater than what could be achieved alone. Cultural synergy is said to occur when two or more people, groups, or nations use their differences in perception to work together for mutual benefit, thereby creating something that is greater in quality and quantity than the sum of individual efforts.

values and other cultural baggage of the former affiliation into the new situation. We should be more aware of this behavioral reality and deal with it, especially by development of greater flexibility and openness to different cultural challenges.

Both the individual and the institution are products of human culture at a particular place and time. In advanced economic societies, we have been conditioned by the industrial age. Preindustrial or less developed countries may be largely hunting or agricultural societies, but even they along with the rest of the planet are rapidly moving toward becoming metaindustrial societies. Soon humans will be challenged to create cultural adaptations suitable for life and work in outer space. Both managers and human systems are in the midst of profound transition. Many people in today's new technology firms are contributing toward what will become tomorrow's metaindustrial organizational culture. As anthropologist Edward Hall so aptly observed:

> It is not that *man* must be in sync with or adapt to his *culture*, but that culture grows out of sync with man. When this happens people go crazy and they don't know it. In order to avoid mass insanity, people must learn to transcend and adapt their culture to the times and to their biological organisms.

This last point is especially telling in relation to corporate culture. Finally, Dr. Jonas Salk and others have speculated that humans seem to develop social systems based on biological models. The body is a marvel of symmetry and synergy. It is a wondrous example to managers of what we should replicate in the corporate body, especially in terms of cooperation and collaboration among the parts. For that to happen we must transcend obsolete organizational cultures and create more relevant ones.

CHAPTER 3   New Corporate Rationale and Identity

A special mystique held sway throughout IBM for decades from the time of its founding in 1924 by Thomas J. Watson. During his reign as CEO, a close-knit camaraderie existed. The corporation and its representatives projected a distinctive "IBM" look. It was expressed in the unwritten dress code, the "THINK" signs in offices to remind employees to "problem-solve," and even for a while in the company song, "Hail to IBM." One might expect this type of behavior in a Japanese firm, but it seems unusual in an American enterprise. Yet such a philosophy helped IBM to create a superb marketing and service organization. Although it did not result in technological leadership, by the 1970s IBM commanded 60 percent of the world computer market. Even though that dominance has slipped and IBM no longer experiences an annual 20 percent growth rate, it certainly possessed a mysterious "something" that helped to propel it to such development. It might be called organizational philosophy or rationale. It contributes to institutional identity and progress in most spectacular ways. Managers should understand this phenomenon better and learn to influence it.

ORGANIZATIONAL PHILOSOPHIES AND BELIEFS
A dimension of any culture that must be analyzed is its belief system. It is expressed in a people's philosophy, religions, or general attitudes. It is the ideals and ideas that a group lives by, that make it distinctive. What is true in macrocultures is also evident in organizational cultures. A corporate culture has a belief system that may be written or unwritten, formal or informal. In a sense, it is the organizational philosophy—the principles and concepts of being, knowledge, or conduct that guide the behavior of people

in that human system. Or it may be thought of as the corporate rationale—the fundamental reasons for the organization's existence. Sometimes manifested in an organization's statement of principles, it is usually translated into stated goals and objectives. It is in any event a powerful, and often neglected or misunderstood, force in organizational behavior.

Consider these corporations and how they manifest their philosophies:

- International Telephone & Telegraph Corporation, where financial discipline demands total dedication.
- Digital Equipment Corporation, where an emphasis on innovation creates freedom with responsibility.
- Delta Air Lines, Inc., where a focus on customer service produces a high degree of teamwork.
- Atlantic Richfield Company, where an emphasis on entrepreneurship encourages action.
- PepsiCo, where today beating the competition, whether inside or outside the company, is the surest path to success.
- J. C. Penney Co., where building long-term loyalty is all-important, so everyone is treated as an individual and openness in the organization is promoted.*

Such beliefs and attitudes often get translated formally into a corporate rationale. This was the case when founder James Cash Penney formulated the company's guiding principles into "The Penney Idea"—a seven-point code. It evoked tremendous employee loyalty and became entrenched in the corporate culture, but now these paternalistic attitudes have produced lower profits. Organizational philosophies need modification, adaptation, and updating if survival and development are to be assured.

The corporate rationale also gets expressed in company strategies, orientations, and even slogans, which may contain code word symbols for the organizational philosophy, such as profits, service, innovate, excel. Slogans may be covert, such as "Don't rock the boat," or they may be stated overtly as in this high-technology firm's motto—"Intel delivers."

William Ouchi and Raymond L. Price remind us that an organizational philosophy serves three functions: (1) It is a mechanism for integrating the individual into the organization, for linking in-

* *Business Week*, October 27, 1980.

dividual and corporate goals; (2) it is a mechanism for integrating an organization into society, for stimulating social approval or disapproval of its practices; (3) it is an elegant informational device for concretizing its values and expressing its management theory and its forms of control. They point out that most Japanese corporations have well-developed management philosophies and their executives often write books on these philosophies. But there can be cross-cultural problems when these philosophies are transmitted to American firms acquired by them. A Japanese firm's U.S. executives complained about the Japanese inability to formulate specific objectives, by which the Americans meant quantified targets. The Japanese corporate president's response to this would be that if the Americans understood the company's philosophy, they would deduce for themselves the proper objectives for any conceivable situation. Ouchi and Price also cite instances of the Japanese management philosophy of service and long-term profitability coming into confrontation in their American subsidiaries where the local cultural mindset was on profits and short-term return. However, in many American firms, this cultural business tradition is changing—instead of just profits, profitable service is now the theme being heard.

The industrial-age culture and its philosophy are disappearing. Rugged individualism is being replaced by team or participative management. The "public-be-damned" attitudes of some corporations are giving way to corporate social responsibility. "Reduce-costs-at-any-price" concepts are giving way to sensitivity to the ecological or human impact of corporate decision making. "Bottom-line-only" considerations diminish in complex postindustrial situations. Now management planners think more in terms of down-line profitability. They wish to build volume sales over longer periods and gain brand recognition. They think of global, and not just local, markets and strategies.

Organizational philosophy is becoming more farsighted and futuristic and less earthbound. Many of the perceptual constraints or psychological blinders that limited organizational leaders in the past are being removed because of increased education, information, travel, and exchange within the world marketplace. Gordon L. Lippitt of George Washington University has summarized the changes under way in organizational philosophies: from mechanistic forms to organic forms, competitive relations to collaborative relations, separate objectives to linked objectives, organizational resources regarded as owned absolutely to organizational resources regarded as also society's.

This noted behavioral scientist believes that such changes are reflected in the new ways organizations are being structured and managed. Lippitt and other organizational theorists see the trend as away from autocracy, so evident in the declining bureaucratic organizations, and toward greater democratization, as indicated in the emerging ad hoc or organic systems that feature more decentralization and collegialism. These systems use as a corporate strategy temporary entities from task forces to project groups.

The shift in organizational philosophies now going on is what Ouchi calls "going from A to Z." He cites Hewlett-Packard, Dayton-Hudson, Rockwell, Eli Lilly, and Intel as trend indicators of the new management philosophies. Whether the corporate philosophy has emerged from the company founders or a survey-feedback strategy, Ouchi maintains it should include the organization's objectives, operating procedures, and constraints. Drawing from the company statements from these metaindustrial firms, Ouchi provides these illustrations of change in corporate philosophies:

> OBJECTIVE: To achieve sufficient profit to finance our company growth and to provide the resources we need to achieve our other corporate objectives....
> To help our people share in the company success, which they make possible; to provide job security based on their performance; to recognize their individual achievements; and to insure the personal satisfaction that comes from a sense of accomplishment....
> To serve as the consumers' purchasing agent in fulfilling their needs and expectations for merchandising and services....
> To provide an attractive financial return to our shareholders....
> To serve the community in which we operate.

In developing such expressions of corporate philosophy, Ouchi recommends that "living" documents be compiled over a period of time with maximum personnel participation. He suggests that management use a culture profile mechanism that takes various categories of organizational culture, such as short- or long-term environment, and then examines where the organization was, what it has done, where it is, and where it wants to go. Such processes for clarifying corporate philosophy also contribute to solidifying organizational identity.

SYNERGY AS A MANAGEMENT PRINCIPLE

New corporate philosophies that foster collaboration and cooperation among employees and their publics are using synergy as a principle of management. Firms or agencies that believe in promoting integration and that operate on the idea of interdependence also manifest synergy. It is a concept that will be a bedrock of organizational behavior in the metaindustrial age.

Descriptions of this innovative idea make its value evident*:

Synergy is combined action which occurs when diverse or disparate people in groups work together. The objective is to increase effectiveness by shared perceptions, insights, and knowledge.

Synergy is the additional benefit that accrues when a number of systems coalesce to form a larger system, so that the whole becomes greater than the sum of its parts.

Synergy is a corporate strategy that produces collaborative benefit, which is generated consciously or unconsciously because people cooperate.

Synergy relies upon joint action by discrete entities to create an integrated solution.

Cultural synergy is like a successful marriage. Two people, two organizations, or two nations come together for mutual benefit to develop a relationship which is different in quantity and quality than the sum of their individual contributions.

A managerial rationale based on the principle of synergy should become a part of a metaindustrial organization's culture. The complexity of our times and technologies, the interdependence of our systems, both natural and human, the nature of our problems and challenges—all demand synergistic strategies and skills. However, the passing industrial culture, of which we are all a product, has conditioned us differently, and we have to be re-educated in teamwork.

The need for this was vividly demonstrated to me while conducting management games. One simulation used in executive development is called "The Blue/Green Game." Its purpose is to convince the participants of the value of cooperation and collaboration. The trainees were divided into two major groups, A and B, and then into four subgroups, A1 and A2, B1 and B2. They were instructed: "You all work for the same organization, and ultimately report to me (as general manager). The object of the game is to get as many points (profits) as possible in the time allotted."

---
* This analysis was developed together with Robert T. Moran.

With everyone working for the same entity, the individual could achieve only when the *whole* organization benefited, and not at the expense of any of its parts. Invariably, some managers in training would forget the goal and get caught up in the idea of personal victory. They exhibited the same dog-eat-dog behavior they practiced back on the job, a product of American cultural competitiveness. They adopted an uncontrolled win/lose approach, sought success at the expense of others, lacked trust, and betrayed others. Only when they pursued a win/win strategy, promoted the common good, and collaborated could they truly achieve. For some, it was a painful lesson in the value of synergy and seeking consensus.

There is enough evidence in both corporate and international life that the way to move ahead in this postindustrial period is through synergy. Behavioral science management research has consistently confirmed its appropriateness, whether we use Douglas McGregor's term of Theory Y, or Blake and Mouton's grid analogy of 9,9 or team management approach, or Rensis Likert's Systems 3/4 terminology to describe organizations with a more consultative or participative management. Chris Argyris of Yale University stated something similar in his organizational mix model. He points up six dimensions to ensure organizational success now and even greater success in the future:

1. The whole is created and controlled through the interrelationship of the parts.
2. The need for awareness of the plurality and patterns of parts.
3. The achieving of objectives, especially among units and subsidiaries, must be related to the whole.
4. Internally oriented core activities, such as structure, roles, processes or objectives, must be capable of change and modification constantly.
5. Externally oriented core activities, such as fluctuations in the society or economy, must be responded to creatively.
6. The nature of core activities are influenced by past, present, and future, requiring vision and long-term planning.

When an organization's philosophy moves it in these directions, it is healthy and can be continuously renewed. A healthy corporate philosophy would encourage:

- Emphasis on cooperation for mutual advantage, and idealization of win/win, or victory for all.
- Promotion of individual and group development, or the common good.

- Fostering of nonaggressive, nonexploitative behavior toward others.
- Utilization of community resources and talents for the development of human potential in all.
- Inculcation of a belief system that is consoling and comforting, in which power is used for the good of the community, while helping individuals and groups to work out or channel hurts and humiliations.
- Development of psychologically healthy members who are open to change and practice reciprocity in their relationship.

Unfortunately these policies don't exist within the broad range of U.S. companies. But as managers and executives, we have the opportunities to exercise synergistic leadership in corporations, government agencies, and associations. We can contribute to the creation of an organizational rationale that will move the system in the new directions that will ensure continued and future success and well-being.

THE CORPORATION AS CHANGE AGENT

What is the role of organizations in society? Some would answer that social institutions are created to serve human needs and to be sources of human creativity and innovation. The modern business corporation is barely a century old, and it is already in transition from a monolithic, bureaucratic hierarchy to an increasingly democratic global enterprise. A rapidly changing social and technological environment has an impact on the organization, and it becomes itself a force for change in external society. Each age has produced its own dominant social institution, and for the twentieth century this has been the modern corporation, especially in its multinational form. Today it is a superb social instrument for channeling human energies into higher goals that can be achieved only through team efforts. The corporation organizes productive patterns and develops creative talents—all toward some performance that results in economic or social good. The nobility of the effort should be reflected in the corporate philosophy, so that it can be implemented in a sensitive yet practical manner.

A recent dialogue* between Charles Fombrun, a professor at The Wharton School, and Reginald H. Jones, chairman and CEO

* *Organizational Dynamics,* Winter 1982.

of General Electric, underscores the need for this. Jones observed that major corporations are socioeconomic institutions whose responsibilities extend beyond their investors: "There's also a responsibility to the employee, to the suppliers, to the customers, and to the public.... We've got to recognize that the greatest asset any public corporation has today is its public franchise—that is, the willingness, the interest of the public in seeing to it that the corporation continues to exist because it is a producer of values." Fombrun responded that what happens in corporations has a lot to do with what's going on in society as a whole, since most of us work in organizations of one form or another: "Therefore, things like human resources systems that are put in place inside corporations help create changing attitudes and values. The criteria we evaluate people on, the criteria we reinforce, the kinds of training programs we provide, the kinds of rewards workers are given—all create the social context." Obviously organizations play an important part in national well-being, and their philosophies or belief systems should reflect that consciousness!

Cornelius Brevoord, dean of the Graduate School of Management in Delft, The Netherlands, has called for the following changes in organizational philosophies: from functional specialization to interdisciplinary approaches, authoritarian decision making to democratic decision making, negative control systems to positive control systems, one task per worker to teamwork, vertical information systems to functional information systems. When these insights are combined with those previously cited by Lippitt, we have a synergistic indication of corporate change that can have profound implications for society. Managers have to be aware that their corporations are indeed changing because of a combination of sociotechnological trends, and also that these organizations then cause change in the lives of their employees, customers, and communities.

The issue is whether such changes shall be haphazard or planned. The corporation cannot act on its own; managerial decisions cannot be made in a vacuum. Apart from government regulatory groups, community organizations—from environmentalists and ecologists to consumerists and feminists—act as a catalyst or a constraint on corporate plans. Active interaction between internal and external environments requires a synergistic interface. Corporate management will be involved in broader social issues and changes as human society makes this rapid transition into cyberculture. Citizens everywhere have great expectations of the modern corporation. Corporate developers have it in their power to reverse urban deterioration and renew cities where politicians fail; to resolve learning problems that baffle educators, to reverse social ills that overwhelm clergy and social workers, to rehabilitate delinquents. Their effectiveness extends beyond national borders, where corporations have often spearheaded community development in Third World nations.

Like it or not, the corporation and its managers are agents of change. According to Brevoord, the new function of management is the structuring and running of organizations that produce wealth (economic/humanitarian/societal) in a scientifically and socially responsible manner. That is, the corporation not only responds in a timely and effective way to environmental changes, but inaugurates creative change internally and externally. Right now high-technology firms are providing us with both miracle chips and a new microtechnology that could transform society itself. The battle over the Falkland Islands demonstrated that microchips are transforming warfare. These changes may reduce human drudgery, cause job loss and the decline of traditional industries, or even make killing more efficient in combat and other social disruptions. It would seem, then, that leaders also have the responsibility to prepare personnel and the public for the effects of the new technology.

Enlightened corporate philosophy in computer software and hardware suppliers, for instance, might result in advertising and educational programs that help the masses to appreciate how the computer can contribute to individualization, to making the mechanisms of supply and demand operate more responsively, to creating unheard-of careers, products, and services. It is not enough to reassure the population that automation can cause new jobs and industries to come into being. The corporate catalysts should be helping the citizenry to make the transition to the new way of life, to reduce the fears and traumas of the transitional experience, and to take advantage of the metaindustrial opportunities. For military planners and decision makers, the technological imperatives are that greater quality in recruitment is essential. Fewer, more highly trained, military technicians will alter the makeup of the "defense" forces in the future. Indeed, whether in private or public sector, if the cybernated revolution can make us wiser, healthier, and even happier, organizational leaders, particularly those in the forefront of the technology, should reduce the culture gap between the technologists and the masses.

CHANGING IMAGES OF ORGANIZATIONS

Corporations spend millions of dollars on public relations programs to improve or maintain their images. Corporate logos, colors, stationery, and brands are part of the process of establishing organizational identity. Advertising and other community relations efforts are intended to produce recognition for the corporate person. Depending on our relationship to the institution, we have different images of the organization.

First, there is the official view, the image the corporation deliberately projects through its public relations, which is reflected by the owner and executives. Then there is the internal view, the one held by employees and other insiders whose perspective is shaped by their daily experience. There is the government's view, which reflects the official dealings in regulatory issues, and finally there is the public view held by suppliers, customers, and others.

In a prophetic statement, editor Don Fabun made this astute comment:

> We live in a world of visions—the concepts we form of ourselves and of the things about us. We constantly strive to reduce complex interactions of ourselves with our environment into well-defined models that have form and substance that we can visualize and understand.

As we grow and develop, we form a self-image that may be accurate or inaccurate. We project that self-image to others, and more often than not, they respond to that *image,* not to the real person behind the image. As we mature, we revise our self-image from time to time on the basis of life experience, education, and feedback. If we accept input from others, we change our image periodically, sometimes correcting distorted projections. When we are comfortable with ourselves, we are said to be *congruent*—our external image of ourselves is in harmony with our inner feelings.

What has all this to do with corporate image? Well, we have many images of ourselves and of others. One of these is role image—for example, as father or mother, manager or executive. And this image must be reevaluated from time to time, if we expect to remain relevant in our situations and to obtain expected responses from those we deal with. It is the same with an organizational image (which will be discussed further in Chapter 7). As times and conditions change, corporations, government agencies, and other associations should update the images they project to the public at large. This is vital, for it is related to the system's sense of self, and it is expressed in organizational philosophy and rationale. After all, as the corporation matures, its multidimensional organizational impressions must be reviewed and revised in order to strengthen its identity and to project a strong image. In a global marketplace many companies' activities are constrained and are less effective because their executives have too narrow or too provincial a view of the firm and its future.

Just as people can have identity crises as they grow and face life's turning points, so too can organizations. These turning points or crises are challenges to grow or regress, and they are experienced by collections of people formed into that entity called an organization. The public utilities industry is experiencing an institutional crisis. Many gas and electric companies have confused their sense of identity and their purpose. Prior to the 1950s in the United States, such firms were well accepted by the populace, esteemed for services rendered, and rarely questioned in their corporate activities, except by the quiescent public utilities commissions. As public consciousness, information, and fear have grown, the utilities have begun to be challenged by environmental and ecological groups on their management decisions about the construction of nuclear and other power plants; by the poor and by senior citizens about the astronomical rise in utility rates; and by young adults who consider the activities and advertising of the average utility irrelevant and wasteful. In a postindustrial world of inflation and energy shortages, power utilities are in a struggle to regain a new sense of identity and to project a more suitable organizational image.

The corporate image needs to be redesigned and recommunicated continuously, and that is a primary management responsibility. Currently, we have an organizational image of ultrastability or continuous change—an energy exchange system constantly engaged in internal and external transactions. In contrast to industrial-age organizations, which sought stability in their structure and processes, metaindustrial systems build change and flexibility into the organizational culture. Such an approach expects a situation of continuous change, ambiguity, and uncertainty, so coping mechanisms for instability are part of normal operations in high-performing organizations. This picture, described by Don Fabun, seems more appropriate to metaindustrial corporations in the new technologies fields:

> A more recent way of looking at corporations is to consider them as energy exchange systems in which there is an input of energy from the

environment, and a patterned internal activity that transforms the energy into output, which in turn provokes a new energy input. The corporation is thus seen as an open system engaged in constant transactions with its environment, which can be visualized as a system of systems. These systems include the subsystems within the corporations (divisions, departments) which are constantly engaged in energy exchanges, and the systems operating outside the corporation, but affecting it—other members of the same industry, members of competing industries, suppliers, governmental institutions, etc. The energy exchanges—transactions—that take place both internally and externally occur in a field of force (visualized ... as a magnetic field) operating in space/time and made up of all the patterned but individual desires and aspirations of all the people who make up both internal and external environmental systems. This way of looking at a corporation offers a picture that is fairly close to modern physical theory and one which should be capable of expression and measurement in scientific, quantitative terms.

Managers seeking to apply this image to their individual companies should consider human energy as one dimension of the energy exchange provided through the organization. Every facet of the management process can be redefined in terms of human energy, both physical and psychic, and what leaders are doing to use it effectively or to waste it. Let's take eight key responsibilities of management and revise our role images in this way:

1. *Leadership:* The generation of energy, human and natural, toward achieving organizational goals.
2. *Motivation.* The directing of energizing forces toward personal/organizational goals and objectives.
3. *Communication.* An exchange of energy between persons and groups.
4. *Change.* The altering of energy priorities for the individual or the institution.
5. *Planning.* The setting of new priorities for energy use.
6. *Control.* Management and record keeping of energy effort.
7. *Conflict.* Disagreement over energy use; should be used and channeled rather than being permitted to undermine effort.
8. *Reward.* Confirmation and reinforcement* of proper energy use.

* Based on the psychological research of B. F. Skinner, *positive reinforcement* is a systematic procedure for reinforcing desired behavior, or rewarding right

With an image of a corporation as an energy exchange system, management would be concerned about minimizing dysfunctional energy and maximizing cooperative energy for the improvement of productivity, morale, and service. Such an image could pervade corporate philosophy and practice. Management might then be more sensitive to the quality of the work environment and its pollution. It might focus more on waste of human energy, especially on the underutilization of creative people, give more priority to the development of human resources, and counter the dissipation of human assets. Management might then insist that corporate planning emphasize the intelligent use of employee energy, that organizational communications be more open and circular, that conflict be confronted and used to improve performance. Management might then use imagination and innovation in job redesign and enrichment, in insisting on people maintenance programs to balance plant maintenance efforts. Human energy conservation programs comparable to those for natural energy might be launched so that unemployed minorities and the poor are not permitted to deteriorate in the community and women would be given equal opportunities for growth and compensation in organizations.

TRANSFORMING ORGANIZATIONAL IDENTITY AND SPACE

The preceding observations can do much to help an organization obtain a new sense of itself. Before redefining corporate identity, there is another aspect of organizational culture to be considered. It is the matter of corporate space, both physical and psychological. Our concept of space is relative, culturally influenced, and multidimensional. For example, an organization's physical space can be considered in terms of its property, buildings, and facilities—the three-dimensional expanse that its objects occupy on the earth, or in the atmosphere above or beneath the surface of the planet. Or the organizational space might be thought of in

---

actions. The rewards may be psychological, physical, or financial, but they are regularly bestowed in a positive manner. Negative reinforcement is avoided. Sometimes called behavior management or operant conditioning, positive reinforcement is a form of behavior modification that can be used successfully with patients and prisoners to change antisocial or destructive behavior as well as with the average person to increase performance and stimulate achievement. Since culture conditions us, this is an attempt to plan the conditioning in a positive manner for more productive results.

terms of its "territory" or "turf"—its markets, its customers, its spheres of influence. Or it might be thought of in terms of relations, a network of connections between the corporation and people, organizations, or objects, such as a unique product line related to certain mineral or natural resources.

The organization seeks to preserve a sense of distance, or uniqueness, between itself and others, especially those companies in a similar industry. To preserve its institutional territoriality, and to distinguish itself from its competitors, a corporation may go to great lengths to delineate its boundaries. Human systems separate themselves from larger environments by establishing physical or psychological barriers between internal and external activities. A company may do this by developing a unique vocabulary. (A hospital accomplishes this through medical terminology and jargon. The computer industry has set itself apart by giving new meaning to words like software and hardware, and by adopting such terms as systems architecture, systems package, data and word processing, and information handling.) In addition, within the organizational space, groups may delineate a subterritory. This may be a professional specialization, like marketing or manufacturing, or it may be a department, a division, or a subsidiary.

The corporation sets these space boundaries to protect the system's identity and integrity, and to avoid being absorbed by the environments outside itself. When a merger or acquisition takes place and two distinct organizational cultures are integrated, the issue of corporate philosophy and space becomes critical. When Pan American Airways took over National Airlines, the latter lost its identity, and its space was absorbed into the larger carrier. Because Pan Am did not carefully plan for the cultural integration of the two systems, it went into a financial crisis and had to sell off its profitable Intercontinental Hotel unit.

Organizational boundaries are set up to delineate not only the physical corporate environment but the psychological environment as well, which also sets the system apart from other systems. Even though the U.S. Marine Corps is a part of the Department of Navy, it retains an ambiance of its own. So too with the auto industry; General Motors and Ford have different psychological spaces, despite the fact they are in the same basic business and even have their headquarters together in Detroit.

The importance of this psychological environment has been recognized by the high-tech firms, while the mature corporations often ignore it and emphasize plant maintenance over people maintenance. Probe the implications of this observation by Apple Computer's Mike Markkula: "My basic understanding is that if you took all the people out of buildings, what you have is a bunch of buildings. The company's worth nothing without these people." Obviously, executives of this type are concerned with the organization's psychological space.

Some organizations provide a space that is relaxed, informal, and comfortable. Their people are productive and the organization considers them important. Others offer a work environment that is stressful, overly rigid, and highly materialistic. Their people are not important; making money is all-important. Many traditional industries now in trouble have mechanistic work environments that alienate workers.

Today, especially in highly technical environments, work space is becoming humanized. In Europe and the United States the trend is away from the assembly-line approach to organizational life. There are widespread experiments in restructuring plants through the use of more autonomous work groups, quality-of-worklife studies, and job enlargement or enrichment programs. Other alterations in work space include more decentralization, participative management, and greater emphasis on organizational and team camaraderie. It is not enough for management to concern itself with the work space from the viewpoint of health and safety. Renewal of older industries or corporations will not happen if efforts are limited to improving ventilation and factory appearance or curbing excessive noise, or by introducing new equipment.

Management must direct its attention to involving workers in the improvement of the company's psychological environment. The metaindustrial firms place less emphasis on executive space, such as privileged dining rooms or parking areas. The high-tech environment puts more emphasis on professional competence and ingenuity.

The rapid introduction of office automation, computers, word processors, and other forms of telecommunications is drastically altering the work space. Some personnel are already working out of their homes because of such advances, and a new type of supervision is being developed for these off-site workers with a different sense of organizational space. Electronic connections and networking are radically changing our whole sense of work space.

Many observers of the contemporary work scene believe that this new industrial revolution will focus more on people, because we will be freed from drudgery and have time as managers to consider employee needs and aspirations when designing work systems. The increasing use of robots not only alters the work space, but brings new opportunities for the smaller number of knowledge workers left in the factory or plant environment. Perhaps we can now design work environments that offer more creative use of human energy and more joy for the inhabitants of that organizational space. Furthermore, the intelligent use of both physical and psychological space within a corporation not only affects productivity and performance, it influences many management decisions. These range from where to locate offices and what to show visitors, to where to hold training sessions and the security provisions in areas containing dangerous substances. This dimension of organizational culture also applies to giving up space, as in plant closings or when a reorganization requires cutting back on allocations or units.

There is also a concept of *invisible space* within an organization, which is more than the intangibles of spirit or atmosphere. Informal and collateral organizations and work arrangements exist that appear nowhere on the organization charts. They are vortexes of power about which top management is sometimes unaware. They are often centered around talented persons who do not have titles of formal leadership. They are specialists, consultants, analysts, researchers, who cut across corporate lines and divisions and often prepare the organization for change in its microculture. Sometimes these informal, but vital, change makers are brought into the corporate space, as when a futures research unit is formally established. The formal organization designs the structure, sets the goals and missions, assigns roles and tasks, dictates rules and regulations. The informal organization creates the social environment so it can all work—it sets the tone and the "real" behavioral norms, provides the group recognition and the support to achieve. It is in the interaction between the formal and the informal organizations that the system and its people move forward. It becomes a beautiful place to work when corporate resources enable personnel to develop their own capacities, so that these personnel can enable the corporation to accomplish its mission. Corporate creativity is best expressed in an organizational environment that fosters both social and economic utility.

CAPSULE CONCLUSIONS

Organizational cultures can be transformed by the people in such systems to meet the metaindustrial challenge. Mere change in technology, processes, or marketing is insufficient. Fundamental alterations are needed in corporate philosophies with respect to why the organizations exist and by what principles they function. The new corporate rationale expresses contemporary concepts of work, the workers, and the work relationship; it must enunciate a new commitment to shared power and participative effort. The new managerial belief system espouses organizational norms that value innovation, candor, feedback, collaboration, and especially competence. In such a context, priority is given to the promotion of synergy in corporate activities and team approaches in management activities. Also the corporate attitude is futuristic; it appreciates planned change, long-term forecasting, and decision making.

With such a philosophy, a corporation can create and project a consistent organizational image that gives it both a unique identity and cohesion. Then human energy can be transformed into meaningful and creative efforts for global benefit. Then the private world of the corporation can positively influence the public world of society. Then the corporation appreciates its social responsibility, so that it combines the maximizing of profits with the enrichment of the quality of life.

The emerging world corporation needs what Canadian consultant Paul Rubinyl refers to as "global management"—the ability to effectively direct, integrate, and control large, complex human and mechanical systems. Such a reorientation to corporate leadership requires a systems approach; that is, an integrated system of interacting and interdependent components.

Perhaps when there is a greater sharing of organizational and management philosophies across macrocultures, a synergy will occur that will enable us to develop management systems that are truly global in scope and content. Then we may be ready for the industrialization of outer space through *supranational* planetary organizations!

CHAPTER 4 Changing Corporate Purposes and Standards

Back in 1958 a little-known Ohio bank got a new CEO who proposed a new goal for the institution. John D. McCoy asked the board of directors to spend 3 percent of each year's profits on research and development. Some of the directors were puzzled as to why a bank needed research, but they agreed to the request. A new mission emerged, and it led also to the adoption of a behavior norm for the organization called "innovate," which values creative solutions. As a result, Banc One is one of the most advanced financial institutions in the United States. It became the holding company of 25 affiliates, *Bank One*, throughout the state; the parent company has also acquired a 30-acre data processing center outside of Columbus. This single-bank holding firm is ranked among the top four in the nation in return on assets.

One of Banc One's innovations was with Bank of America, which now uses Banc One as a clearinghouse for its national credit card system. As the third-largest credit card processor, Banc One serves 160 financial institutions. It also became the first financial organization to install cash-dispensing automatic tellers, and joined with Merrill Lynch's Cash Management Account (CMA) to provide banking services. Money-fund customers are thus allowed to write checks or use their VISA cards against CMAs with brokerage houses. With nearly 400,000 accounts the CMA business is now worth $25 billion, and it is spreading to other brokerage firms.

Banc One's pioneering efforts are being cloned in the industry—an industry that is being revolutionized by one company's leadership. McCoy's latest venture into the financial future is the bank-at-home business, so that customers can pay bills through a computer terminal hooked up to their television sets. Bankers throughout the world now come to Columbus, Ohio, to study the pace-setting systems of Banc One. This actual case underscores the importance of corporate *goals, values, and norms* in helping a company to be successful.

As in society at large, human behavior in organizations is usually goal-oriented. Within the unique environment of a corporation, agency, or association, behavior is normatively regulated. That is, it is based on the values of that human system; thus standards for performance are established. Yet these behavioral goals, values, and norms are a product of culture. First, they reflect the external macroculture of a particular people at a particular time and place. Thus, in North America today, a manufacturing firm resonates not only its country's particular culture, but twentieth-century industrial culture. A multinational corporation's manager operating abroad communicates a culturally biased set of objectives, priorities, and standards that may or may not be in tune with the host culture. A manager in the international market also conveys the corporation's internal culture.

Each of us transmits a unique perception of reality—my world, your world. The enterprises with which we are affiliated influence that perception. Therefore, as Rhinesmith reminds us, both our macrocultures and our microcultures condition the manager concerning:

Nature orientations—the relationship of the human being to nature, or whether we are to control and influence the physical world around us, or live in harmony with nature....
Temporal orientations—our perception of time, its importance, and the emphasis to be placed on past, present, and future....
Abstract-concrete orientations—the ability to translate ideas and conceptualizations into pragmatic results and benefits that are quantifiable or measurable; the emphasis to be placed on seeking concrete outcomes and empirical evidence in contrast to concerns for intellectualization, quality of life, moral principles, or spiritual implications....
Unlimited/limited goods orientations—the amount of goods or resources (e.g., physical comforts, needs satisfaction, friendships, relationships) that can be supplied to one's pursuit or problem. Is it unlimited or limited energy? Some cultures would hold that through hard work anything can be attained. Other cultures believe that goods and resources are allocated or proportionate.

These four cultural orientations explain somewhat why corporate goals, values, and norms are so highly influenced by national culture. In the global marketplace, a Japanese or a Chinese business might have objectives, priorities, and standards that puzzle its North American or European competitors or suppliers, and vice versa. Organizational self-perception, culturally influenced, affects answers to such critical questions as: (1) Why does this corporation exist and whom does it serve? (2) What is important in the corporate environment? (3) What is acceptable corporate behavior and appropriate performance by members?

TRANSFORMING ORGANIZATIONAL GOALS AND POLICIES

A Dutch conglomerate coped with the trials of Nazi occupation to become one of the leading multinationals in the field of electronics. From Eindhoven, the N. V. Philips holding company has spread across the world, and its trade name has become a household word. What are the goals of such an enterprise? In his biography, company chairman Frederik Philips provided some inkling of them when he wrote that industry provides an opportunity for people to work in teams and without endless tensions, and that the purpose of industry is to serve the community of which it is a part. With that as a context, he sat down with company social affairs people in 1969 and drafted a document about which they sought feedback from industrialists and unionists. In 1975 this resulted in a statement of corporate purpose, which the Philips board of management adopted as the guidelines of the company's aims. It includes such ideas as these:

The industrial enterprise fulfills an important economic and social role in society. Its primary function consists in the production of goods and the provision of services. It thereby creates employment and income and opportunity for personal development for the many people in and outside the enterprise. The market economy in which it operates is a stimulus to the development of new products and techniques and new forms of organization. Its research, geared to the possibilities of the future, contributes to the scientific potential of society. All these factors have enabled the industrial enterprise to have a positive influence on the growth of prosperity and well-being.

From such a premise, the Philips people then developed basic goals for their own enterprise, which include such concepts as the ensuring of continuity through profitability; the company's responsibilities toward employees, including optimal use of talent; safety and security; adequate information to promote two-way communication; relations with society and others outside the organization, including social development. From such considerations, executives create corporate policy—the course of action and procedures to achieve objectives. Thus another dimension of organizational culture is manifest.

Essentially, human systems translate their organizational philosophy or ideology into goals and objectives that energize member performance. But such statements of purposes constantly need reevaluation and revision, lest they get locked into the past and become irrelevant. Many businesses today have goals and objectives appropriate for the disappearing industrial culture. Their missions are out of touch with social, economic, and technological changes. Their corporate aims are based on an obsolete view of the world and capitalism—the old culture of consumption, acquisitive materialism, and exploitation of the environment. These companies need to come to terms with the postindustrial reality and develop new conceptualizations of their purpose and functions. Carl Madden suggests that corporations need to be:

Dedicated to what might be called "humanistic capitalism" pursuing limited but well-defined social and economic purposes, developing measures of social and economic costs and benefits, and making profits distributed to a very wide group of owners, far wider than today, with a much more responsive process for the exercise of management trusteeship.

For metaindustrial organizations, it is important to formulate synergistic goals and objectives—that is, socially responsible purposes that consider the needs of people and their environment, and that promote the common good of the organization and its employees, as well as of the consumers and the community. This means that corporate aims should be emphasizing cooperation and collaboration within and without the organizational culture.

The research of James E. Post of Boston University suggests three coping patterns in corporate policy setting: (1) *adaptive*, which emphasizes organizational reaction to external events, (2) *proactive*, which is an attempt to initiate changes in, to alter, or to moderate some of the effects of the prevailing environment, and (3) *interactive*, which recognizes that corporate purposes and practices are both changing and should be in harmony with the trends in the external culture. Today, corporations must formulate multiple purposes to fit a multinational and multicultural market. To sell the world, metaindustrial planners cannot afford to be enthnocentric; their outlook must be cosmopolitan. Goal setting should reflect diversity and decentralization, while seeking unifying principles or themes in complex organizations. The following list summarizes ten corporate objectives for organizational survival and development drawn from the stated purposes of two firms in tune with postindustrial reality—Hewlett-Packard in the high-technology field and Dayton-Hudson Corporation in retailing. From these illustrations of William Ouchi, a synthesis of metaindustrial objectives can be ascertained.

1. To achieve sufficient profit to grow and effectively utilize our resources, while satisfying shareholders' concerns for return on investments.
2. To provide quality, reliable, and profitable service (and/or products) to customers which satisfy their needs, while gaining their loyalty.
3. To share our success and profits with employees as consensus is attained relative to the most acceptable means for this, based on recognized performance and accomplishment.
4. To manage in a fiscally responsible and creative way, utilizing initiative and the latest management processes and technologies.
5. To innovate in new fields and endeavors when we can make a profit and a technical or social contribution.
6. To provide personnel with personal and professional growth opportunities through meaningful work, study, and career experience.
7. To exercise corporate citizenship in the community in a manner that is socially responsible and responsive for the mutual benefit of all.
8. To be alert to changing consumer needs, intelligence, and feedback.
9. To cooperate with industry peers, civic and government agencies, universities, and other social institutions to improve the environment in which we all function.
10. To operate in the global marketplace with cultural sensitivity to differences in human needs and perceptions, development and adaptations, while striving to improve the human condition.

Mature industries use behavioral scientists to help them plan systems renewal, particularly with reference to goals, values, and norms. Such organization development technology is employed by either internal or external consultants to assist industrial-age organizations in coping with rapid transitions. Metaindustrial organizations use professional futurists and technological forecasters to help them get a fix on the decades ahead, to better ascertain probable alterations in their markets, products, and services. Then they make adjustments in their corporate goals. Theirs is a long-range horizon based on future environmental scanning. Whether they use a nearby university futures studies center or an internal futures research division, they examine tomorrow's corporate environment. The following is a profile of future-oriented organizations that fine-tune their culture to anticipate new realities.

Focus Issues
- New interpretations of fundamental concepts regarding changing families, quality of worklife, work ethics, transitional management, etc.
- Future values that may be most different from today.
- Impact interrelationships as trend indicators of future crises, markets, etc.
- World trade interdependences that may spawn new cooperative services, merger possibilities, collaborative research, etc.
- Decisions today that could shape the future.

Organizational Culture
- Philosophy of active anticipation and systematic design of the corporate future.
- Image of the corporation as a subsystem in a macro environmental system, with which it is interdependent.
- Atmosphere that encourages and accommodates exploration and experimentation.
- Management that is oriented to the future and that values planning for change.
- Norms that confirm innovation, flexibility, and long-range views.
- Processes and methods for early warning systems, forecasting, and assumptions' revisions.

Futuristic Technologies
- Trend monitoring: identify trend, track its progress, and alert management about significant shifts.
- Long-range forecasting: projection studies of industry thrusts and developments; monitoring likelihoods by extrapolation, econometrics, demographics, and simulation model building.
- Impact evaluations: in terms of current trends and long-range forecasts by technology assessments or environmental impact studies.
- Image creation: imagining alternative futures for the corporation by means of scenario building.
- Change mechanisms: design, implementation, and evaluation of continuous change processes that facilitate corporate adaptation to possible, probable, and preferable business futures (e.g., force field analysis methodology for assessing driving/resisting forces for/against a change).

Interestingly, a corporation based in Western culture is more likely to be futuristic than one in an Oriental or Middle Eastern culture and to value change and futures studies. Some examples of future-oriented company efforts are: (1) General Electric's 30-year study entitled "The Future of the Business Environment" into the year 2000 and its periodic follow-ups, (2) Security Pacific National Bank's report: "2000: Tomorrow Begins Today," which examined early warning signals in a growing world, American mobility and prosperity, changing life/work/house styles, and tomorrow's scenario for business and the electronic information society, (3) the Diebold Group's emerging social issues program and automated office program for its *Fortune* 500 company clients, and (4) Sears, Roebuck's "Monitoring and Forecasting System" to minimize future risks by examining external forces that have an impact on the business they are in, the mix they sell, their customers, the geographic areas in which they sell, the ways in which they sell, and the markets to which they sell.

Even the U.S. Chamber of Commerce, under Chief Economist Carl Madden, issued reports through its Council on Trends and Perspectives. In 1969, it forecast dramatic alterations in the industrial world as entire new industries came into being based on technological advances, services, and human needs. And in the 1980s, businesses were founded on high technology, space technology, and genetic and medical technologies. The Chamber of Commerce accurately predicted the challenges business would face with the emergence of the postindustrial society. One wonders how many of its members listened and altered their goals, values, and norms as a result of this prophetic information.

Some firms provide futuristic input into the organization through professional or trade associations. The corporation may send representatives to special conferences or seminars and bring back reports and other information that influence organizational goals, values, and norms. One such example is the Third General Assembly of the World Future Society in Toronto, Canada, which included many corporate executives and consultants. It produced in 1980 a conference volume, *Through the 80s—Thinking Globally, Acting Locally* (available from the World Future Society Book Service, 4916 St. Elmo Avenue, Washington, D.C. 20014). Similarly, Omicron, The Center for Systems Humanics (202 Johnson Road, Morris Plains, New Jersey 07950) held a conference in May 1982 for information scientists and professionals from *Fortune* 500 companies on the themes of the metaindustrial work culture and the information technology environment. The insights which senior management gains from such exchanges will eventually be translated into changes in corporate purposes and standards.

In summary, a future-oriented corporation is both goal-oriented and people-centered. It values informality, intimacy, collaboration, and flexibility. Its norms encourage participative decision making, readiness to change, creative risk taking, supportive power use, learning from failure, authentic and open communication. Its goals reflect the system's philosophy and rationale, respond to new knowledge, perceptions, and needs, and retranslate themselves into new policies, strategies, objectives, and targets. Its values express a unique view of the world and external reality. They emphasize what is important by setting priorities, extrapolating on the basis of changes and shifts in society, its industry, and markets. Finally, goals, values, and norms interact to energize personnel behavior.

TRANSFORMING ORGANIZATIONAL VALUES AND NORMS

All humans value certain qualities, experiences, things, and people. Their values stem from their needs system and reflect their private world and life experience. Some of these values, whether known or unknown to the individual, get translated into attitude and behavior patterns. Thus the person who values sports or cultural activities devotes much time and energy to such undertakings. People in groups and organizations develop a collective value system that influences member behavior. These institutional priorities not only produce actions but affect those individuals and institutions who interface with that organization.

The values and norms of an organization echo those of its macroculture. A Latin American or African firm, for example, might place emphasis on family relationships and loyalties, so important in their native cultures. Family connections might therefore become a factor in the firm's recruitment, selection, training, and promotion policies. Corporate values and norms pervade every aspect of managerial activity from planning, organizing, and controlling to leading, communicating, and problem solving.

Organizational needs determine the values or priorities in operations in order to ensure that entity's survival and development. After the creation of a corporation, for instance, a value system gradually emerges regarding the customs, practices, and activities that corporate persons esteem. Whether positive or negative, written or unwritten, these measures of worth have a powerful influence on employee behavior. They determine the relative merit attached to working hard, doing one's duty, observing the rules, teamwork, reliability, customer service, and other value indicators. This value system and its maxims are reinforced by established standards for worker behavior and performance. Such norms may be found in managerial guidelines, personnel manuals, performance criteria, union contracts, work conventions, and so forth. Adherence or resistance to them affects job retention, career development, profitability, and even organizational excellence. The corporate values and norms are evident not only in member behavior but also in company slogans, mottos, logos, and other communication symbols.

The importance of values and norms within society is the subject of the following astute comment by business school deans K. Black and R. O. Wilson in their analysis of the impact of science on culture:

> It is ... the scientific revolution that is changing people's beliefs about what is valuable. People's values ... are centered in their culture. When a culture is challenged by change, the group's population is checked and the culture is fragmented or a new culture is developed. Social change, as the anthropologist sees it, is inherent in the basic fabric of civilization. There are special situations known as "culture crises." Our present culture crisis is associated with the breakdown of the existing industrial world view in the face of new knowledge.

To illustrate the impact of changing values on the organization, let us examine the traditional value of honesty. During the industrial age, there has been an erosion of that value in terms of increasing employee theft. But in a knowledge society, the integrity of personnel requires innovative standard-setting and security systems. In the metaindustrial work scene, computer and information theft and misappropriation take on completely new dimensions with staggering implications. In 1981, Burns International Security Services estimated that of 2,000 computer thefts, only 15 percent of the crimes were detected by employers. In Silicon Valley, stolen chips have become a hot item, often with the collusion of organization members. The very small size of these bits of silicon, the brains of the computer, make them a target for thieves both internal and external. In one holiday weekend, 498,000 chips worth $2.7 million were stolen from Sunnyvale's Monolithic Memories. Does the laid-back, open atmosphere of some of the California high-tech firms make them vulnerable? Should the corporation develop approaches that encourage employees to be more protective of valuable hardware and software? Can an ex-

Changing Corporate Purposes and Standards 63

amination of values in the metaindustrial work culture delimit such crime without destroying the sense of trust and colleagueship?

There is even a fringe of people in computer technology who have become addicted by their machine, so amoral and alienated from people that they take it as a game to defraud, misinform, or steal data. Cracking computer codes is considered legitimate. Corporations and industries will have to join together to confront such misuse of computer power and to protect privacy and trade rights or property. Employees should be included in any new expression of such values, while issues of morality, the rights of others, and the common good are considered more in in-service training. Rewarding and reinforcing both honesty and integrity helps. Developing profiles of deviancy in the high-technology culture may be useful. Reevaluations of traditional values, standards, and security approaches are in order.

Behavioral scientists in this century have been studying the implications of ongoing social changes for organizational culture. A summary of their research is provided here with the trends moving from the left column to the right:*

Social Values

- Property ownership to guarantee individual rights.
- Product orientation, and rights of manufacturer.
- Limited government when market mechanisms fail or are nonexistent.

- Membership/cooperatives—social legislation guarantees rights.
- Community orientation—needs of common good and consumers.
- Increasing government intervention—regulations and public programs.

Human Values

- All people are alike—workload is structured and everyone shares it equally.
- Rugged individualism—emphasis on individual success, income, status.

- All people are different—capitalize on particular abilities, characteristics, and potential.
- Participation — achievement through teamwork and participative management or group endeavor.

* Amplification of the research of Eric Trist by professors Gordon Lippitt and Cornelius Brevoord.

- Economic production and performance emphasis, work ethic.
- Educational elites and ignorant masses; learning limited to upper classes.

- Self-realization through personal and professional development; quality-of-life emphasis.
- Lifelong education for all who seek it; knowledge society with better-educated populations and higher expectations.

Work Values

- Loyalty to the organization — seek achievement through opportunities it offers.
- Self-control on the job; obey rules and follow directions of superiors.
- Independence — everything depends on own hard work and efforts.
- Endure your lot.

- Self-actualization through a professional or trade affiliation, with loyalty to oneself and peers.
- Self-expression and -regulation, partially realized through team participation and consensus.
- Interdependence — personal goals can best be achieved through cooperation and collaboration with others.
- Enjoy your life.

To keep organizations relevant and to counteract institutional obsolescence, leaders must take into account such social trends. In this era of transition, there is a clash between the industrial and metaindustrial views of reality and appropriate human behavior. Thus a continuing revision of goals, values, and norms is necessary to ensure people's adherence. Managers lose credibility if they are locked into an industrial mindset where they decry the decline of the traditional work ethic while upholding the value of unlimited competition. Such an administrator still believes in total loyalty to the organization, but is confused by a new breed of workers with a different set of values. Maintaining an archaic value system in a changing social setting is a questionable posture. It can distort perspective on the importance and potential of a particular process, technology, or piece of equipment, as well as on what qualities to seek in new hires or for promotion.

A future-oriented leader struggles to continually update both self and associates on attitudes, perceptions, and values in order to make timely business decisions and carry on productive organizational relations. Such a manager tries to stay in touch with the real issues behind social change. In particular he tracks what is happening in the thinking and actions of today's youths who are tomorrow's workers.

The revolution in values in society at large is reflected in changing organizational cultures. The disappearing industrial culture valued efficiency, diligence, orderliness, punctuality, frugality, and honesty. To find out the values of today's workers in the U.S., the Opinion Research Corporation (Princeton, New Jersey) surveyed 175,000 employees in 159 companies from 1950 through the 1970s. Among the findings, these researchers discovered that in general employees seek (1) opportunity for advancement, (2) a feeling of being respected by the company, (3) confirmation that the company listens and responds adequately, (4) a sense that the company treats one fairly, (5) and on-the-job satisfaction of self-esteem needs facilitated by the company.

For metaindustrial managers who wish to ensure that their corporate values and norms are in harmony with contemporary employee needs and values, there is a powerful message here. The industrial-age workers' focus may have been on lower levels of the human needs hierarchy—seeking satisfaction of physical and security needs. Since values or priorities flow from needs, it is becoming clear that the needs of postindustrial employees are centered more in the self-esteem and ego areas. Recent college graduates indicate that they seek intrinsic satisfaction from their work and expect adequate financial compensation in the process. Corporations should recognize these new realities and design work environments that satisfy changing employee needs and values. Many of the high-technology firms have proved they can succeed by doing just that!

Metaindustrial organizations value employee input and do not believe that all the wisdom resides in management. Not only do they favor group decision making, they seek out employee and consumer ideas, attitudes, and opinions by means of survey instruments, opinion polling, and other forms of human factor data gathering. This information is then analyzed, reviewed with management and employee representatives, and then used in the formation of new strategies, norms, and policies. Many high-performing companies are learning to use the high-achieving employees to diagnose organizational health and to solve persistent personal problems. Formalizing this process into a performance management workshop with top performers on videotape has been found to be a powerful feedback mechanism to management and to create new norms of top performance. The participants become behavior models to average workers when their videotapes are used in the training of others.

Behavioral scientists have done significant research in the last part of this century on the importance of group norms. Whether behavior is appropriate or inappropriate in an organization is largely determined by group standards. Whether employees cooperate or compete, perform effectively or ineffectively, innovate or maintain the status quo—all can be traced to organizational norms. What a corporation sets out in personnel directives or union contracts as general behavior standards gets reinterpreted, reinforced, or rejected by the subsystems within the operation. Managers and members of departments, divisions, and subsidiaries may carry out or undermine such organizational guidelines and even develop their own unique group norms to regulate their own behavior. Nadler, Hackman, and Lawler suggest applying the term *norm* only to overt behavior—what people do or say about their attitudes, beliefs, and performance. They characterize norms in terms of the *amount* of a given behavior exhibited by members and the *degree* of approval or disapproval that members attach to the behavior. Their research shows that groups with high social needs can develop and enforce norms that facilitate or obstruct productivity. Managers would be well advised, then, to ensure that the design of work affords satisfying social interaction, that positive group performance is rewarded, and that the group is related to as a social unit.

The importance of values and norms in organizational culture, as well as the need to revise them periodically, is seen in the experience of the Amdahl Corporation, a computer manufacturer based in Sunnyvale, California. Recently, Amdahl has enjoyed a boom that is impressive even by the standards of this volatile industry: In 1976 it had 770 employees and revenues of $92 million. In 1978 it had 3,000 employees and revenues of $320 million.

As Amdahl's sales of computers soared, so did its demand for semiconductor chips. Early on, it bought chips from two suppliers—Motorola and Advanced Memory Systems (AMS). Amdahl required a custom-designed chip and tried to convince both suppliers that they would quickly recoup the costs of retooling for production. AMS chose instead to get out of the business, and Amdahl looked elsewhere for a second supplier. "If AMS had stayed with us, our purchases from them would be equal to their entire sales at the time they abandoned the business," commented Amdahl's chairman, Gene White. "But they couldn't wait." So the new supplier who enjoyed the surge in business was a Japanese firm.*

At the heart of this critical incident is a corporate value based on short-term planning and profits versus long-term planning. It also involves inadequate risk venture norms on the part of AMS. Unlike its Japanese competitor, AMS apparently did not value creative risk taking, nor did it have regard for long-range profitability. These are two essential qualities for corporate success in a complex postindustrial world.

The values and norms which are emphasized in the meta-industrial organization and its work culture appear to be the following: quality work, productive behavior, competent performance, creative risk taking, team entrepreneurship, profitable service, participation, power sharing, collaboration, flexibility, innovation, ultrastability, long-term perspectives, R & D emphasis, informality or nonhierarchy, and sensitivity. The sensitivity is to the human aspects of technology; to community concerns, especially about ecology; and to cross-cultural factors in both the market and workplace. These terms are self-explanatory except for "ultrastability," which we previously defined—coping mechanisms in a system or lifestyle that provides for continuous change, uncertainty, and ambiguity, while we learn to deal with relativity and instability.

CAPSULE CONCLUSIONS
Changes under way in macrocultures are the driving forces for alterations within microcultures. In the United States, for example, there has been a dramatic shift in this postindustrial period to a service economy, which now employs almost 70 percent of the labor force. Traditional agriculture and manufacturing are rapidly being replaced by service industries for everything from information processing and communication to education and retailing. For the profit-making corporation, such trends imply changes not only in functions and personnel but also in philosophy, goals, values, and norms. Corporate social responsibility and involvement are no longer extras; they are an essential part of doing business in these turbulent times. David Rockefeller put his finger on

* "American Industry: What Ails It, How to Save It," *Atlantic Monthly*, Sept. 1980.

this issue when he stated that business leaders "have no choice but to respond by becoming themselves reformers, making a conscious effort to adapt the market system to our changing social, political, and technological environment."

Such thinking by the former chairman of Chase Manhattan is not radical or unique. Walter Wriston, when he was chairman of Citicorp, commented that new ideas and values are not always welcome in society. He urged that world corporations become agents of change, not merely by erecting new facilities or introducing new processes, but by bringing new ideas and values into the community, such as upward mobility for all based on competence. Wriston praised the development of multinational managers who recognize that no profitable market can exist where poverty is a rule of life, that color, sex, and other traditional barriers to career development are obsolete and talent should be the only criterion, that a global perspective in business is essential because human and natural resources everywhere are interdependent. These corporate perceptions are indicative of the profound transition under way in business rationale, purposes, priorities, and standards.

This is the direction in which emerging metaindustrial organizations are moving. They are concerned about the ecology of both the social and the work environments, about improving the human condition both outside and inside the corporation with their products, services, and profits. Their company objectives, values, and norms reflect this understanding and commitment. Despite the growing introduction of automated systems and robots into an increasingly technological work culture, these metaindustrial managers want to improve the quality of life for those humans still left in their offices, plants, and facilities, as well as for the community affected by their innovations.

The metaindustrial organizational culture places high value on knowledge and information. They are viewed as vital resources and tools for communication, decision making, and institutional well-being. They contribute to the functioning of a more open society and to greater democracy in the workplace. This postindustrial corporate culture also values its people more, especially as assets to be capitalized on for their own benefit as well as for the benefit of the organization and the community. Instead of tolerating unemployment and underemployment, the new technological enterprises may become instruments for better utilization and channeling of human energy and creativity.

CHAPTER 5　Transforming Corporate Look and Style

An organization's culture can help to turn its people on or off. That is, it can energize personnel, so that they accomplish, achieve, and produce. Or it can undermine employee morale, so that they are apathetic, uninvolved, and unproductive. The trend today is toward a work atmosphere that is informal and friendly, as well as stimulating and meaningful.

CREATIVE CORPORATE ENVIRONMENTS
The high-technology firm epitomizes somewhat the new business environment—more flexible, less concerned with titles and the trappings of rank, managers and technicians who are low-key and modest, usually non-unionized, and comfortable with team approaches. These companies operate in a context that is technical and automated, and in a market that is internationally competitive and noted for volatile growth. Its people are energetic and entrepreneurial, as well as imaginative and creative.

Here we will elaborate on four aspects of creative corporate environments: physical appearance, psychological climate, personnel composition, and distribution of power.

Physical appearance. Industrial-age factories were known more for their utility than for their beauty. Often they were located in congested urban areas where they could attract the cheapest labor in the greatest numbers. In contrast, metaindustrial organizations seek out knowledge centers, often locating near universities and research facilities. They consider the quality of life that a particular community can offer to employees before deciding to locate there. When these plants are newly constructed, they often resemble a college campus. They are attractively designed and landscaped and they look like pleasant places to work. In the United States many corporations have moved out of congested urban areas to suburban or smaller communities. In the East they center around places like Armonk and Stamford, where one can view miracle miles of attractive facilities for *Fortune* 500 companies like IBM and Union Carbide. In the West they congregate in the Palo Alto area near Stanford University or in Southern California adjacent to the University of California-San Diego. They flock into beautiful industrial parks called Torrey Pines or Campus Point. Here, in charming locales, they erect or lease eye-catching buildings of glass, brick, or wood. Some, like General Atomic Corporation in La Jolla, offer a campus on a rolling hill with exercise facilities for employees that may include a pool or tennis court. Signal Companies and E. F. Hutton Insurance headquarters overlook the Pacific Ocean, providing a comfortable work atmosphere inside and out. Many of these alluring facilities house the companies of the future—those engaged in contract R&D, such as IVAC, Science Applications, Maxwell Laboratories, and Systems, Science and Software.

Local communities seek out the new "clean" businesses to emphasize the "lifestyle" advantages they can offer to knowledge workers and their families. The new businesses, often service- and information-oriented, seek pollution-free surroundings and are environmentally responsible. Their interior workplaces feature modern design, brilliant colors, greenery, as well as office automation. All in all, the physical look of the metaindustrial organization prompts a positive response from worker or visitor.

Psychological climate. More important than the changing physical appearance is the internal atmosphere of the postindustrial organization. The change is from mechanistic assembly-line formats to responsible, autonomous work teams. As Emily Coleman of AT&T has observed:

> The psychic emphasis of individuals in the work force is shifting. It is shifting from a negative, fear of want, to a positive—a "quality of work life"—in which employees can attain or maintain a self-image of responsibility for their lives and a distinction between what they are doing and what could be done by a machine.... Personal satisfaction and a sense of accomplishing something of importance to the enterprise, of a contribution made to which a person can point with pride, [are] coming to rival money and assigned status as individual incentives.

The metaindustrial organization's response to such personnel concerns ranges from introduction of more flexible work schedules to job sharing and networking. Some employees affiliate with the company by electronic connections and work out of their homes, while other have a consulting relationship. The climate in such corporate cultures encourages innovation and risk taking, as well as venture capital and experimentation. It reflects a management philosophy that believes material, financial, and human resources should be organized for both economic and social ends. Management is committed to providing organizational conditions and operational methods that enable people to achieve their own goals while contributing to the objectives of a productive enterprise.

Personnel composition. Diversity in the makeup of the workforce is characteristic in these new organizations. Women, minorities, and foreigners are very much in evidence at all levels of operations. Although fewer in number, personnel are more intelligent and better informed—competence is the only norm for inclusion. The new look in employees may also feature a wider age span. This may happen when the new corporations do not automatically force out seniors but instead make retirement a matter of choice and performance. Although the initial emphasis in the metaindustrial organization may be on technical personnel, it may draw increasingly on generalists and other professionals. In the quest for mission accomplishment both on this planet and in outer space, no ethnic, racial, or national group is excluded.

Distribution of power. The sharing of authority is another feature of the metaindustrial organization. This is most often accomplished through a team management approach or through problem-solving groups like the quality circles that have been established to increase productivity. A new balance is being struck between control and initiative. Competence is held in higher regard than rank or status. Increasingly, organizational power lies with those who have information and know how to use it intelligently. The participative corporate style extends to goal setting, decision making, and control, as well as to motivation, communication, and leadership. It enables women to get into the executive suite, and blacks and Hispanics to enter management. Power, when exercised, is based on the concepts of collaboration and reason, not coercion or threat.

The most significant force transforming organizational look and style today is people. Table 1 presents a profile of this metaindustrial knowledge worker to which corporations are responding, and by which they are being changed. When such persons

TABLE 1. Profile of metaindustrial knowledge workers.*

Characteristics	Competencies	Attitudes	Concerns
Professionals or career persons; single people and dual-career couples; primarily age 25–45	Highly media-educated and computer-oriented	Seek freedom of choice and control over life space; live for today	Self-fulfillment, talent utilization, physical appearance, and wellness or fitness
Median individual income of $18,000+; seeking identification through work roles	All with high school diplomas; most with one or more university degrees	Want instant gratification and conveniences, as well as high expectations of entitlements†	Instant cultural opportunities (from travel, arts, media, and gourmet experiences)
Motivated by involvement, responsibility, and meaningful work	Greater coping capabilities; more traveled and mobile, more environmentally aware and systems oriented	Relaxed toward work and seek leisure as form of compensation, as well as early retirement for second careers	Enhancement of quality of life; more personalized jobs and ad hoc work experiences or collaborative relationships

* I am grateful to the Futures Research Unit of Security Pacific National Bank in Los Angeles for some of the insights offered in this table.
† Workers feel entitled to benefits once viewed as an outcome of the collective bargaining process; what once was seen as a valuable fringe benefit is now considered an indispensable right.

move into leadership positions, they further alter the manner in which the company operates.

The new look in today's successful organizations is multidimensional. Inside, it offers a creative work environment. Outside, it demonstrates socioeconomic concerns. As Peter Drucker wisely commented, "The new demand is that business and business persons make concern for society central to the conduct of business itself. It is a demand that the quality of life become the business of business."

CHANGING ATTITUDES TOWARD APPEARANCE AND TIME AT WORK

In part, cultures can be studied in terms of the people's appearance and dress, as well as their time orientations. People set themselves apart by their garments and adornments or lack of same. With regard to time and time consciousness, macrocultures can be analyzed as to whether their sense of time is exact, casual, seasonal, or approximate by sunrise or sunset, and their planning long- or short-term. In a microculture such as the military, all this becomes evident by analysis of the uniforms and their special markings, or by noting the 24-hour system of telling time and the synchronization of watches. With respect to organizational culture, such factors contribute to the creation of a sense of organizational identity.

Traditions in the industrial work culture in these areas are gradually disappearing. Very careful rules and regulations were spelled out in personnel manuals. There were also unwritten customs regarding employee dress, appearance, and behavior. Some organizations still require uniforms, or business suits and ties for the males and dresses of specified lengths for the females. Many companies were concerned about the length of men's hair, or the wearing of company blazers or jackets, or the use of certain dress and equipment for safety or hygiene. Some professions may continue to distinguish themselves by their garb, such as the white medical smock. Other corporations maintain social distinctions by mandating that supervisors wear white shirts and ties, or that blue-collar employees wear certain work clothes. Obviously some jobs will continue to require a very specific clothing to prevent contamination or other injury. The banking industry has been famous for its unique code of dress—which has recently undergone much change. The impeccably dressed president of a large Manhattan bank tolerates the rumpled hair, sport shirt, tweed jacket with the elbow patches, and canvas shoes of the vice president of computer operations because he is very competent in his field and essential to the bank's operations. "Computer people are different—they talk mostly to machines. So in order to get his services, we had to relax our executive dress policy. As long as he stays away from the customers and provides us with accurate data, we can live with his dress deviations," said the bank president. That statement says a great deal about the changing work culture and its norms.

Metaindustrial organizations seem to be more colorful, diverse, relaxed, and casual in their approach to dress and the appearance of personnel. The unwritten rule seems to be *appropriateness*—wear what is comfortable for you and others in this work setting, as long as it is appropriate to the company environment. Knowledge workers, even at the executive level, are more egalitarian and collegial in their approach to one another. They resist having creativity and competence stifled by institutional pomp and structure, so metaindustrial companies make accommodations in such matters of dress and work schedules. In some board rooms of high-tech corporations even jeans are acceptable. Yet, after an entrepreneurial genius founded Atari and the video company got into financial trouble, a Harvard MBA-type was brought in to restore tight management practice and to see that revenue increased. One of his first acts was to reinstate business suits and ban casual dress.

During the postindustrial transition, there will be variations and fluctuations in dress, between the traditional and the "far out." The general trend in the work culture is toward a more comfortable, confident, creative environment. Dress will reflect that atmosphere, so flexibility is required. As we industrialize outer space, we can expect the twenty-first-century look to influence our earthly business and professional garb and adornments.

Our concept of time, of course, is relative. Managerial activities are influenced by the macroculture and its temporal orientations. In North America the emphasis is on the future and influencing it. In Asia a manager's perceptions of time may be cyclical or oriented to past traditions. Peoples undergoing rapid economic and technological development tend to be more present-oriented. Some organizational cultures place a high priority on promptness and preciseness, while others are more approximate in their time frames and target setting. A workday in the industrial culture is different from what it was during the agricultural period. The 15-hour factory day of the nineteenth century is now the twentieth-century eight-hour day. And the work week is down from 70 or 80 hours to 35 or 40.

A major study released in 1981 by the Work Institute of America predicts that by 1990, the standard work week in the United States will be 36 hours, and that 25 percent of the workers will be on flexible time schedules, in contrast to 10 percent today who enjoy that privilege. The institute further predicts that 28 percent of all workers will share work assignments with others, or voluntarily take part-time jobs. According to this same report, the unprecedented changes under way in American culture will alter not only family structure and workforce composition, but also the work schedule itself. By 1980, 10 million U.S. workers were already using some type of flexible work schedule and compressed work week. That is, they were putting approximately 40 hours into four days or less. Some firms have been experimenting with a 25-hour work week with two 12½-hour weekend shifts or two 12½-hour workdays. No wonder that Robert Zager, one of the directors of this Work Institute study, commented: "Employers have literally tossed out time clocks, shredded time cards, and are taking a whole new look at the old concept of employment."

Perhaps this is an idea whose time has come none too soon. Such an enlightened approach may help to cut down upon the annual $20 million time theft economists estimate occurs in the U.S. workplace. That is the projected cost of bored, underutilized, and badly managed workers who now steal time on the job for personal purposes.

In contrast, the metaindustrial organization permits some latitude relative to work time, allowing employees more freedom and initiative in setting their own work schedules. So long as they meet team objectives, they can design a work-time plan more in keeping with their personality and lifestyle. Such tolerance reduces stress between family and job, and makes time pressure at work more manageable. These organizations want talented personnel, so they allow time accommodations to obtain professionals who may be working mothers or part of a dual-career family, or who seek more leisure for personal and professional development.

Many high-tech firms report that their people are not clock watchers, that they think in terms of getting the job done well and reasonably on time. Many of them are so interested and involved in their work that the time devoted to it is greater than traditionally expected. The fine line between work and leisure time is eroding.

Advanced technological societies seem to be fast-paced. Young, bright managers are said to be on "the fast track." One attempt to curb stress and tension, while working more productively, is in the area of time management. Seminars and books help metaindustrial leaders to work smarter, faster, and better. Time management will assume more importance since the metaindustrial culture will provide us with less time on the job and more time for personal use. The challenge will be to use the personal time for growth and *re-creation*, developing untapped human potential.

Our sense of a day is also changing. From the agricultural workday of sunrise to sunset, we have moved to the 24-hour time span. People now work in shifts around the clock with the help of electric lighting and other modern conveniences. Space and computer use now demand a round-the-clock day, which may bring about a three- or four-work-shift approach. One problem is that so many economic, social, and recreational services are still locked into the 8-hour daytime work schedule. Just as banks have been extending business hours and offering round-the-clock automatic tellers, so too will government agencies, social services, and educational institutions have to become more time accommodating to meet the needs of metaindustrial workers.

Yet, the emergence of the 24-hour workday has its hazards. When we depart from the standard day work, shift work may lead to personal problems that include low job performance, ill health, and disruptions in family life. A new field of research called "chronobiology" investigates the daily rhythms on which human life operates. One of the pioneers of the field, Charles Ehret, a senior scientist at Argonne National Laboratory, has been studying the impact of shift work in the power industry.* He suspects that the interruptions of normal body rhythms by shift work may explain, in part, the problems of work crews involved in the Three Mile Island nuclear accident and a 1979 Western Airlines crash in Mexico City. Ehret believes that better shift rotations, improved eating patterns, and a better working environment can reduce such harmful effects. Workers permanently assigned to night shifts are especially prone to difficulties when their internal clocks

---

* *Los Angeles Times,* May 27, 1982.

are out of sync with their families and friends. Ehret advocates shift rotation by phase delay—one week of morning shift, one of afternoon shift, and a third of night—to adjust the internal clock more slowly. Such adjustments, plus employee guidance in chronohygiene, may help to humanize the metaindustrial workplace. A dehumanized work experience not only contributes to making the employee mentally dysfunctional, but undermines safety and productivity.

On the positive side, the information society will buy more time for individuals *to be*—that is, to pursue self-fulfilling goals and to become what they are capable of becoming. A new value and right are emerging in determining how one's time is to be used in the pursuit of such life-enhancing goals.

FOOD, FEEDING, AND FITNESS HABITS AT WORK

International executives and business representatives are well aware of the cultural differences around the world regarding food preparation, eating habits, and sense of bodily health. They are fascinated by the ways local people everywhere demonstrate their uniqueness in the selection, preparation, and presentation of food, and in their dining procedures. They take advantage of international cuisine everywhere, and swap stories about the feeding habits in foreign cultures. They are aware that one country's pet may be another's culinary delicacy, from dogs to ants. Since humans have learned to cope anywhere on this planet, their food preferences, cooking skills, eating utensils, and practices at table vary widely. So while managers overseas are usually aware that Europeans hold their forks differently from Americans, they may not be conscious of ethnic and minority food differences within their own society. While they may be aware that class and social status influence the dietary practices and beverage choices of labor and management, they often ignore the food dimension in organizational culture.

In industrial work culture, much emphasis was placed on the length of lunch and coffee breaks, where employees eat in contrast to where management eats, or even how they perform this ritual (e.g., eat "on the run," "brown bag" lunch and discussion, or "two martini lunches"). In mature companies, the number, care, and quality of fast-food and beverage dispensers, the condition of the lunchroom and allowances for overtime dining, and provisions for certain foods on the menu (from soul food to diet food) might become issues of union negotiation. Position in the organizational hierarchy has often been reinforced by type of eating facility, such as the executive dining room. Such cultural factors sometimes have a powerful influence on employee behavior and morale.

All this is changing in the metaindustrial work culture. High-tech firms resist structure and prefer informality, usually having one cafeteria where all personnel gather regardless of rank. While on a consulting assignment with The Western Company of North America, I witnessed the new trend. Corporate headquarters in Fort Worth, Texas, were modern, attractive, and comfortable; the tasteful dining area reflected the whole atmosphere in this petroleum supply and maintenance firm. When a breakfast meeting was scheduled with the chairman of the board, it was a welcome surprise to accompany Eddie Chiles, the millionaire and principal stockholder, through the cafeteria-style line. He and workers greeted each other in a warm and friendly manner. Increasingly the new corporate look extends from including health and natural foods on the company menu to displaying artworks and plants in the dining area. Music, wines, and even gourmet dishes may be available in corporate dining facilities these days. Time for food and drink is not grudgingly provided, but offered as a means of refreshment and as an opportunity for discussion with colleagues.

The old sage who held that a sound mind exists in a healthy body would find support for this belief in metaindustrial organizations. The personnel and medical staffs in such enterprises are concerned with reducing stress and improving safety for employees. The new look includes corporate preventive health, or wellness, plans. The new corporate attitude encourages fitness programs for all personnel. If it cannot provide facilities for exercise programs while at work, such corporations often pay for memberships in health spas and athletic clubs or allow company time for fitness endeavors. Rather than waste money on negative efforts to curb absenteeism or legislate sick leaves or provide extra hospitalization insurance, the new approach invests in positive and preventive efforts that keep employees physically and psychologically healthy and happy. New compassionate strategies may range from guidance on nutrition to saunas in the workplace. For people suffering from abuse of drugs, alcohol, or tobacco, rehabilitation may extend from Zen lessons to behavior modification. The message is clear: This organization cares about its people and their well-being.

The proliferation of stress-management seminars in industry is another indicator of changing organizational cultures. In an era of profound transition and rising mental illness, it is good business strategy to help employees, especially senior management, to cope more effectively with rapid change and the tensions of these turbulent times. A long-term study of European executives by two British researchers on management stress is already beginning to reveal some interesting data. In a recent survey of 500 British executives, Andrew Melhuish, a medical adviser, and Cary Cooper, a management professor, revealed that only 16 percent were regular smokers; 24 percent reported having one or two alcoholic drinks a day (which other researchers indicate might not be bad for the heart and tension reduction); 30 percent admitted to taking tranquilizers daily (18 percent because of work stress); 74 percent said they got frequent vigorous exercise. With regard to stress itself, 56 percent blamed work, while 44 percent cited family problems.

Response to Melhuish and Cooper's annual questionnaire uncovered one area for improvement in leadership—34 percent of the managers surveyed stated the main cause of stress centered around *their relationships with their immediate supervisors,* a crucial variable in both health and job satisfaction. With such behavior models, one can only wonder how much stress those surveyed cause their subordinates. The other reasons for stress are also the very issues that metaindustrial organizations are now addressing—frustrated career aspirations, excessive time away from families, and the tendency to be a "workaholic." A significant finding of the research was a feeling that company management structure is usually dominated by competition rather than by mutual support and teamwork. The British investigators have identified two key contributors to managerial stress: work environment and executive personalities. It is hoped that such research will be expanded with American executives, especially those in the new technologies. Since stress can be both a positive, as well as a negative, the energized person maintains a balanced or manageable stress level.

CHANGING LEADERSHIP STYLE
The contrast in industrial and metaindustrial work cultures is nowhere more evident than in the exercise of authority and power. The epitome of past viewpoints was revealed in the April 1980 *Fortune* magazine article "The Ten Toughest Bosses." It described

traditional CEOs like Harold Geneen of ITT, Maurice Greenberg of American International Group, Donald Rumsfeld of G. D. Searle, Alex Massad of Mobil Oil, Richard Dayco of Dayco, and others. The group's leadership style was characterized by such terms as: demanding, capricious, arbitrary, vindictive, unrelenting, abrasive, intolerant, rough-tongued, controlling, tireless, threatening, ambitious, blunt, and belittling. These tough bosses are classic examples of the dying Theory X manager. Despite their dedication and devotion to the "bottom line" and profits, they seem to rule at other people's expense and with little regard for subordinates. A few quotations from this feature about various CEOs will make the point:

Of Thomas Mellon Evans, chairman and CEO of Crane Company:

No question he is a genius.... has his own ideas and pursues them.... doesn't listen well, so he is frustrating to work for.... [His] most glaring trait is his lack of feeling for people.... He's the toughest man I have ever known.

Of Robert Stone, executive vice president, Columbia Pictures:

Known as Captain Queeg when he ran Hertz.... A galley master who, hearing that rowers would die if the beat were raised to 40, would say, "Make it 45."

Of William Ylvisaker, chairman and CEO, Gould, Inc.:

Uses Marine Corps boot-camp approach ... creates aura of power and wealth and reminds people it all flows from him.... They won't go to the bathroom without his permission.

The story offers some other quotes that summarize traditional leadership styles:

Robert Malott, chairman of FMC Corporation, once told a group of his managers: "Leadership is confirmed when the ability to inflict pain is confirmed."

Wallace Rasmussen, former chairman of Beatrice Foods, told an AMA meeting of company presidents: "Running a corporation is a twenty-four-hour-a-day, seven-day-a week job." When asked by participants about duties to wife and family, he is said to have replied, "Get rid of them if they get in the way."

Yet the feature did also describe a sort of transitional leader, Andrall Pearson of PepsiCo, the quintessential professional manager, who also has had a long career at McKinsey & Co.:

He thinks and talks in terms of systems, processes, leverage points, and yardsticks.... [He] will negotiate standards with us for an outstanding performance.

Finally, the author, Hugh Menzies, research associate at Seth Cropsey, concluded that there was no evidence that the methods of tough bosses really paid off in profits. He observed, "It very well may be that a tough boss can attract and keep quality managers only as long as his methods keep making them winners." Menzies also emphasized the high turnover from this type of leadership.

The Society for the Advancement of Management recently provided a clarification of the terms *managing* and *management*:

Managing—designing and maintaining an environment for effective and efficient use of resources and performance of individuals working together in groups toward accomplishment of preselected missions and objectives.

Management is both a science and art; as a science it is organized knowledge—concepts, theory, principles, and techniques—underlying the practice of managing; as an art, it is the application of organized knowledge to realities in a situation, usually with a blend or compromise, to obtain desired practical results.

In the context of the changing complex organizations of today and tomorrow, the standards outlined in these definitions indicate that the leadership style of traditional executives—the "tough bosses"—would prove increasingly inadequate, if they ever were really adequate.

Western business leadership seems to be in crisis. In the large, mature industries, executives are often afraid to take creative risks of investing in plant renewal or ventures; they prefer to put liquid funds into acquisitions and mergers. Productivity is not increased, nor is the economy improved. David J. Secunda, corporate vice president for the American Management Associations, addressed the issue in this way:

It is time ... that management take its share of the blame. I predict that the productivity revolution of this decade will occur in the executive suite. I think that 80 percent of the reasons for productivity being down on the plant floor can't be blamed on the plant workers.

Secunda believes foreign competitors are outperforming many American top managers, who are musclebound, sluggish, and apathetic. They seem more willing to suffer events than mold them. Even the prestigious Conference Board has complained that companies need better management and that traditional financial measures of corporate performance are no longer satisfactory. What, then, are some of the new trends in leadership and where can they be found?

For more than 30 years behavioral scientists have been providing clues, based on research, to the directions management should be taking with their leadership. A benchmark was the publication of *The Human Side of Enterprise* by Douglas McGregor. In contrast to the classical style, he proposed Theory Y management based on these assumptions about workers:

- Expending physical or mental energy at work is as natural as play or rest.
- Employees will exercise self-direction and self-control toward achieving objectives to which they are committed.
- Such commitment is the function of rewards associated with achievement, including self-actualization and esteem.
- Most people are capable of a relatively high degree of imagination, ingenuity, and creativity in solving organizational problems.
- Industrial life traditionally has utilized only part of the average person's intellectual potentialities.

McGregor, like subsequent behavioral science consultants, then advocated a leadership style that created a corporate environment that offered more opportunity for employee self-regulation, participation in goal setting and decision making, exercise of flexibility and creativity, and consultation with supervisors. Experience has since confirmed the wisdom of such a management philosophy. So have executive studies. For his doctorate in business administration at United States International University, Harry Gillespie, CEO of a furniture company, obtained data on leadership style through interviews with the top executive officers and their subordinates in several hundred companies.

Gillespie confirmed a change in this postindustrial period to more participation through delegation to second- and third-level subordinates. Gillespie, now counseling with other top managers in The Executive Committee (TEC) in San Diego, found that chief executives in smaller companies tended to be less participative, while those in large corporations, above $25 million, became more participative. His research demonstrates a shift in business attitude toward participation based on a management style that is holistic, knowledgeable, and sensitive to many needs and wants.

The new leadership style can be seen in mature industries, such as Westinghouse, where key executives like William Coates and Thomas Murrin promote participative management, especially through the use of quality circles and a council of managers. Coates, when interviewed by *Fortune,* observed, "We spend a lot of time trying to get a consensus, but once you get it, the implementation is instantaneous." The new style can be best seen in the high-tech firms, such as Intel, where the three chief executives, Noyce, Grove, and Moore, actually share leadership and provide an "open-office" physical and psychological involvement that invites personnel to share authority. Hewlett-Packard's John Young epitomizes the CEO style in the new-technology firms—informal, low profile, and open-minded.

The new executive styles can also be viewed in companies that have adapted Japanese managerial insights, or are owned abroad by Japanese. In a recent book, Richard Pascale and Anthony Athos describe, for example, Bowles and Company, which has offices around the world. CEO John M. Bowles is employing the successful structure, style, and operations of the Japanese trading companies: "Our idea is to recruit offshore, and have satellite subsidiaries. We don't expect to sit here in Menlo Park and call the shots in Singapore," he said. Numerous books and articles have extolled the Japanese managerial insights. These have ranged from long-term performance and profit emphasis to employment security and attention to quality control. The new management synergy has brought adaptations of the Japanese "bottom–up" and lateral communication, consensus decision making, quality implementation of decisions, the use of ambiguity as a management strategy, and the sharing of recognition with others.

Pascale and Athos contrast the interdependent and cooperative approach typified by Matsushita Electric Co. with the toughguy stance of ITT under Harold Geneen. They suggest that both American and Japanese management styles deal with the Seven "S's" but differ in their emphasis: Western management stresses the three hard S's—structure, strategy, and systems—while Eastern management puts more focus on the four soft S's—superordinate goals, skills, style, and staff. These latter have to do with the people in enterprise—their values, uniqueness, talents, and processes, which when shared not only motivate personnel at all levels but lead to a collective vision. Pascale and Athos maintain that a number of American firms—among them IBM, Procter & Gamble, 3M, Texas Instruments, Hewlett-Packard, Delta, and Boeing—now emphasize the soft S's.

Perhaps the new look in leadership style can best be summarized by enumerating some of the approaches that metaindustrial managers emphasize and some that they avoid:

Emphasize	Avoid
○ Human resources as assets to be developed and utilized.	○ Manipulating and exploiting employees.
○ Involving personnel in the management processes of goal setting, decision making, and problem solving.	○ Autocratic, unilateral, and secretive approaches to management that exclude subordinates from power and authority.
○ Innovation, creativity, intuitive thinking on the part of all, as well as a futuristic orientation.	○ Perpetuating the status quo, the tried and true policies and procedures, and advocating the safe way we have always done it.
○ Open, circular, authentic organizational communications; positive listening.	○ Shielding top managers from unpleasant news, telling them only what they want to hear, and using mainly downward communication.
○ Examining alternative strategies and solutions, and seek unconventional answers or markets.	○ Offering single options for decisions, seeking simplistic solutions, and encouraging only proven strategies.
○ Calculated risk taking, brainstorming, decision trees, and simulated forecasts or modeling.	○ Insistence on orderly and traditional decision making, limiting input and participation in problem solving.
○ Energizing managers as behavior models open to creative deviancy from previous norms and who use the collateral or informal organization when feasible.	○ Managerial vacillation and inertia; focusing on standard adherence and rational policy making; listening only to those with status in the hierarchy or the community.

- Using tentative and temporary solutions and arrangements, such as task forces and project teams, that permit flexibility and fluidity.
- Results performance accountability, and system.

- Insistence on rigid schedules, permanent solutions, solid structure, and following the chain of command or precise steps in operations.
- Gamesmanship, politics, activity emphasis.

IMPROVING QUALITY OF WORKLIFE

The dramatic efforts under way to improve the quality of worklife (QWL) are testimony to the changing corporate look and indications of tomorrow's organizational environment. In mature industries, QWL strategies are aimed at revitalizing the traditional approaches to productivity and assembly lines. In the new technological industries, QWL strategies are endemic to their operating styles. In both cases, the purpose is to humanize the workplace, and to assist people to *work together* for a common purpose. The outcome is personnel *working smarter*, which Walter Fallon, Eastman Kodak's chairman, defines as "imparting a strong sense of teamwork and giving employees more say about how they do their jobs." Even union leaders, once scornful of labor-management partnerships as in Europe, are beginning to endorse QWL programs, as in the case of the United Steel Workers and the Communication Workers of America.

As the rhythm and ethos of the industrial age break down and the fragmentation of job tasks proves unsatisfactory, managers are forced to experiment with new work arrangements and to apply the findings of behavioral research. Since the 1950s, managerial ingenuity has been put to the challenge of reforming work. The results have provided a variety of tactics from improved collective bargaining and worker representation on corporate boards or councils to employees deciding how work will be organized and offering solutions for improved performance and productivity. The last is the strategy of the quality circles.

Ed Yager of Consulting Associates in Southfield, Michigan, defines quality circles:

A Quality Circle is a voluntary group of workers who have a shared area of responsibility. They meet together weekly to discuss, analyze and propose solutions to quality problems. They are taught group communication process, quality strategies, and measurement and problem-analysis techniques. They are encouraged to draw on the resources of the company's management and technical personnel to help them solve problems. In fact, they take over the responsibility for solving quality problems, and they generate and evaluate their own feedback. In this way, they are also responsible for the quality of communications. The supervisor becomes the leader in the circle and is trained to work as a group member and not as a "boss."

A Quality Circle is a small group of employees doing similar work who voluntarily meet for an hour each week to discuss their quality problems, investigate causes, recommend solutions and take corrective actions.

A circle is primarily a normal work crew—a group of people who work together to produce a part of a product or service.

Circle leaders go through training in leadership skills, adult learning techniques, motivation and communication techniques. The Quality Circle itself is trained in the use of various measurement techniques and quality strategies, including cause and effect diagrams, pareto diagrams, histograms and various types of check sheets and graphs. More advanced circles move on in their training to learn sampling, data collection, data arrangement, control charts, stratification, scatter diagrams and other techniques.

A typical Quality Circle includes five to ten members. If the department requires more than one circle, then a second leader is trained, and a second circle is formed. The circles then call on technical experts to assist in solving problems.

Circle meetings are held on company time and on company premises. Where companies have unions, the union members and leaders are encouraged to take an active role in the circle, to attend leader training and to become fully aware of circle principles.*

The QWL concept can be practiced in many forms. There is no quick-fix method that is successful in all cases. It implies commitment to long-term organizational change and to a creative process of people involvement that may bring unexpected and undreamed-of results. Don Scobel, now director of the Creative Worklife Center in Mentor, Ohio, has recently written a book describing the efforts over the last decade by the Eaton Corporation to transform the environment in its multinational entity. When this manufacturing company opened its Kearney, Nebraska, plant, a series of events took place, some by plan and others by serendipity, that positively altered workplace culture. It is a case study in how to improve the nature, effectiveness, ground rules, joy,

* Reprinted with permission of the American Society for Training & Development, 600 Maryland Ave., S.W., Washington, D.C. 20024.

and fruits of worklife. Scobel provides rare insights into how an MNC can have a constructive impact across cultures and on a global basis. Essentially, Eaton used pragmatic strategies for promoting trust, involvement, and participation on the part of its people. It also fostered a collaborative process and volunteerism. Furthermore, synergistic cooperation between management and unions was successfully realized.

The spread of industrial democracy and the demand for enhancement of the work culture is a worldwide phenomenon. Changes may involve improved evaluation and promotion procedures, lifetime employment guarantees, collective decision-making processes, or nonspecialized careers and lateral transfers. Whether it is a push for co-determination, pension-fund socialism, or lifetime income security plans, it signifies a fundamental change in the character of work. Some companies have even moved beyond profit-sharing plans to permitting workers to become shareholders. Perhaps the ultimate outcome is now emerging with the creation of worker cooperatives in which workers own and run the enterprise. The many factors involved in the QWL quest are summarized in Figure 5.

CAPSULE CONCLUSIONS

Changes in society, in the marketplace, and in the worker are stimulating a transformation in organizational cultures. Corporations manifest this new look and style in a variety of ways. The construction and interior design of new facilities demonstrate sensitivity to the needs of both employees and the community. But the transformation under way in the corporate environment is psychological as well as physical.

The metaindustrial organization looks different in terms of the diversity among its personnel, especially the knowledge workers. Opportunity for all based on competence is the growing norm, and the barriers that once selected out so many citizens from career development are being eliminated. A *new associative person* is present in many companies and agencies. Composed of varied, competent people of all races, sexes, and creeds, they use their energies in the pursuit of goals and self-actualization. These mobile, self-motivated individuals take economic security and fringe benefits for granted, seeking instead personal and professional development. Often working in temporary groupings or teams, they look on managers as coordinators, facilitators, and re-

FIGURE 5. Quality of worklife.

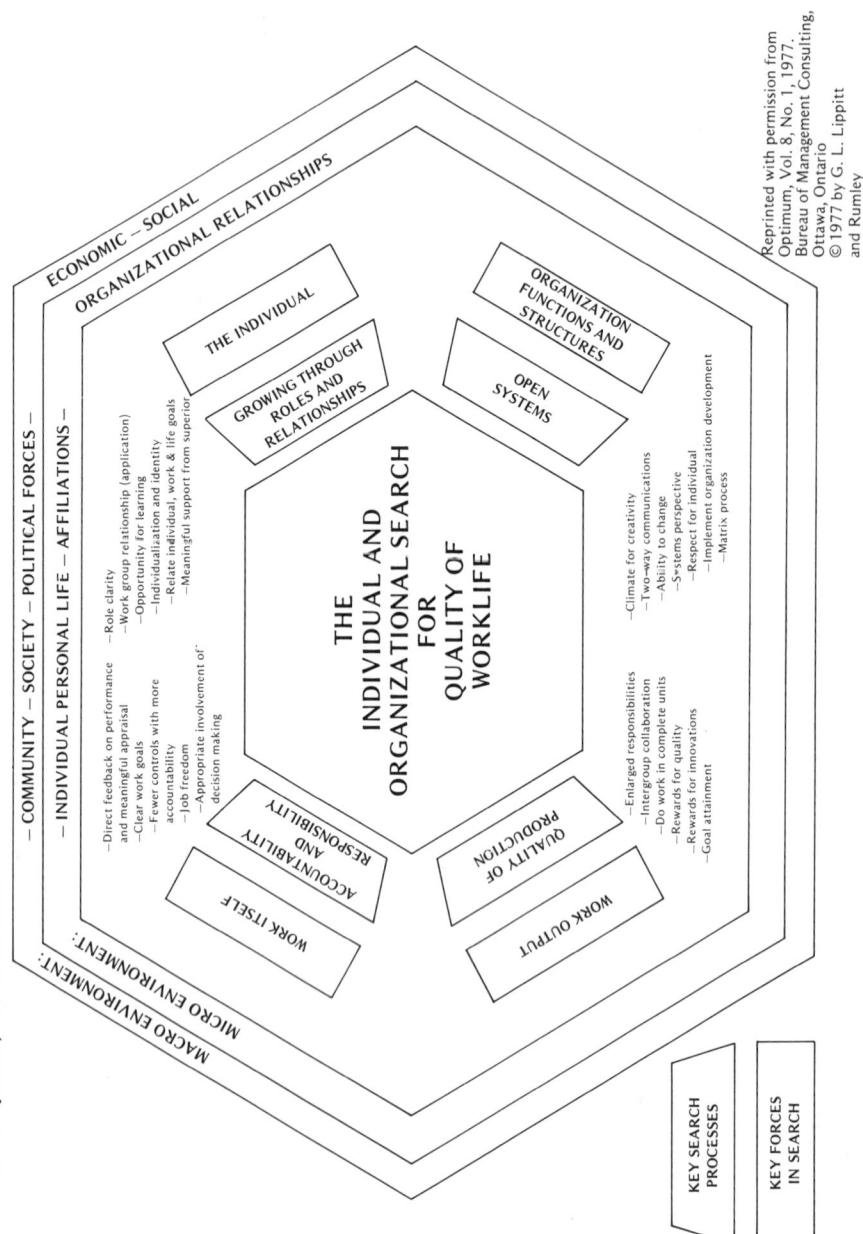

sources. Operating in complex, frequently technological, settings, they are comfortable with matrix management and practice flexible coping skills in situations of uncertainty and ambiguity. They are capable of intense short relationships. And they believe in quality production and service, as well as in planned change in their personal and organizational lives. These learners value entrepreneurship, synergy, and interdependence. They are unafraid to enter the new career fields and markets and are ready to promote the industrialization of outer space.

As we have seen, the rigidity in standards of business dress and appearance is going. Appropriateness to local custom and comfort is the current criterion. Work schedules are also characterized by variety. The amount of time devoted to the formal work week is shrinking, and more provisions are being made for job sharing and for part-time and contract work. Such changes are also contributing to a more healthy worker, who lives a longer, more pleasant life. Personnel policies now support employee fitness and nutrition programs. Corporations are concerned not only with the traditional occupational health and safety practices but also with improving mental health and decreasing stress.

Organization development also involves new leadership styles that are more humanistic and concerned with utilizing and developing people's potential on the job. Sophisticated metaindustrial management struggles to (1) promote integration in complex systems by seeking holistic solutions and strategies, (2) cope with increased diversity of products, services, markets, and people needs, and (3) support the individual while encouraging more synergistic employee behavior. The whole movement in business, government, and nonprofit organizations to improve the quality of worklife is intended to stimulate both productive performance and increased job satisfaction for workers. In these efforts, the following trends are clear:

- Increased experimentation with innovative organizational forms to delimit bureaucracy in favor of more responsive, relevant organizations.
- Expansion of relatively autonomous work groups that share management authority and power, while offering members opportunities for individual growth and development.
- Advances in information processing and related technologies, which can further decentralization, local autonomy, lower-level responsibility, and human resources accounting

and development systems, while promoting the more effective integration of the whole organization.
- Furtherance of self-designed work tasks, compensation plans, work-at-home schemes, and worker-owned businesses.
- Rapid introduction of automation and robotics into the total organization, transforming the traditional roles and relationships of people in organizations.

The changes will result in more variety in organizations, more options for personnel, and more emphasis on marketing involvement by all employees. The new leadership and personnel styles will favor more responsibility and flexibility, and more emphasis on dealing with the whole person, whether employee or customer.

CHAPTER 6   Revolutionizing Corporate Processes and Activities

Different cultures organize their learning, work, and even play in distinctly unique ways. Anthropologist Edward Hall maintains that the mind is internalized culture and that this influences how a group assembles and processes information so as to achieve its goals. Dictionaries define the term *process* as a systematic series of actions directed to some end, or a series of changes taking place in a definite way. In human enterprises worldwide, a variety of basic processes are undertaken that result in specific managerial activities. Businesses may engage in financial, technological, manufacturing, or marketing processes. Our focus here is on that aspect of organizational culture designated as managerial processes and information processing. We will examine the revolution that is under way in management processes and activities in this postindustrial society. Special emphasis will be placed on the current phenomena of office automation and team management. The work processes of the metaindustrial corporation are markedly different from those of industrial corporations. It is vital that those in leadership positions comprehend the profound transitions taking place.

WHY A MANAGEMENT REVOLUTION?
The inability of some managers to change their managerial philosophies and processes has led to major administrative crises in many human systems. To use the analogy of a ball game, far too many managers are playing in the old ball park, by the old rules, and still think they have the same kind of players. Consultant Peter Drucker underscored the issue when he observed that all the assumptions on which management has been based for the last 50 years are obsolete. As we make the transition into the

twenty-first century, leaders have to develop a new set of assumptions not only about the nature of workers and work, but also about business and management itself. Out of these new assumptions will come the managerial processes and practices of the metaindustrial organization. Experimentation is already evident in the mature industries that are going through planned organizational renewal, as well as in the companies involved in the new technologies. Just as the Industrial Revolution had an impact on the industrial age, so the Metaindustrial Revolution influences our period and causes a major alteration in the way in which people are managed.

In a speech to the U.S. Chamber of Commerce in 1981, Commerce Secretary Malcolm Baldrige blamed American management for being "too fat, dumb, and happy," as U.S. exports fell behind imports. He berated poorly run industries that cannot survive foreign competition and predicted that economic systems that foster waste and inefficiency will fall by the wayside in the eighties. The former CEO of Scoville, Inc., Baldrige commented:

> I don't think it's labor productivity that's a problem. It's management. And I speak as a former manager.... Management hasn't been sharp enough or hungry enough or lean enough.*

The problem is not confined to the United States. *Pravda*, the Russian Communist party newspaper, has criticized Soviet management of business and industry as incompetent, inert, and unimaginative. Yet there are organizations that, sensing the needs of the times, have learned to build profits through corporate change. Roger Howe, vice president of human resources in the Donaldson Company, has written of ways to create a plant environment that improves productivity at all levels, while enhancing teamwork and employee morale by accomplishing more with the people now employed. Similarly, Vough and Asbell have described how IBM reduced labor hours by 65 percent and costs by 45 percent while improving quality through an incentive program that increases the productivity of self-motivated employees. Furthermore, by fostering cultural sensitivity and synergy among the management approaches in different countries, international business can be advanced.

In the electronics field, San Diego–based Kyocera International, Inc., a subsidiary of Kyoto Ceramics, holds 70 percent of

---
* *Los Angeles Times*, October 1, 1981.

the market in ceramic housings for integrated circuits. Its CEO, Arthur Jonishi, reports that in its California plant, it utilizes Japanese-style consensus decision making, avoids overdepartmentalization, and stresses standards of efficiency obtained through common agreement. Kyocera uses the "amoeba system," which makes each operating unit a profit center responsible for generating those profits. This planned change and participative atmosphere result in decentralization of authority, lower turnover, and greater entrepreneurial spirit in workers, as well increased identification with the company.

Traditionally, the management activities have been planning, organizing, recruiting, selecting, leading, communicating, relating, problem solving, decision making, negotiating, conflict utilizing, training, controlling, rewarding, evaluating, and even innovating. But management is more than this and it is subject to continuous change. For example, R. Alec Mackenzie, former vice president of AMA's Presidents Association, takes a three-dimensional view of the management process. Figure 6 reproduces Mackenzie's remarkable conceptualization, which centers around these basic elements of management activities: *ideas*, which create the need for conceptual thinking; *people*, who create the need for leadership to influence people to achieve desired objectives; and *things*, or material resources that create the need for administration. Three functions permeate the work process: problem analysis, decision making, and communication. From these components the other aspects of management noted in the diagram flow. Successful management is the integration of all the parts without the neglect of any function.

Mackenzie sees a sequential connection among many of these elements: First, the objectives of an undertaking have been clearly stated, then planning and organizing follow, which lead to the need for staffing, directing, and controlling in terms of the dynamic plan. The cyclical approach to management provides a unified concept for fitting together the management activities, as well as for distinguishing leadership, administrative, and strategic planning functions. It is likely that circles of activities could be added within this basic model, as changes require them.

Organization theorists have elaborated on the ongoing management process. Vincent Bozzone, a New York consultant, analyzes the management cycle in terms of three major functions. The first is *planning* for the future, including "precontrol" activities such as gathering information, technological forecasting, setting objectives, establishing timetables, determining resources,

FIGURE 6. The management process.

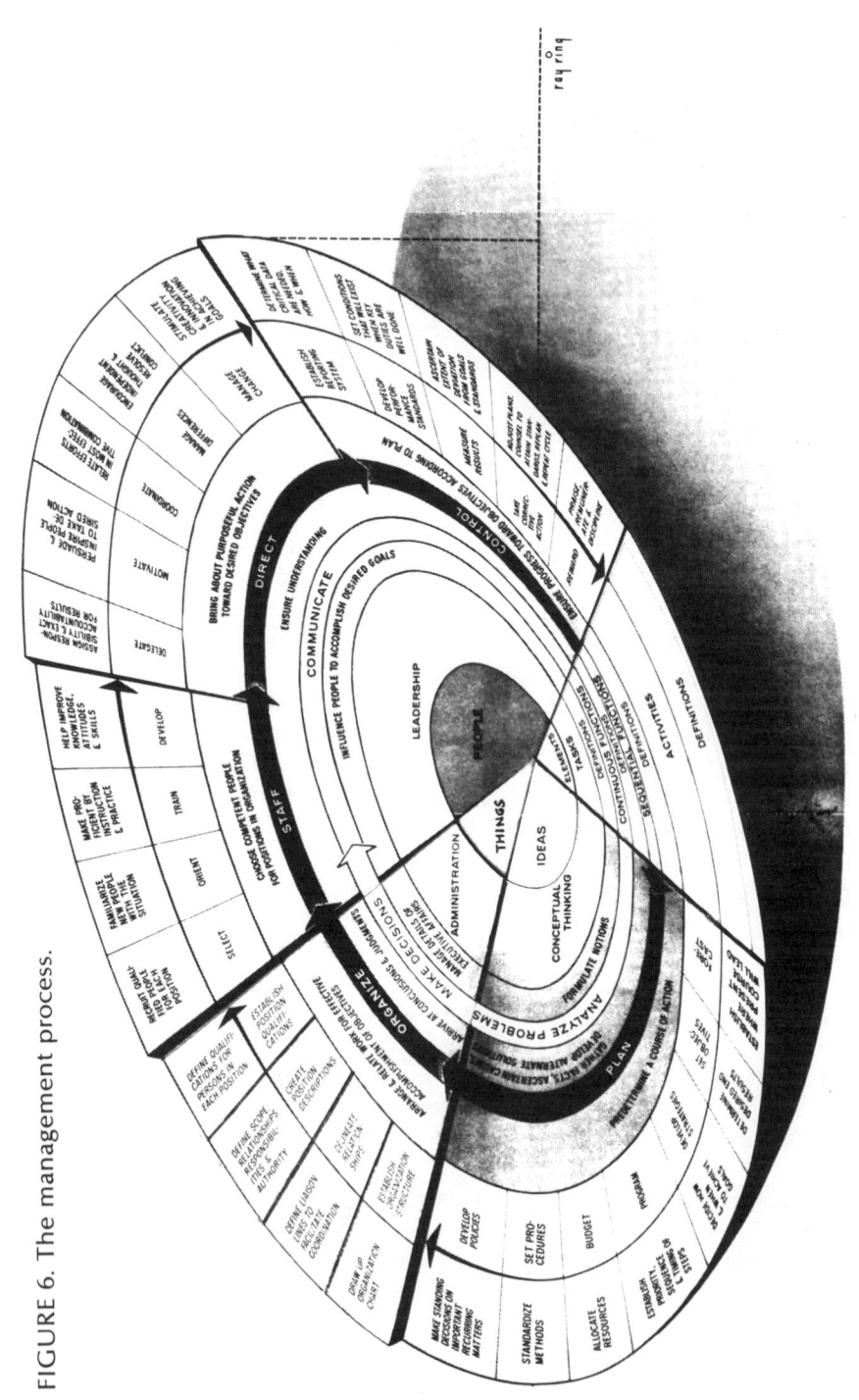

Reprinted by permission of the *Harvard Business Review*. An exhibit from "The Management Process in 3-D" by R. Alec Mackenzie (November/December 1969). Copyright © 1969 by the president and Fellows of Harvard College; all rights reserved.

and action steps. The plan on how to make things happen has to be checked for scope, relevance, and accuracy. The second is *implementing* in the present, which involves "ongoing controls," communicating the plan and expectations, producing and corrective action, and reinforcing. Such activities make actions happen and then check on the actions in case corrections are necessary. The third is *evaluating* the past as to what has been accomplished and how. Such "postcontrols" involve inspecting or performance appraisal, comparison of actual results, self- and group evaluation, learning, and actions to improve the next cycle. This step enables management to know what has happened, and whether the planning was appropriate. Finally, there is continuous reporting back as these three functions occur, so that plans can be revised or expanded as needed.

However, each element in the management process is culturally conditioned. Thus managerial activities or interpretations of basic functions may differ from culture to culture. This is why business schools offer courses in comparative management, and why companies like National Semiconductor have several versions of supervisory development for their overseas programs. National's international training and development coordinator, Eve Majure, reports that management preparation in eight Southeast Asian countries includes culture specifics on the nation in which a plant operates and adapts management education and concepts to the particular culture.

Stephen Rhinesmith has detailed some of the cultural differences for each of the major management activities in terms of value orientations—that is, culturally conditioned perceptions of the world, oneself, subordinates, motivations, relationships, and activity. For example, a people's orientation regarding man-nature relations should be examined. If the people believe that nature is dominant, then the management activities of planning, evaluating, and innovating are irrelevant because people cannot predict the future, nor understand the meaning of change; fatalism would then prevail among management planners. If the value was that people should act in harmony with nature, then management would need to consider the ways things are and initiate change only within the context of nature's established order in the universe. If, like many Westerners, the culture teaches that people are to control nature, then goal setting, planning, evaluating progress, and innovation are all appropriate. In such a cultural view, when old ways appear insufficient for coping with new environmental demands, new approaches must be created. Optimism pervades managerial planning, as is evident in so many North American organizations.

Every dimension of the management process is affected by culture, both in its macro and micro manifestations. A people's temporal orientations, their ability to think in abstract or concrete terms, to perceive in terms of the individual or the community, their attitudes toward dependence and independence, their need for affiliation or achievement, their emphasis or lack of emphasis on family and social relationships, their approach to being and doing—all these and many more aspects of culture have an impact on such managerial activities as leading, decision making, and problem solving. Participative management, for instance, is relatively easy for cultures that support collaboration to learn and more difficult for cultures whose norm is aggressive competition.

Although cultural changes were gradual in the past, during the past three centuries the rate of such changes has accelerated. This includes changes in organizational cultures. Although the industrial work culture developed over the past three centuries, the last three decades have witnessed profound alterations in corporate cultures. American organizations, for instance, are suddenly more open to worker participation in the management process, to team management and collaborative decision making. With the growth of multinational corporations, management has had to become more flexible and adaptive to meet varying needs within a transitional environment. Transnational enterprises have had to transcend ethnocentrism, and develop strategies based on alternative management forms and activities. A new corporate culture has evolved that helps bind members together while facilitating internal communication and decision making. In the metaindustrial organization, high performance in both the individual and the company is valued and encouraged. The emphasis is on promoting member identification with the organization and setting broader goals. The concept of responsibility, for example, is extended outward from management to employees to customers to community. Shared values and ideals are the new energizers for metaindustrial personnel.

Because the objective reality surrounding the corporation changes so rapidly, metaindustrial managers value entrepreneurial innovation and use knowledge to become more productive. Today, according to Peter Drucker, all institutions are accountable for improving the "quality of life," so economic and social development are the result of effective management.

Currently, there is a fundamental shift under way in business from the traditional manufacturing of the industrial age, to the new technology and information processing of the postindustrial period. William Christopher reminds executives that, in coping with this transition:

> all successful companies create their successes through a *continuing process of renewal*, through a continuing process of modification in purpose and structure. This is done by a monitoring process that constantly renews purpose and objectives as appropriate to both internal and external environmental change.

To promote such organizational development, new configurations must be designed in both structure and management. Christopher maintains that in addition to the need to set more specific objectives and devise a system for measuring progress toward goals, a new concept of control is necessary. He would design operations so that at all decision points actions will be taken that result in attainment of key performance objectives. Thus effective control becomes self-control through feedback.

There are numerous instances of companies struggling to renew their processes and activities. In the restructuring of IBM, three groups were formed. One is a single marketing and service entity for all products; another handles development and manufacturing for larger computer systems, including semiconductor components; the third concentrates on development and manufacturing of smaller processing systems.

Sometimes the redesign involves more than the reshuffling of divisions, and the organizational change has to be almost forced on the company. Faced with economic disaster, Pan Am made four fundamental changes to survive. (1) It scaled down service by eliminating unprofitable routes. (2) It persuaded personnel, particularly pilots and flight engineers, to take a pay reduction. (3) It shifted an increasing proportion of flights to larger aircraft, which meant lower unit labor and fuel costs. (4) It sold profitable subsidiaries, such as its international hotel chain, to improve its cash situation.

Even the young metaindustrial corporations are not exempt from the need for continuous renewal. To increase office productivity by 30 percent, Intel inaugurated a technique for simplifying jobs. Under the leadership of Joseph Nevin, the firm examined each administrative procedure, first laying it out in meticulous detail, then eliminating unnecessary work and putting it back together in a more simple, rational manner. To prevent employees from feeling threatened by such changes, this was done with worker involvement and without firing anyone. In essence, Intel has simplified office work by charting the steps it takes to accomplish something and removing as many of these activities as feasible. It is another example of building *the management of responsibility* into the system by examining the critical payoff functions of the job and relating the job to the duties of other employees. When group consensus is achieved on job essentials and a productivity index is established, workers work more intelligently and more simply, and they are more satisfied because they were involved in the change process.

MANAGERIAL SYSTEMS STRATEGIES
Modern metaindustrial management is being affected by the twin concepts of systems and strategies. First, let us analyze the idea of *system*, which can be traced back to the ancient Greek scholars, such as Mencius, who in 500 B.C. recognized the need for systems and standards, and Aristotle, who in 300 B.C. viewed the world as a whole and people as *social* beings. Systems theory was first successfully applied to biological and social systems. Dr. Jonas Salk believes that humankind replicates biological models in the creation of social systems. A system has been defined as a group of related elements organized for a purpose, a whole that functions by virtue of the interdependence of its parts. In accordance with the science of cybernetics or general systems theory (GST), studies have been undertaken to classify systems and the methods by which they function. In discussing an organizational system, for example, one would distinguish its boundaries, purposes, tasks, and interrelated arrangements or subsystems.

Industrial and management systems can be analyzed similarly in relation to growth and stability under possible future alternatives through simulation modeling. Systems analysis is the first stage in presenting large tasks to computers before they can be programmed and coded.

The father of modern systems theory, biologist Ludwig von Bertalanffy, described these characteristics of systems: (1) the study of the whole, goal-seeking organism; (2) the homeostasis of the organism, or the organism's tendency to maintain an equilibrium; (3) the openness of all systems, with the result that the organism is affected by its environment and vice versa.

By the mid-twentieth century, MIT professor Norbert Wiener

was writing and lecturing on *cybernetics*—the science of control and communication in animals and machines. At the dawn of automation, Wiener stated that all systems could be designed to control themselves through a communications loop that provided feedback to allow the system to adjust to its environment—the very basis for the functioning of electronic machine systems such as computers. Systems theory, though still in its infancy, has had wide application in explaining the interrelatedness of people and their environments, and in the construction of theoretical models.

In the past 20 years, the use of a systems approach in the management process has become more and more popular. Some theorists maintain that organizational survival depends on a symbiotic relationship between an organization and its external environment. Johnson, Kast, and Rosenzweig have applied the systems approach to planning, organizing, controlling, and communicating. In that context, management is the primary force in organizations for coordinating the activities of subsystems and relating them to the environment. Then Voich and Wren used the systems approach to integrate the management process. These researchers believe the systems concept facilitates an understanding of the whole organization and its parts, permits analysis of resource flows toward objectives, describes managerial tasks in terms of resource allocation and utilization, relates environmental forces to decision making, and requires a more synergistic view of the organization and its use of human and physical resources.

The systems strategy has offered management a broad frame of reference for analyzing many activities both inside and outside the organization. It has enabled us to create the image of the organization as an energy exchange system interacting with its environment. Now as organizations become more global, complex, and technological, the systems framework permits executives to see the interrelationships of parent corporation to subsidiaries, especially valuable in an age of corporate mergers and acquisitions. it also enables management to get a better grasp of the subsystems within the operations, such as the human resources management system, which can include recruitment, selection, role assignment, counseling, relocation of employees, personnel record keeping, compensation and rewards, performance measurement and evaluation, outplacement, retirement, and second-career planning. Writing about human resources management in metaindustrial organizations, Miles and Rosenberg use systems terminology to describe the situation:

The system will be led by entrepreneurially oriented managers at the top and operated by entrepreneurially oriented work groups at the bottom. In the middle, small consulting groups of managers and professionals will be on paid call to both the top and bottom of the system. In other systems (within the organization), matrix structures will provide business-oriented growth opportunities with the likelihood that entire work teams will be moved from project to project in line with their increasing technical and managerial skills.

The systems approach is both a way of thinking about the managerial process and a powerful management tool. Howard M. Carlisle reminded an assemblage of management consultants that although a system consists of interdependent parts, all are not of equal importance and their individual importance cannot be properly comprehended without understanding the whole. This professor of management at the University of Utah suggested that relationships in supraordinate and subordinate systems may be vertical, horizontal, or multidirectional. Subsystems display characteristics of the broader entity, while boundaries and interfaces determine how effective the unit is in its exchange with its environment. Organizations as open, organic systems must be adaptive, while experiencing both growth and decline and conflict and dissonance.*

Organizational microsystems, such as finance or marketing, may cut across traditional departmentalizations. The classical managerial differentiations have been according to function, process, product, geography, or customer. Thus, in companies like Boeing or Ford, separate plants are often assigned different products, and their interdependence as a total system is pooled in the perceptions of the corporate general management. In emerging metaindustrial organizations, departments, when they exist, are less formalized, more flexible, more self-sufficient, and better integrated into the whole. New management information systems permit organizations to be less hierarchical, more loosely coupled, and better coordinated at a lower cost. High-technology firms demonstrate less concern for formal structure, clear authority, and rigid controls, while operating more comfortably with some ambiguity, dual or matrix supervision, and dynamic interactions.

In Figure 6, the management of differences was defined as "encouraging independent thought and resolving conflict." Metaindustrial systems seem better able to integrate differences

---

* See R. Lippitt and G. Lippitt, eds., *Systems Thinking.*

in skills, disciplines, expertise, input, and backgrounds. Rather than causing fear, these differences are welcomed as synergistic solutions are sought to complex problems. Such organizations synthesize both human and technical systems through the managers and computers acting as integrators. Their managements exercise a new form of power in terms of both systems understanding and information utilization. Furthermore, they use systems thinking not only to predict the future but to arrive at a more preferred future.

Strategic management is the planning and combining of resources and activities to obtain specified, long-term goals. Managers must consider contingencies, alternatives, and methods of maximizing results in given circumstances. A Japanese consultant for McKinsey & Company, Kenichi Ohmae, recommends that strategic planning be done in terms of the corporation, the customer, and the competition. Using the mind of the strategist, modern managers, according to Ohmae, seek superior performance relative to competition, while matching corporate strengths with changing market needs. He cites the case of Casio, a manufacturer of watches and pocket calculators, which is clever in its strategy of accelerating and shortening product life cycles. It introduces a new item, brings down the price fast, then makes it obsolete by introducing an improved model.

Strategic management in metaindustrial organizations may involve the use of simulations, scenarios, assumptions testing, and multiattribute decision making for the better analysis of business problems. To improve systems effectiveness, various forms of analysis are employed, such as environmental scanning, financial ratios, forecasting techniques, and options evaluation. The fourth merger wave of this century now under way is a result of strategic planning. The fluidity and the complexity of an economic market in transition stimulate metaindustrial organizations to employ managerial systems strategies. Chapter 12 will provide further comment on this vital management process.

THE IMPACT OF AUTOMATION

The most distinctive feature of metaindustrial organizational culture is the changes in information processing brought about by computerization. Here we will focus on the implications of office automation. In Chapter 9, we will examine the issue of robotics. Both phenomena will revolutionize management, as well as jobs and work relations. The outcome will be heretofore unimagined organizational designs, structures, processes, and procedures by the end of the century.

Although over 200 vendors now promote office automation systems, the office of the future will likely evolve gradually over the next 20 years. Integrating any new technology into a working environment involves management strategies of planned change. PACTEL, a London-based international consulting firm, estimates that capital investment per office worker will rise from $3,000 in 1980 to about $15,000 in 1990. Their senior vice president, Harry Bunn, predicts that worldwide expenditures for office automation equipment may reach $80 billion over the next ten years. Confirming the investment payoff, Booz, Allen, and Hamilton conducted an exhaustive study and concluded that companies that aggressively pursue office automation can achieve a 15 percent improvement in productivity by 1985.

Most of the products and services involved in this office revolution involve information—its processing, retrieval, and transfer. Computing power will be facilitated by the electronic work station and the local-area network. The decentralization of data processing results in an office of the future that Joe Brancatelli has described as follows:

> Experts now agree that it comprises a highly automated office environment that performs most clerical chores electronically and encourages dramatic improvement in the productivity of managerial and professional personnel. Voice and video teleconferencing* services, using telephone lines and communications satellite links, will increasingly replace person-to-person meetings and interstate travel. Memos and letters typed on paper will give way to computer-controlled electronic mail and calendar-date books displayed on video screens, while

---

* *Teleconference* or *telemeeting* is a generic term to describe electronic communications among three or more people at two or more locations. Increasingly, this involves video, as well as audio, interaction and can be mixed for two-way audio/one-way live video. In some arrangements the audience is at multiple sites, receiving a transmission from a central point of origin, and participation is through a telephone hook-up. Often this requires the use of satellites in outer space; the use of "uplink" or transmission of a TV signal to a relay satellite, of a "transponder" or broadcast satellite system for video meetings, and of a "dish or earth station" to receive the satellite broadcast. A "turnkey program" is a coordinated teleconference system that includes hardware, satellite time, and production and receiving site elements. A related emerging field is private television networks, such as for a hospital or a multinational corporation, which permits education, entertainment, and videoconferencing by satellite.

clumsy and bulky hard-copy filing and photocopying systems will be replaced by sophisticated electronic and microform systems for information storage and retrieval. Office workers will have easy-to-use computer terminals that will perform localized data and word processing functions. Almost all these new services will be integrated into compact, executive work stations that look much like today's video terminals.

Between now and the year 2000, the changes in office operations, processes, and equipment will astound the manager and radically alter roles. The minicomputer and word processor will be at the heart of the technological transition. By connecting networks of processors, letters and reports will be transferable from one location to another. Communicating office copiers can be linked to computers and word processors. Advancements in remote dictation equipment will increase the amount of work managers do outside their offices. Laser-powered telecommunication systems will bring us into the age of phonics, carrying communication on pulses of light, rather than by electric signals, so that offices will benefit from improved, low-cost voice, data, and video services. Computer graphics and computer-assisted printing techniques will permit simulated pictures, charts, and illustrations of superior quality. Digital image processing will open up new possibilities for improved designing, modeling, marketing, and advertising.

With access to a computer library of digitally stored documents, the manager's research capability is enhanced. Now it is possible to scan electronically for information from reports, investigations, and other documents, so that the needed data can be printed on demand. CAMIS (Computer Assisted Makeup Imaging System) is already available for this purpose. On-line bibliographic data bases will give the manager instant entry into the world's libraries. A new volume on videotext informs us already of the coming revolution in home/office information retrieval.*

We will have to learn new techniques and their uses—for example, audiographics and micrographics. Audiographics is a new form of organizational communication that involves two-way voice interaction through the exchange of drawings, documents, graphs, and other information via facsimile graphic transmissions. Micrographics, the process of miniaturizing images on film in full color, will reduce the need for file cabinets and other paper-storage equipment and facilitate information retrieval. The 3M mi-

* See E. Sigel, ed.

crofiche reader/printer combined with computers is only the beginning. It will permit data access and display at phenomenal speeds, photographing of images for selective printouts. CIM (Computer Input from Microfilm) is already being used in business for oil exploration by reading seismographs, in hospitals to read electrocardiograms, and for automatic optical reading of texts. The developments in micrographics permit managers to limit the purchase of books and to utilize facsimile transmission of documents. In fact, every office now has the possibility of becoming its own publisher by computer editing, composing, printing, and distributing reports, manuals, and even books, with endless retrievals of the original possible for reediting at will. The manager can expect new applications of communications technology to advance organizational effectiveness, as the next chapter will further detail.

New information networks will permit the transfer of electronic mail and the streamlining of business operations through computer program storage. Then the office will be able to be its own travel agent, receive investment and financial analysis and world and business news on a 24-hour basis, conduct an electronic personnel search for full- or part-time or contract workers, share training software, and more. Simply by paying a subscription, the office can be turned into a business information center with entry into virtually any field, from advertising and zero-based budgeting to genetic engineering and space colonization. And this can be accomplished in seconds, as Lockheed's Dialog Information System reminds us.

Proponents claim that the cost of gaining access to such information services will gradually decrease as users increase. Supposedly the expense of traditional paper processing will be reduced. On the subject of paper, John Connell, director of the Office Technology Research Group in Pasadena, California, states: "Paper is the nemesis of the modern office. It is the most expensive medium one could select to store information. The costs of moving paper from one executive to another executive and then filing it later are staggering." Nevertheless, Henry B. Freedman, director of research for the Policy Studies Corporation in Springfield, Virginia, maintains that the computer and micrographics enhance, but only in some cases, substitute for paper. Although paper use may diminish, the new technology will increase the quality of printing and paper reproductions. Freedman predicts that an electronic-paper hybrid will create new industries and stimulate new sectors of the economy. He believes business will still require paper-based communications, but they will be custom-made documentation that is carefully selected from electronic storage: "Human verification requires hard copy," according to Freedman. In any event, electronic printing of paper will both cost and save money for managers. Already the traveling executive can purchase from Sony Corporation a briefcase with a six-pound portable printer, enabling him to produce copy while flying on an airplane!

But what will the impact of this new technology be on people in government or corporate offices? First, there will be managers who oppose these changes. Just as the introduction of the typewriter and telephone into the office met with resistance, so office automation will be opposed, even by administrators. It involves unfamiliar concepts and technology; people normally fear change in the status quo. Managers who are experienced in traditional communications tools may feel threatened by telecommunications and computers if they have no background in using such technologies. These innovations will also be thwarted by the *existing* corporate culture!

Managers are supposed to delegate clerical tasks and record keeping to secretaries and support services. Automation requires the substitution of traditional managerial status symbols, such as secretaries, for strange and sophisticated hardware, and this involves management retraining and persuasion. Until voice-activated or touch-sensitive video screens are available, current computers will require managers to use typing skills and learn new computer languages. Already there is a generation gap between the young managers and professionals raised on television and computers. Mature managers may have to be sold on office automation, and new equipment may have to be introduced as a reward to the best and brightest performers. Brancatelli suggests some practical strategies for introducing the new technologies into the work space and culture:

> It's axiomatic that changes, especially major changes, rarely happen overnight or unattended by difficulties. True to that adage, conjuring up the office of the future requires time, patience and planning. Technological barriers have rapidly diminished; resistance from managers and office workers who feel overwhelmed or threatened by the automated office revolution has not. The following guidelines can help steer your organization as steadily and painlessly as possible toward a sophisticated and efficient office of the future.

○ Start small. Introduce new technology on a department-by-department or division-by-division basis. Don't overwhelm employees with a vast, company-wide change.

○ Proceed gradually. Phase in new automated systems and services rather than introducing them all in one indigestible lump.

○ Introduce office automation technology only into those areas where benefits are immediately needed and will be immediately evident.

○ Integrate the new technology into your existing system and office structure. Present new equipment and services as aids to increased productivity, not replacements for secretaries and support staff.

○ Select an automated system that is compatible with the needs and preferences of your employees.

○ Consult the potential users of the new technology before you start. Let them have a say in the system they will be using.

○ Provide heavy and continuous training in the use of the new products and system both during and after the introductory phase.

○ Integrate new equipment into the "corporate culture" as one of the trappings of executive power. Managers will want an executive work station more if it is a benefit awarded as a symbol of success.

○ Don't force anyone to use equipment he or she doesn't want to use. If the majority of your managers and professionals are using the new equipment, resisters will fall in line as they realize that their refusal places them at a disadvantage.

○ Allow each person to adjust to the new system at his or her own pace. You can't rush the learning process.

○ Be prepared to wait out a possible "generation gap" between older or longer-tenured managers, who are more likely to resist the change, and younger or newer ones. If possible, target the latter group for the earliest transition, since it is usually more familiar with automated equipment and more flexible or more eager for the change.

○ Start immediately. Moving into the automated office of the future takes time for phasing in and adjustment. The sooner the transition is made, the sooner the return of higher productivity will show against the investment of time, effort and money.*

As managers seek to integrate the new technologies into the metaindustrial work cultures, diverse attempts are made to humanize the process. In Europe, *ergonomics* has come into being, the study of the relationship between humans and machinery. Office technology can be designed to be more compatible with human needs and to reduce people's resistance. Keith Wharton, a

* Reprinted with permission from Special East/West Network Report by Joe Brancatelli, "Office of the Future—The People Factor," in *United Mainliner*, October 1981.

London consultant, reports that Germany and Sweden are applying ergonomics to create tiltable video screens, increase screen brightness and readability, determine whether keyboards should be integrated or be independent of terminals, and ascertain other ways of making people more comfortable with the equipment. Similarly, in America, *systems humanics* has emerged—the human issues raised by the introduction of the technologies like word processing machines, computers, lasers, robotics, and such inventions. James Webber and Howard Rothman, partners of Omicron, have established in Morris Plains, New Jersey, a center for this purpose. They are concerned that the new media technology is moving faster in development than the capacity of people and their human systems to absorb it effectively. Their program provides a forum for *Fortune* 500 senior information executives to deal with the human element, and to plan the physical and psychological relationship of people and the new technologies.

The second people factor in the office revolution will be in human occupations. The global work patterns in economically advanced countries will be away from traditional manufacturing industries and toward information technologies. The U.S. Department of Labor reports that the number of computer-related jobs doubled in the 1970s and will probably double again by the 1990s. At AT&T, as well as in major banks, already 70 percent to 80 percent of the employees use computers. Such trends contribute to the increase in the numbers of white-collar and women employees, drawing heavily on the younger, best-educated generation in the history of human development. *The Economist* (March 1981) of London ran an article predicting that jobs of the future will be found:

- In occupations not yet formally categorized (e.g., small businesses and self-employed, providing specialized services with the help of machines and related to new technologies).
- In the dramatic electronic growth area where the silicon chip has created enormous demand for programmers, electronic engineers, and computer-skilled people.
- In satellite-based telecommunications for both home and office, including the production of labor-intensive earth stations which should prove a boon to developing countries.
- In biotechnology that encompasses genetic engineering and monoclonal antibodies which will have an impact on engineering, chemistry, and agriculture in particular.

- In traditional health, education, and professional fields that increasingly will employ computer-assisted technology.

The effects of cybernation and other forms of automation on organizational cultures will be immense and profound. Future-oriented managers will get themselves and their subordinates ready now to cope more effectively with these challenges!

CHANGING CONTROL AND DECISION MAKING
The ways in which management maintains control of operations and engages in decision making are being radically altered in metaindustrial organizations. The first obvious trend is toward more internal, and less external, regulation of the job. This means more local plant and group autonomy and more self-regulation by workers. Improved professionalism, higher education, new technologies, and complex systems all are forces in the direction of such changes. Furthermore, the introduction of cybernated systems into business and government makes mechanical regulation feasible by means of feedback control. As human enterprises extend beyond their borders into the international market, and eventually into space industrialization, such supranational activities often are outside the control of national governments. Through its Commission and Center on Transnational Corporations, the United Nations has been studying this new phenomenon and is seeking to work out appropriate arrangements for the operation of such corporations, especially in developing countries. Some predict that supranational regional authorities will become the source of such regulation, involving active participation by the world corporations themselves.

The trend toward self-regulation in humans and machines by feedback is characteristic of metaindustrial organizational cultures. Among managers and workers, self-regulation is often accomplished through organization development (OD) strategies. Diagnostic human factor studies and process consultation are two principal ways for accomplishing this planned, continuous change in human systems. Diagnostic studies of organizational health may be used by internal or external OD consultants, or by managers themselves. Data are systematically sought and analyzed, then fed back to management to increase organizational effectiveness, especially among groups. The data may come from workers, customers, contractors, managers, or consultants.

The objective is to satisfy human needs, improve the work environment, and enhance human performance. The intention of feedback data is to help individuals and groups gain greater control over their own work space, processes, and relationships. Works groups and management teams are thus liberated from onerous supervision and may design their own approaches to achieving results. With the new concepts of control, personnel view one another as resources to be called upon in the process of problem solving and goal attainment. Self-motivation and peer pressure replace pressure from above. The data are collected and allowed to speak for themselves. With knowledge workers, information, expertly gathered, analyzed, and presented, becomes the new criterion for excellence. Positive data are used to reinforce right behavior, while negative data are used for change. The contrast between the current condition and the desired business result becomes the focus of group discussion and solutions.

Peter Drucker advocates that managers engage in systematic studies of principles, organized knowledge, and human performance, including their own. Diagnostic studies can be made of every aspect of the management process described in Figure 6. Management consultant Walter Mahler calls this "experimental-mindedness" and recommends data collection, analysis, and reporting to define problems or opportunities, to stimulate action and determine priorities, to identify alternative solutions and possible obstacles, and to provide useful benchmark measures and targets for change. Many behavioral scientists recommend that corporations and agencies include climate surveys in their data gathering process. The Organizational Culture Survey Instrument provided in Appendix A has been developed for this purpose.

The "process consultation model" is another means for continuing organizational improvement. It is a third-party intervention to identify processes requiring modification, to develop client diagnostic skills, and to involve personnel in generating remedies for their own difficulties. Again, consultants, internal and external, or managers outside the group participating may become the mechanism for making this helping relationship function. Applying the model may mean the use of diagnostic instruments or simply a group facilitator or both. The model can be used for job redesign, to probe new markets or innovations, and to deal with team functioning. It always involves the use of objective feedback, assessment, and creative problem solving. Its purpose is to increase human productivity and self-regulation. In the metaindustrial organization, all work units are encouraged to look on other groups as their clients. Thus, in an R&D center, the various project teams or laboratories become one another's clients. Such strategies have been used successfully by the U.S. Air Force, NASA, TRW Systems, and Texas Instruments. The outcome is the building of trust in the corporate environment and the creation of an open, problem-solving climate.

There are also new plants with team work stations that use computer-connected television to project data on production and to improve quality control. Feedback on the number of assemblies in comparison to projected schedules again stimulates team performance. Such groups monitor themselves and eliminate the need for supervisors. Even in conventional industrial manufacturing, such approaches have proved successful, as has been demonstrated at Sweden's Volvo plants. At Kalmar, the work teams organize themselves and work at a speed of their own choosing as long as they meet production goals. Employees work harder and in an improved environment.

Previously, we indicated how computers and other forms of information technology can be used to improve decision making and to increase participation. Industrial-age managers frequently made decisions "by the seat of their pants." Metaindustrial managers can use electronic data processing to benefit from past experiences and to forecast the future based on several alternative decisions. Simulations, modeling, and micrographics give managers a wide range of options to increase the effectiveness of their business selections. Decision trees and systems have been designed to fix responsibilities for choices, to apply time frameworks, and to tie together many elements related to the decisions. Metaindustrial work culture aims to move responsibility closer to the problems and to balance authority for the decisions. It seeks multiple inputs for analysis before decision making. It is based on the premise that decision making and problem solving should be located as close to the information sources and relevant resources as possible. Group decisions arrived at by collaboration and consensus are characteristic of such organizations.

The metaindustrial corporation is more cosmopolitan in its management. It incorporates from different management systems and cultures what is appropriate in particular places and situations to get the job done effectively. Thus it will learn from the

Japanese ringi system of decision making about the value of letting subordinates initiate ideas, about means to promote coordination among functional units, about consensus orientation. It will develop synergistic strategies of decision making that may include: leader/group sharing of decision responsibility, circular consultation for initiation and coordination, flexibility in consideration of long- and short-term implications of decision planning, alternative-choice participation and consensus, rational/intuitive analysis as a decision criterion, open communication that operates on both the cognitive and the affective levels. In this manner, management processes move beyond cultural constraints as the best solutions are sought.

A unique feature of metaindustrial management is participation, especially in decision making and change. Those who have to implement the decisions are always involved in the process. What today's European, and to a lesser extent American, workers are pressing for—democratization of the workplace by sharing in organizational processes—is an integral component of metaindustrial work cultures.

The case of Texas Instruments may put the observations made here in a more practical light. TI's strategic management system is suitable for large-scale complex organizations. TI built on its technical competence in "close coupling" with computers to coordinate technical specialties among diverse experts around a central goal. It made structural changes within the company, such as the development of the Product-Customer Center (PCC) and the OST System (Objectives/Strategies/Tactics). Team management was supported by reporting systems, group delegation, and encouragement of technical innovation. Procedures were specified, recorded, and replicated for a shared frame of reference and shared perceptions, supported by administrative systems that direct attention to data collection and interpretation. The management of strategy has been systematized, broad participation is the norm, constructive criticism is sought to improve the systems, and superior coordination among delegated tasks is evident. These are some of the management factors that have helped Texas Instruments to maintain its leadership in its industry.

MATRIX/TEAM MANAGEMENT

Another feature of the metaindustrial work culture is the prevalence of team management. Contemporary project, product, and matrix management experimentation builds a bridge to the managerial styles of the future. In contrast with the disappearing bureaucracy, this approach encourages dual reporting functions and even multiple supervision, work organized around temporary groupings that may involve both permanent and temporary authority lines, and group collaboration and coordination. Such cooperative management facilitates the accomplishment of complex technical tasks by the synergistic use of "brainpower." This aspect of the new organizational culture is evident today in the high-technology firms that pool the human resources of many skilled specialists to achieve their objectives. Figure 7 illustrates the process.

In an era of rapid technological advancements, the computer and management information systems facilitate such team synergy. This management strategy permits more timely, shared decisions, more effective use of human and financial resources, more flexible and adaptive responses to changing market situations. To succeed, managers must be trained in both the technical and interpersonal dimensions of such team operations. Knowledge workers need to learn new ways of relating and working together to solve cross-functional problems. For managers conditioned by experience in hierarchical organizations, team-building sessions will help them to better understand group dynamics and the way in which technical specialists can be coupled across specialties.

After experience in aerospace matrix and grid management, Robert F. Smith became an innovator in team management applications to the advertising industry. While CEO and chairman of Phillips-Ramsey, Inc., a San Diego–based marketing and communications firm, Smith experienced the challenges of interdisciplinary work teams that created and delivered products and services for individual clients. As a member of AMA's Presidents Association, he wrote in its newsletter that the systems-oriented account team worked on the assumption of keeping a client for life and that this stimulated general management development. The teams were formed before a client contract was made, were involved in the marketing effort, and continued to participate through creation and execution of advertising campaigns, while operating as individual companies within the total enterprise. The executives in charge of functional disciplines stabilized the system, while account executives learned on the job to take on the regular activities of general managers. Smith's experience demon-

FIGURE 7. Matrix organization.

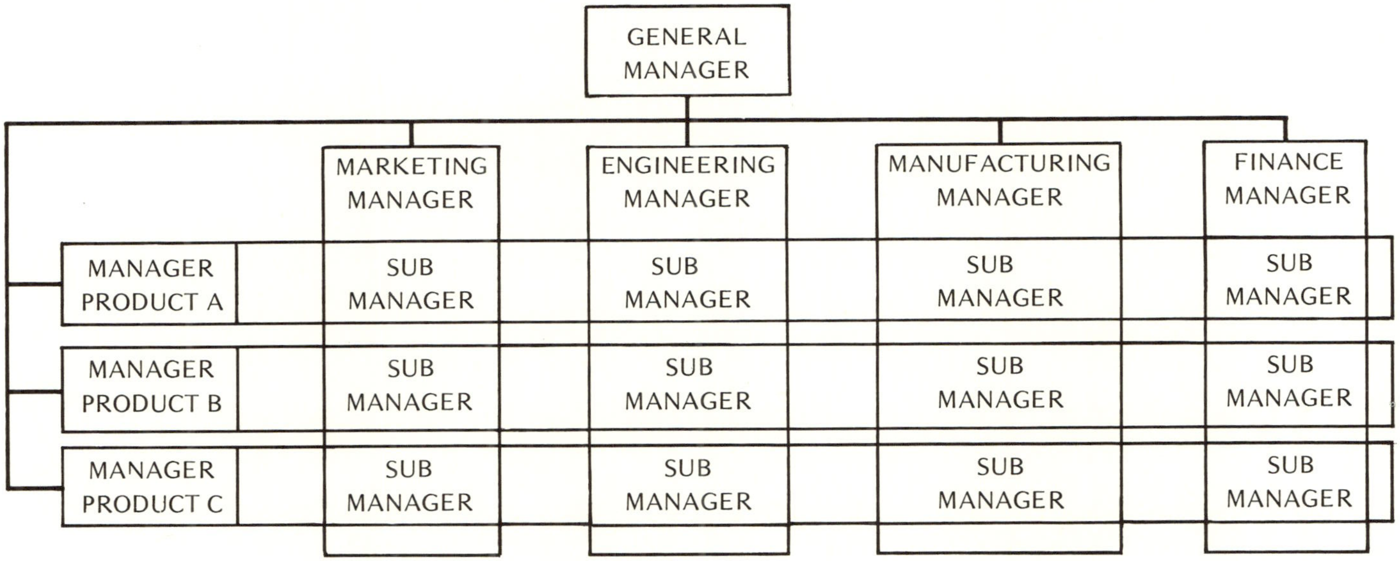

Courtesy Dr. J. Gordon Baugh, *A Study of Decision Making Within a Matrix Organization*, 1981. Unpublished doctoral dissertation, U.S. International University, SanDiego, Calif.

strates how team management can be used outside of technical fields. His insights are worth noting here:

People living in our matrix, I think, are always pressing, feeling overworked, and liking it. We seem to be meeting the personal needs of staff members at all levels for interesting work, clear goals, a part in planning, a voice in decisions, feedback on results, and recognition for jobs well done. Make no mistake, the matrix structure requires maintenance. A continuing education effort is needed to prepare new team members who have previously worked only under the unity-of-command doctrine, but now report to one functional head and three or four, even five, team bosses. . . .

The matrix structure demands a special capacity for making swift changes and accepting critical feedback. High-quality performance under pressure is quickly visible, but so is failure. It's a fast track.

Phillips-Ramsey learned that team management requires (1) careful selection of personnel who can grow and prosper under this approach, (2) extensive time for personal and group communication, (3) tradeoffs between functional and team managers, and much negotiation among them so a win/win approach is maintained, (4) bilateral decisions and group consensus, and (5) coordination and support services. They also found that such management involves frequent discussions on member and client satisfaction levels, employee workloads, and clarity of assignments, as well as on planning systems and skills, position descriptions and accountability charts, standards of performance and results measurement, reward and correction feedback, consultative leadership, and decentralized authority. Above all, team management demands open communication, backed up by systems and paperwork that facilitate accomplishment.

When metaindustrial organizations, especially those operating on a global scale, use team management, they should be aware that it is a different culture of shared values and assumptions, as well as new patterns of acting and thinking. In some parts of the world, this approach will be contrary to traditional local culture. The research of André Laurent at INSEAD in Fontainebleau, France, tends to confirm this observation. At this management center, which brings managers together from all over Europe, his studies of their attitudes revealed that those from Latin cultures (France, Belgium, Italy) are likely to have mental barriers to new management strategies like matrix organizations. Although such managers can learn to work effectively in the team situation, it may take special training or reconditioning to accomplish what may come naturally in other national cultures.

Successful team culture is characterized by members who are able to:

- Tolerate ambiguity, uncertainty, and some lack of structure.
- Give and take feedback in an objective, nondefensive manner.
- Demonstrate interest in member and group achievement.
- Establish intense, short-term relationships and disconnect when projects are completed.
- Create an environment that is informal, relaxed, comfortable, nonjudgmental, innovative, and open to change.
- Seek group participation, consensus, shared decisions, and creative problem solving.
- Keep group communication on target and on schedule, while valuing effective listening, confrontation and leveling, and conflict utilization.
- Encourage member expression of feelings and concerns about group morale and maintenance.
- Foster trust, confidence, and commitment to the group and its goals.
- Clarify continually roles, relationships, and responsibilities.
- Link the group to other work units, and be supportive of its functions within the total operations.
- Make the most of internal and external resources within a context of realistic expectations.
- Synchronize efforts for their maximum synergistic effect.

Team management is needed for dealing with knowledge problems demanding high-quality, creative solutions with rapid processing and high output. It is essential in the metaindustrial culture, where both life and its challenges are *less* structured, quantifiable, and definable, and past experience is unreliable.

CAPSULE CONCLUSION

In this postindustrial age, humankind is inventing social organizations that are more responsive to current human needs. The new entities call for managerial behavior, processes, and activities appropriate to the altered situation. This means changing some classical attitudes toward structures, roles, and authority, as we reconceive both the manager's and the organization's place in the metaindustrial society.

As André Laurent has said, leaders possess mental maps or implicit theories about the management of organizations which are strongly influenced by national culture. In addition, they are influenced by the industrial work culture that dominated our lives until the end of the 1950s. We have examined why a management revolution is under way during the transition to metaindustrial organizations. We have reviewed some of the dimensions of that emerging corporate culture that differentiate its processes and activities—managerial systems and strategies, office automation, differences in control and decision making, and matrix/team management. As we proceed, we will cover other factors in this management revolution that will see us transform the workplace by the twenty-first century.

CHAPTER 7 Transforming Organizational Communications

Humans are the most versatile communicators of all creature life on this planet. We send messages verbally and nonverbally, using an incredible variety of media for transmission, including our own bodies. We are always inventing new ways of communicating, and new ways of revealing our inner selves. With our inventions for human exchange, we also change the world around us. One of the most effective ways to study a culture is by analyzing its communication systems.

We also express culture symbolically, and culture is altered when communication symbols and technology change. Communication systems have always been a way of distinguishing one macroculture from another. The same symbol has different meanings attached to it in different cultures. American executives in England had to learn, among other things, that a "loungesuit" to the British is a business suit. It is quite a challenge for a North American multinational manager in India to communicate with the local people—apart from the common language of English, the Indians also have 15 other major languages and 500 dialects. The meanings a different culture has for simple gestures are often the reverse of ours; Greeks shake their heads up and down to indicate "no." Even when different peoples speak the same language, they may have unique versions of it, as well as different accents. Witness the use of English in the Commonwealth nations, where accents and vocabulary uses may baffle English speakers from other places. Abroad, wherever English is the principal language, Americans find the forms distinctively different from their own. And of course it differs regionally within the United States.

Within national cultures, many subcultures exist, each with its own complex variety of communication systems. In institutional microcultures, the signal systems, professional jargon, technical languages, and in-company terms offer a way to distinguish one group from another. People outside the particular group often have difficulty comprehending the specialized vocabularies, acronyms, and abbreviations. Communication is also a clue to personal status within organizations—blue-collar speech and writing differ from that of managers and supervisors. At lower levels of organizations, some employees excel at nonverbal communication, while at upper levels the emphasis is on word power. The cultural orientation of a corporation, its formality and informality, may be indicated by its emphasis on titles, or in its use of first or last names. The changing organizational culture is evident in the new, nonsexist job titles and work vocabularies. Communication is indeed the major characteristic for analyzing organizational culture. And the management information system (MIS), a reservoir of important communications and means for conveying them, may often be the critical factor in ascertaining the degree of success of one business over another.

THE ELECTRONIC INFORMATION SOCIETY
As we prepare to enter the twenty-first century, we are formulating an electronic information society (EIS). It values knowledge and the interchange of data that is rapid, relevant, and comprehensive. This, in turn, has an impact on organizations, not just those that are the source of the new EIS technology, but all the enterprises that use the new media to conduct business more effectively on a global basis.

The transformation under way in organizational communications is more than technical. It involves an attitude change about human interaction in the work culture, as well as the expansion of the man-machine interface in offices and factories. In the meta-industrial culture, organizational communications are even more complex and sophisticated, serving, as they must, global and interterrestrial needs.

The rapid development and extent of the communications revolution is illustrated in Figure 8. Graham Molitor explains that "as new communications technologies are introduced, older, more traditional ones wane in importance. And as these supplementary media take hold, people are exposed to ever-increasing amounts of information. The acceleration of change is dramatically accentuated by advances made in the twentieth century alone. Modern communications technologies, in particular, are

FIGURE 8. Innovation and dominance in communication.

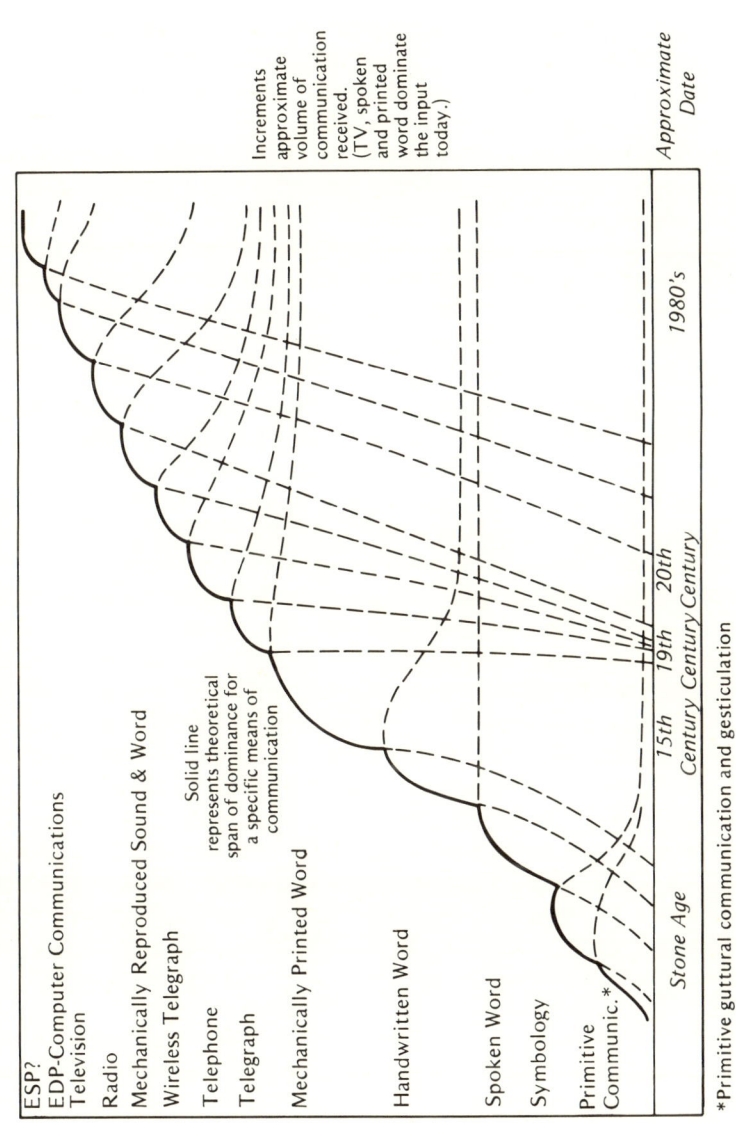

ESP?
EDP-Computer Communications
Television
Radio
Mechanically Reproduced Sound & Word
Wireless Telegraph
Telephone
Telegraph
Mechanically Printed Word

Handwritten Word

Spoken Word
Symbology
Primitive Communic.*

Solid line represents theoretical span of dominance for a specific means of communication

Increments approximate volume of communication received. (TV, spoken and printed word dominate the input today.)

Stone Age | 15th Century | 19th Century | 20th Century | 1980's

Approximate Date

*Primitive guttural communication and gesticulation

Source: *The Futurist*, April 1981. © Public Policy Forecasting, Inc.

not only restructuring our economies but reshaping our lives. The major resource and business of the postindustrial period is *knowledge*. Molitor reminds us that "Intangibles have replaced tangible goods as the dominant factor in commercial enterprise, the central assets, the primary source of wealth and power. A new set of 'knowledge industries' are on the rise."

Old companies, such as Exxon, are getting into the new communications businesses, and new corporations are springing up to get their share of the 15 percent growth rate in this field. In 1981 alone, close to $62 billion was spent on information processing equipment, supplies, and services. Such industries are causing drastic changes in organizational communications and are fast becoming a decisive factor in national productivity. The United States is the current leader, with over $30.5 billion spent just on information equipment. But its closest national competitors in the new information industries, at over $8 billion each, are Japan, France, and Germany, whose governments are already formulating national policies to ensure technological leadership in the communications businesses.

The basic French strategy is to become the world leader in the combination of telephone and computer—"télématique" as they call it—so they have established a telecommunications authority (PTT) to coordinate manufacturing efforts and product promotion. Their plans call for the replacement of telephone directories with electronic visual display terminals and the introduction of "mass fax" or desktop facsimile machines, that is, electronic mail. Japan Inc. has openly avowed its goal of world domination of telecommunications, both electronic and optical.

Hank Koehn, the in-house futurist at Security Pacific National Bank in Los Angeles, California, contends that the electronically interlinked society is changing the very nature of communication and information gathering. He believes that telecomputing with visual images and voice interaction alters the formation of opinion, creates a new social consciousness, and fosters emergence of telecommunication networks as a new social "nervous system." Koehn says that we are transcending the physical limitations of time and space, as well as the perceptual limitations on seeing the world from a fixed position!

Within organizations, this has meant more people working in the information sector and a MIS shift from central to distributed data processing. With the advent of microcomputers, greater control over information flow and faster access to relevant data are now possible. Distributed processing alone is enough to revolutionize organizational communications. Interlinked systems and microprocessors facilitate communication among geographically distant localities. The future will bring a breakdown of the telephone monopoly, and we will see more computer applications and information transport, data generation by voice and other means of sensory input, and new means of transmission from microwaves to light frequencies by fiber optics. Government regulations will have to change to deal with the phenomenon of crossbreeding of data communications and telecommunications. Public knowledge will become more accessible and diverse. It will also become the object of economic production and consumption.

Koehn states what is common knowledge among professional futurists. He predicts that by the year 2000, we will have in common use,

- Home communications centers with videophone of multipart conferencing, computer and terminal which can access or mail information anywhere and any time, multichannel television with feedback controls for two-way communication over fiber-optics cables, and video recorders/players.
- Teleprinting via teleprocessing networks with more producers of messages and freer flow of information.
- Telecomputing networks that eliminate one's need to be near traditional centers of transportation and communications, so both individuals and institutions will have greater freedom of location.
- Development of ad hoc groups for communications planning around products, not organizations—once developed and installed, the groups will disband and new ones will form to meet the next technological challenge.

Over the next two decades, business, industry, and even government will be the center for such research and development, the precursors of communications possibilities to be shared with the masses by the turn of the century.

Metaindustrial managers keep abreast of such organizational communications advances through conferences, reports, and networking. The significance of all this was borne out by a series of European Economic Community conferences beginning in 1981 in Dublin, Ireland. Organized by the EEC's Forecasting and Assessment in Sciences and Technology (FAST) Commission on "Information Technology: Impact on the Way of Life," the concern was information services as a resource for individuals and groups, and their effect on lifestyles. The FAST program examines computing and telecommunications systems based on microelectronics in relation to (1) changes in work organization and environment, (2) regional and local use of the new technologies, (3) developments in education and mass media, (4) redefinition of occupational roles, (5) access to information technology, (6) telecommunications, transportation, and new urban forms.

Similarly, the World Future Society devoted its Fourth General Assembly in July 1982 to consideration of the theme: "Communications and the Future." Its reports and videotapes deal with the expansion of communications technologies into all areas of life. The conference concluded that "these new technologies may increase complexity and create problems, but they also have the potential for enhancing many areas of life." Two quotations from their announcement brochure are worth reproducing here, for they are by eminent futurists and are most insightful:

Only during the past seventy lifetimes has it been possible to communicate effectively from one lifetime to another—as writing made it possible to do. Only during the last six lifetimes did the masses of mankind ever see a printed word.
—Alvin Toffler

In the closing days of 1958, a human voice spoke for the first time from space.... It marked the dawn of a new age of communication, which will transform the cultural, political, economic, and even linguistic patterns of our world.
—Arthur C. Clarke

It is from perspectives such as these that one should analyze organizational communications and their effect on a corporate or agency culture. There is one other element to be considered. In past centuries, cross-cultural communications were limited by our capacities to exchange information across borders, or over the various boundaries within a nation that separated one group from another. Now most communications can be intercultural because of the diffusion of new communications technologies, products, and services. This causes a convergence of cultural insights in global communications—the art of understanding and being understood by parties of another culture. Yet at the very time that we are forging a world culture, international business communicators would be well advised to be more aware of cultural influences on their own concepts of self, management, and organization, as well as more sensitive to the relative differences in perception by those from other cultural groupings. This is valid not only for our commercial dealings with foreigners or with minorities within our own country, but in communicating responsibility with those from differing microcultures, whether it be another profession, or industry, or corporation. With intercultural awareness, sensitivity, and skills, metaindustrial leaders will be able to use the new technologies for more appropriate and meaningful human interaction.

CHANGES IN ORGANIZATIONAL COMMUNICATIONS
Back in the 1940s, then president of the American Management Associations, Alvin Dodd, observed that "the Number 1 management problem today is communication." Four decades later the situation has not changed much, despite a multitude of seminars and courses attended by managers, and numerous books and articles read by them—all on the subject of improving management communications. Films and videotapes have been produced on the topic, and great advances have been made in new communications equipment and systems. All this can be confirmed by research reports on the issue, which are summarized in six volumes of *Organizational Communication.** The conclusion is comparable to the sage comment of W. H. Whyte of *Fortune:* "The great enemy of communication is the illusion of it." Perhaps the place to begin is for the reader to engage in a self-analysis of his or her own communication skills as a manager. Appendix B provides an inventory for this purpose.

Human communication is both complex and multidimensional. It is complex because it is both verbal and nonverbal, involving vast differences in oral, written, and body language. It operates on different levels—cognitive, or "I think," and affective, or "I feel." It is influenced by culture, which changes the meanings ascribed to communication symbols among different peoples and in different places. In attempting to transmit messages, we have a vast array of media that increase continuously in scope and impact. The media can range from words, pictures, signs, sounds, gestures, and numbers to mechanisms of mass communication such as the telephone, computer, radio, television, and satellites. Since the creative human mind keeps discovering new means for both fostering and complicating interpersonal, group, organiza-

* See H. H. Greenbaum and R. L. Falcione.

tional, national, and international interaction, humankind has an array of choices and opportunities for rapid and global communication. We are even engaged in attempts at interterrestrial message exchanges.

Metaindustrial managers seek to become more professional, sensitive, and aware communicators. Operating in the world market, they also increase their skills in cross-cultural communication and negotiation. Since they are a part of the technological culture, they advance their knowledge of new tools for management information systems, both hardware and software. They strive to develop their comprehension and expertise in interpersonal, group, and organizational communication. Since they realize that productivity and employee/customer relations are best advanced through improved business communication, they search out ways to facilitate personnel growth in this critical area of management.

Metaindustrial leaders espouse new values in business interactions, such as trust and integrity, openness and authenticity. Yet they do not abandon old, but valid, values and business practices that are essential to human interchange. Giving one's word, whether orally or in writing, should still be held sacred. This is what Admiral Hyman Rickover complained about in testimony before a joint Economic Committee of Congress (January 28, 1982): "It used to be that a businessman's honor depended on his living up to his contract—a deal was a deal. Now, honoring contracts is becoming more a matter of convenience." At the same time, in certain situations and cultures, candor or informality may be inappropriate. Generally within organizational exchanges, circular communication, in contrast to one-way or downward interaction, is preferred. Metaindustrial managers regard feedback highly, not just in computer systems, but in human interchanges. In the process of sending and receiving messages, they are attuned to the "silent language" of facial expressions, voice tone, emotional involvement, and gestures. In the metaindustrial work culture, the informal systems of communication are utilized as much as, or even more than, the formal ones. Problem-solving teams are formed on a continuing, but temporary, basis to promote understanding of organizational goals, foster collaboration, and reduce duplication.

In group meetings, concern today is expressed for both the task and maintenance levels of communication, so that team morale is placed on equal footing with getting the job done well. To avoid information overload, metaindustrial managers reduce the paper exchanges and increase the personal interface, be it face-to-face encounters or encounters through new technology from videophones to teleconferencing. The emphasis is more on moving the brain than the body. Postindustrial leaders eschew communicating with people in terms of categories, and seek to break down the communication barriers between blue- and white-collar workers, between labor and management, between unions and companies, between nationals and foreigners, between industries and disciplines. The focus is encouraging synergistic communication, convergence of perceptions to gain the greatest insight and input to manage complex problems and challenges in an interdependent society. Thus organizational communications are supportive of more pluralism, equal opportunity, and affirmative action for women, minorities, and foreign nationals.

SYSTEMS APPROACHES TO COMMUNICATION

The systems orientation of metaindustrial management is most evident in the area of communications. Every system has a purpose, a structure, control principles, and variables. But it is the communication channels and relationships that hold the system together. The system interacts with its external environment while creating an internal environment that facilitates a human energy exchange or communication. The interface and interplay of the many variables in the system depend on feedback, so that outcomes can be compared to objectives, and inputs can be modified to ensure convergences of goals and results. Organizational communications involve a dynamic energy exchange to gain information and insight, to maintain stability, and to respond to changes. Metaindustrial systems even seek to promote ultrastability, so that the organization is more fluid, building innovation and continuous change into this system. Effective global managements design systems that integrate the parts into a whole, that foster a balance between the autonomy of operation centers and the requirements of corporate headquarters, that incorporate all the organization's publics, that encourage coordination between operating units and levels of management, that regulate the flow of information so that decisions are relevant, comprehensive, and participative. The interaction of the organization with its external environment is a critical concern of metaindustrial management.

In attempting to analyze organizational communications from a systems perspective, the paradigm provided in Figure 9 may be helpful. Using the analogy of a cube, which is multifaceted, the manager may view communications from the position of the for-

FIGURE 9. Metaindustrial organization communication systems.

FORMAL

EXTERNAL	Letters ( )
	Press releases ( )
	Publications &
	  Reports ( )
	Telephone/Telex ( )
	Telecommunications ( )
	Community/Public
	  Relations ( )
	Marketing/Advertising
	  Programs ( )
	Client/Customer
	  Relations ( )
	Open House/Visitor
	  Programs ( )
	Community Service/
	  Field Work ( )
	Microfiche/Electronic
	  Mail ( )
	Environmental Scanning
	  Studies ( )
	Others _____
		Letters/Memoranda ( )
		Reports/Studies ( )
		Signs/Posters ( )
		Organization Charts/Manuals ( )
		In-house Publications ( )
		Bulletin Boards/Announcements ( )
		Telephone/Intercom System ( )
		Closed circuit TV/Radio ( )
		Directors/Staff Meetings ( )
		Project Teams/Task Forces/
		  Committees' Meetings ( )
		Word Processors ( )
		Office Copiers ( )
		Facsimile Transmission ( )
		Micro forms/Films ( )
		Computers/Graphic ( )
		Videotexts/Tapes ( )
		Teleconferencing ( )
		Management Work
		  Stations ( )
		Others _____
			INTERNAL

	A | B		
	C | D		

	Plant/Office Environ-
	  ment/Appearance ( )
	Employee Community
	  Participation ( )
	Grapevine/Rumors ( )
	Union Relations ( )
	Visitor/Guest/
	  Suppliers Relations ( )
	Others _____
		Work/Social Relations ( )
		Car Pools ( )
		Company Clubs/Teams ( )
		Grapevine/Rumors ( )
		Networks ( )
		Employee Group Hobbies/
		  Projects ( )
		Bag lunch Meetings ( )
		Others _____	

INFORMAL

mal and informal systems, as well as from the external and internal systems. It is then possible to further examine communications from a combination of these four basic components. Thus one may review the formal/external communications (System A), the formal/internal communications (System B), the external/informal communications (System C), and the internal/informal communications (System D). This conceptual model should not be used rigidly, for there are some communications activities that cut across or integrate the subsystems. But it does provide some convenient categorizations, and we have suggested some media possibilities in the context of these major four dimensions. Put a check in the parentheses to the right of each item that is present in your organizational communications, and add other items as appropriate.

To further analyze a communication system, managers would do well to identify the various publics with whom the enterprise interacts. Another useful benchmark is the flow of the information—is it largely downward, upward, sideways, or circular? Again, one might ascertain how management communications are accepted by personnel, and how accurate their content is. In addition, a leader should examine the organizational environment to determine whether it is rigid or relaxed in its communication modes. For example, how does the organization view the chain of command with regard to information input and distribution? David Brown, professor of management at George Washington University, reminds us that the institutional communication chain may be too slow, especially in emergencies; too myopic or insufficient; too closed or punishing to permit "leveling" or telling it "like it is"; too protectionistic or fearful of risk taking. Creative managers may have to circumvent the formal channels of communication and use the grapevine, action hotlines, and other informational networks. Metaindustrial leaders do not regard the official channels as sacrosanct; they rely on informal communication systems as well.

In Chapter 6, we referred to general systems theory (GST) as an example of a force that is revolutionizing the management process and managers' perceptions. This is especially valid relative to organizational communications. James Grier Miller, head of the Hutchines Institute in Santa Barbara, has observed in a recent tome that has significance for corporate systems and their interchanges:

- The corporation interacts with all parts of itself and its environment, and boundaries in the old sense are not of major importance.
- The external environment is responsive to corporate actions, while the corporation is, in turn, affected by outside actions.
- Corporate activity, spontaneous or planned, is central to its

purpose, and like living things, it must produce to survive, grow, and evolve.
- The corporation entraps and harnesses new information to do this, and feedback is essential to the process, so that the organization may adapt and change to continue.

Openness to information and responding to such input is a measure of organizational health. Metaindustrial managers use a systems approach to communication to increase organizational effectiveness.

Consultants, both external and internal, can facilitate organizational communications. They can provide more objective perspectives and helping relationships, as well as link the organization with external resources or with various levels of management and internal resources. Consultants can further the communication process among personnel by clarifying problems and opportunities, getting involvement and participation from members, transmitting ideas and decisions vertically and horizontally, creating an internal environment that motivates employees, negotiating consensus, and diagnosing communication needs or effectiveness. Their greatest contribution may be in fostering understanding of the human dimensions of corporate communications.

BEHAVIORAL COMMUNICATIONS

The concept of behavioral communication, which was discussed in Chapter 3, is most important in organizational communication. It has to do with image making and influencing ourselves and others. To best envision this, think of a series of concentric circles. At the center is *self-image,* or our self-perception, which we then project to others. Next is *role image,* whether that be as an executive, a manager, a professional, or a technician. Then there is *organizational image.* Essentially, as we conjure up these images in our minds and then project them outward, we influence the response we get from others. Thus, if an individual has inferiority or superiority feelings, it is likely that the projection of such images will produce negative reactions about the individual in others. On the other hand, if the person has a positive self-image, the receiver of that image is likely to be more accepting of the sender. So the sender, in a sense, sets up the response produced in others; the exception to this is when there is preexisting bias or prejudice in the receiver. Similarly, one may have adequate or inadequate, relevant or obsolete, views of a work role, such as an MIS manager or an account executive. Projection of such images then affects the behavior of colleagues and subordinates. Finally, the organizational image may be archaic or too narrow, or it may be misperceived by employees or customers. Corporations give considerable sums of money to advertising agencies to engage them in projecting to the public better institutional images of the organizations or better impressions of their various products and services.

The first implication of this concept is that we create and affect these images, which produce responses in others. Second, it is important for our growth that self, role, and organizational images be *reevaluated* from time to time. Just as the lens on a camera has to be focused so that images internally and externally are in harmony, so the internal and external organizational environments have to be synthesized periodically. Our images require continuous reexamination and reassessment based on new input or feedback, changed circumstances and people.

Until mid-century, humans had a traditional image of the role of women in society and at work. Now with the women's liberation movement raising our consciousness about appropriate and inappropriate conceptions, managers must revise their image of women's place and potential. We can be constrained or enhanced by our images. For millions of years, humankind thought it was earthbound, until we actually landed a man on the moon. Now we have to take off the psychological blinders that once limited us and explore our new potential in the universe.

The next implication of this vital concept has been provided by an advertising executive, Robert F. Smith of Phillips-Ramsey in San Diego. Building on the research of Dr. Bert Hayward, Smith believes that individuals and institutions each have three images that need to be integrated for effective performance. At the core is the self-image, or how we perceive ourselves as people, companies, agencies, or associations. Then there is the growth image, or how we would like to perceive ourselves in the future. By planning our growth steps carefully, we can actually achieve this goal. Finally, there is the public image, or how people on the outside perceive us. Smith urges his clients to set organizational objectives, strategies, and plans that will permit the growth image to be realized. With regard to the public image, he advises examining two dimensions related to a company's products or services. One is what we guess the public thinks, possibly based on intuition; the other is the reality, which we discover from marketing research, opinion polling, and other means for obtaining feedback. Naturally, it is important to synchronize these views. Otherwise, we might end up going out of business!

We have suggested that managers perceive their organizations as energy exchange systems. With such an image, we would then be concerned about effective utilization of both natural and human energy in an enterprise; we would launch conservation programs for both psychic and physical energy to ensure that employees' efforts are fully utilized for greater productivity. When we act on obsolete images or stereotypes of "those people in marketing or manufacturing," or of "those academic types in ivory towers," or of "those foreigners," or of "those minorities," we demean people and underutilize their contributions to increasing organizational effectiveness. Again, going back to our traditional images of women, we must ask whether there are so few women in the executive suite of organizations or on boards of directors because of those passé images of their role.

In trying to improve organizational communications in the near future, managers will probably turn to technical and hardware solutions. But perhaps they should explore the many other dimensions that could facilitate systems interactions, such as those that follow.

Foreign language studies for personnel. The United States has been described as a "deaf and dumb giant" because most of us speak only English. We send millions of managers, sales representatives, technicians, government officials, missionaries, and even educators abroad without the slightest grasp of the language of the host culture. Yet language is the key to understanding foreign cultures. It is such a national scandal, affecting defense security, that a Presidential Commission on Foreign Language and International Studies was established. In its 1979 report, the commission noted the stake of American business in international trade and finance, but reminded us that the nation's welfare depends on perceptive visions of the world beyond our own borders, and that in the global village of instant communications, it is important that more of our citizens be able to converse with foreigners in their own language, without the distortion of interpreters.

Apart from support of foreign language and international studies in the schools and media, the commission urged business and labor to give more priority to such training for their own staffs, and to make it a factor in selecting employees for overseas assignments. Companies would be well advised to fund foreign language training of personnel and to use the latest technology and methods for such instruction, such as the new TPR or "Total Physical Response" to language learning.

Mergers and acquisitions. As we ride on the fourth merger wave of this century, the studies of Malcolm Salter and Wolf Weinhold of Harvard University indicate that these corporate acquisitions are larger and more complex and involve blue-chip giants. Since 1975, there have been fewer mergers than in the past, but they have been greater in scope—companies being taken over often listed assets of $100 million or more. The building of today's diversified conglomerates may lead to the emergence tomorrow of truly world corporations.

Another phenomenon in the merger business is the intensified activity of foreign companies to go beyond their borders to take over firms in other countries. Such activities point up new problems and challenges in organizational communication. First they occur in the negotiation process of acquisition and then in the actual endeavors to integrate the newly merged entities. If synergy is to occur and profits to be realized, executives must recognize that multiorganizational cultures are involved, each with its own unique systems of communication, and these cultures must be synthesized. If but a portion of the funds invested in financial and legal strategies for the takeover were diverted to improving communications among the entities after the merger, the positive results would be dramatic.

Ethics and privacy in multinational communications. The rapid global advance of new technological communication has proved the obsolescence of industrial-age legislation in both national and international mass communications. Panicked government officials around the world have sought new constraints on the media, which invade their borders with more power than any armies. The UN and UNESCO have been petitioned, especially by Third World nations, to curb the mass media, particularly those supported by advanced, technological societies. The grand scale of information gathering, especially personal data about individuals, through the means of giant computers raises the issues of the right to privacy, who has access to such data banks, what the information is used for, and the adequacy of security systems to counter unauthorized retrievals. The electronic information society raises many new ethical concerns which conferences of corporate executives should confront. Already there have been charges that a major airline used its computer system to put a competitor out of business because the latter was dependent on the former's reservation system. When business firms buy time or services from larger computer systems, what are the moral responsibilities of the *owner* relative to the information acquired and dispensed? What are the obligations of the owners and controllers of major computer systems to protect the privacy and privilege of information entrusted to them? How can the operators of mainframe computer systems be made more accountable for the access and security of their information banks?

These are public issues that should cause international business leaders to be more proactive and less reactive in confronting the ethical matters involved in their global corporate communications policies and procedures. This means facing up to unpopular practices like bribery or graft, political pressures, and requests from external sources for financial information about a company, its employees, and its customers. Various industry, trade, and professional associations of business persons would seem to be the best forums for developing the new strategies, policies, and voluntary ethical codes by trying to cooperate with government entities seeking to regulate public officials.

For example, 24 nations in the Organization for Economic Cooperation and Development formulated an intergovernmental code that dealt with bribery, political communication, and economic reporting. Few multinational corporations took guidance from this statement to develop their own comparable corporate codes. Kenneth Harwood, professor of communication at the University of Houston, believes there would be many areas of general agreement between multinational enterprises and governments if the regulated and the regulators would realize they have more to gain by collaborating in resolving some of these communication problems, and became more aware of each other's needs.

A smorgasbord for corporate communicators. As a final indicator of new directions for managers to turn their creative attentions to in improving organizational communications, we will cite four gold mines to explore:

1. Small-group communication research. Professionals in the field of communication theory and research have done some interesting studies on communication in small groups. With all the staff meetings, project conferences, and team management emphasis, some of these insights have implications for business leaders who wish to be on the cutting edge of the transition now under way. Dennis S. Gouran of Indiana University states that past research in this regard reveals the facilitative and inhibitory

influences that affect group performance. He suggests that research in the 1980s focus on authority relations, pressures for uniformity, status effects, disruptive behavior, and member goal orientation. The results of such investigations can usually be found in scholarly journals, such as those of the International Communication Association (5205 Leesburg Pike, Falls Church, VI 22041), or in unpublished theses and dissertations (available on microfilm from University Microfilms International, Ann Arbor, MI 48106).

2. Directories. These can be a source of worthwhile information for organizations (e.g., to find consultants or other knowledge workers), and every librarian can lead managers to the ones that are the most relevant. The most prolific publisher of these directories is Gale Research Company (Book Tower, Detroit, MI 48226), but alert managers should have a computer system for tracing smaller, newer directories, such as *World Information Sources* (130 North Road, Vershire, VT 05079) and *The Directory of Human Resource Services and Practices* (2355 E. Stadium Boulevard, Ann Arbor, MI 48104).

3. Networks. Whether formal or informal, computer or associational, networks are the fast way for metaindustrial managers to gain up-to-date information. They range from groups of scientists, technicians, and other professionals to futurists, women managers, and hobbyists. Electronic technology has increased the scope of such information exchanges and has resulted in such books as *The Network Nation: Human Communication by Computer*, by R. Hiltz and M. Turoff,* and a "Global Voluntary Information Network," by Yoneji Masuda.† Transnational enterprises are only beginning to tap the communication resources within their own far-flung facilities: for example, organizing human resources development specialists around the world into a single multinational network—or financial specialists and planners, or project managers and marketing directors.

4. The U.S. Chamber of Commerce has established a clearinghouse of information on corporate and organizational-sponsored communication efforts in business and economics. For details of this *Contact* program and its directory of successful communication examples, call John Sullivan at the Chamber's Clearinghouse (202) 659-6183.

---

* Reading, Mass.: Addison-Wesley, 1978.
† President, Information Society of Japan, 4-14-11 Jingumae Shibuyaku, Tokyo, Japan.

NEW MIS HORIZONS

Metaindustrial organizations are very dependent on comprehensive and responsive management information systems. New communication technologies have literally revolutionized this aspect of business. The transition from the dominance of centralized data processing to distributed information systems, especially through managerial work stations with combined word/data processing and video/voice capability, have opened up undreamed-of opportunities for improving organizational communications. There are both challenges and pitfalls in the new MIS:

- Reducing administrative costs by computer over paper-based systems.
- Installing million-bit memory chips by 1985, and total chip/wafer integrated systems by 1995.
- Coping with direct sensor-processor interface, and smart convivial systems during the next decade.
- Choosing between multiple-option systems, while fostering economy-of-scale in distributed systems.
- Coping with increased policy changes and intrusions into MIS, especially by government regulators.
- Making the most of communications subsystem components and machine/computer components.
- Changing over equipment to make way for innovative hardware, especially that which is more portable, less costly, and more sophisticated.
- Using new capacities triggered by the convergence of telecommunications with computers.
- Taking advantage of the linkage between telecommunications and telex, the integration of text and graphics and document production.
- Using the new communications technology to link and integrate workers in both offices and homes.
- Creating new MIS procedures that guide data manipulation and provide for continuous updating.

These are but a few of the new management communications issues that MIS specialists from both sides of the Iron Curtain considered recently at the 42nd Conference of Diebold Europe. When I was asked by this group to address the topic "Managing Cultural Differences in Cohabitation," I was puzzled. The term cohabitation referred to synergy between the *computer profes-*

sionals—analysts, designers, and programmers—and the *users*—operators, office managers, and administrative staff. The institutional subcultures of both groups were being brought closer together by the shift from centralized to distributed processing.

Just as all managers' approaches to organizational communications are conditioned by their macroculture, so the interaction between general managers and staff specialists is influenced by their microculture. Thus it is important for the computer specialist, for example, to enter into the organizational space of the sales manager, who is a user of the systems, in order to meet that user's needs. Similarly, as general managers become more educated and comfortable with computers, they are in a better position to enter into the perceptual field of the MIS professionals, who seek to provide managers with better communication tools. There is a need for more creative interface and empathy between line and staff, between generalists and technicians in the organization. The synergy of their perceptions will permit more scientific decision making based on accurate and relevant data. In dynamic organizational environments, the information specialist helps to define the architecture of organizational communications, to set standards, and to support development and operations. Divisional and senior managers should join with corporate EDP personnel in personalized planning of the management information system. Managers cannot simply be happily involved with their own microprocessors; they must contribute to identifying task structures, manipulating systems procedures, modifying information inputs and scope, and redesigning the centralized information system. Some highlights of the key issues facing MIS for the 1980s that emerged from the 1979 Diebold Europe Conference in Brussels, Belgium, are:

A. Data Communications
   1. How can the trends and alternatives of communications technologies be best predicted to enable management decision making?
   2. What are the critical areas, in a distributed environment, that software technology should address?
B. Acquisition Policy
   1. To what extent should users select equipment and services?
   2. Should we take advantage of special purpose computers?
C. Methodology and Standards
   1. Will methodology and standards in the future systems environments change the role of the systems analyst?

2. Can current methods deal with the unstructured part of the information resource?
3. Can methods and standards enable the end user to develop and maintain information processing applications?
4. How can we measure effective MIS performance?

D. Security
1. Is an autonomous corporate authority the only way to provide security and/or privacy?
2. Can we achieve cost-effective security levels?
3. How do we best protect the transport and flow of information?

E. Personnel Planning
1. How should we develop the interface between the user and the technician?
2. How can we prepare the necessary numbers of skilled technicians to take advantage of advanced technology?
3. How do we best ease the potentially negative effects of job displacement?

F. Organization
1. How should we evaluate the success of our MIS organizations?
2. What level of control should MIS have in a distributed environment?

In the 1980s, metaindustrial managers will be challenged by hardware that is going down in both size and cost. Very large scale computer system integrations are now possible because of magnetic bubbles and microminiaturized computers that contain chips with more than 16,000 circuits and fit into the palm of one hand. Already conventional silicon technology is being transformed. Gallium-arsenide chips have many advantages over the former for greater speed, and may eventually replace electronics with light pulses in computers. Researchers at Fjitsu in Japan have constructed circuit switches using GaAs (gallium-arsenide) chips that can be turned on and off in 17 trillionths of a second. They hope soon to reduce that to 10 trillionths. At the same time, American researchers are trying to develop supercomputers by redesigning today's silicon chips to work at superconducting temperatures to increase transmission speed. The conclusion is that metaindustrial managers plan for *continuous* hardware changes to improve the processing of information. Their problem will be that such technology often outstrips the organizational culture's capacity to absorb such new wonders.

The software for these sophisticated computers and word processors will be scarce and will rise in cost. But a more basic concern is the people who use the technology. Thus, the 44th Conference of Diebold Europe in Paris focused on "The Human Aspects of Information Systems." One problem will be the shortage of information professionals; another will be the need to develop a new generation of information resources managers. Speakers from all over the world confirmed that the relationship between the user and the computer specialist will lose its archaic distinctions as knowledge of formal computing operations becomes more widespread among management. Furthermore, many general managers will be drawn from among EDP specialists. L. Duverger of Diebold France envisioned the "generalization of the information sciences"—not just more universal understanding and use of the computer, but increased appreciation of its ability to do more specific tasks in a variety of fields. Systems engineers will design for undertakings and specializations for which there are no computer applications today. Speaking at this Paris convocation, I anticipated that MIS personnel will become more cosmopolitan, eventually becoming professional organizational communications consultants.

In 1964, John Diebold wrote prophetically about the metaindustrial work culture:

> Today's business machines result from a newfound ability to build systems which process and communicate information, translate from one language to another, respond to the human voice, and devise their own route to goals that are presented to them; machine systems which improve their performance as a result of encountering their environment.... In short, machine systems which deal with the very core of human society—with information and its communication and use. There are developments which augur far more for mankind than changes in manpower, more or less employment, or new ways of doing old tasks.... This is a technology which vastly extends the range of human capability and which will fundamentally alter human society.

Fred Casmir, professor of communication at Pepperdine University in Malibu, California, reminds us that communication is a major survival tool for any organization, and especially for the people in it. For him, information management is more than the capacity to store and retrieve; it is the ability to make meaningful and adequate use of what is provided by information technology. After all, data becomes information when it is used effectively. To be utilized in that manner, it should be derived from multiple sources and integrated. The role of the information coordinator is critical to the metaindustrial organization.

Such resources managers must be both creative generalists

and specialists. In fact, personnel are being recruited from outside the data processing department for this function so as to provide a more objective view. Information professionals must become *bridge-builders* among diverse peoples, organizations, and nations. Within the complex multinational organization of tomorrow, information resources managers will be needed as:

- *Linking-pins* of human minds and diverse systems in global enterprises;
- *Systems consultants* who use information to facilitate transnational data flow, processes, products, and services;
- *Energizers* who provide information leadership so that the metaindustrial organization can achieve its business mission;
- *Synergizers* who use information and its technology to promote collaboration and cooperation among disparate elements in both organizations and society, thereby creating something better than existed in their separate entities;
- *Integrators* who can add bits and pieces to produce holistic information, thus enlarging management perceptions and improving decisions;
- *Cosmopolitan communications consultants* who can move beyond specializations and ethnocentric positions to facilitate human interaction worldwide.

As the possessor of information, as well as the key mechanism for its distribution, the information professional has increasing power within complex organizations. By changing their images of their role and exercising the authority of competence, information resources managers can ensure that data transmission is used for improving *communication,* the very core of our humanness and civilization.* Metaindustrial organizations would be well advised to create a new breed of information managers, who are creative generalists and specialists, capable of serving as linking pins in organizational integration.

CONVERGENCE OF COMMUNICATION TECHNOLOGIES
Developments in the field of communications are so rapid and continuous that they constitute an effective argument for the

---

* I am indebted to two clients, their conferences and reports, for many of the insights in this section: that is, The Diebold Group Inc. of New York City, and Omicron, The Center for Systems Humanics, in Morris Plains, New Jersey.

concept of ultrastability in metaindustrial organizations. Robert M. Metcalfe, founder of 3Com, which makes transceivers for Xerox's Ethernet, perhaps put it most graphically when he complained: "Defining the product is a bitch when you're sitting in the middle of technologies that change every minute." This is what is happening in communications, and it has a dramatic impact on the organization.

Previously, we referred to the concept of ultrastability as building change and innovation into a human system so that it becomes a behavioral norm for people to incorporate continuing change. Technically, in the cybernetic terminology, it means the capacity of a system to maintain equilibrium (homeostasis) after being agitated or disturbed by unknown, unanalyzed forces. It is a management strategy for coping with the unexpected. Ultrastability seems most appropriate for organizations attempting to deal with the merger of computer science with telecommunications. The concept may help when attempting to treat information as a resource that is measurable and controllable. It may facilitate the integration into organizational communications of such innovative tools as laser, xerography, holographics, and image processing. It is a useful idea to recall when introducing teleconferencing, extending computing power down through the corporation or agency, or expanding transmission media for large-scale, high-speed transfer of voice, data, video, and facsimile. Furthermore, the data processing function is merging with office automation. While such communications advances may foster a higher degree of managerial control over information, the pace of these changes will be traumatic for most personnel.

What is happening in office and plant communications is but the prologue to a larger social metamorphosis. Business communications are the laboratory and battleground for what later will explode into the home communications market and center. The old distinctions between office and home are already eroding, and commercial travel has been reduced, as workers increasingly "go to work" at home and deal with management and company staff via two-way video and voice facilities, or send and receive reports through printers. Managers who wish to make sense of the bewildering array of useful communications technologies might first think in terms of integrated communication systems. Whereas in the past we focused individually on office activities, such as data or word processing, today we seek to integrate and maximize the contribution of such functions.* Planning for the new technologies on a total organizational basis is critical.

Once decisions are made as to what directions a company will go in terms of software and hardware, the introduction of these communications innovations should be accomplished in stages. By involving all relevant personnel in this process of planned change, an organization will ensure the humanization of both the technical and structural aspects of the new information systems. The organizational communications of the future will be designed to take advantage of these anticipated developments in the near future:

1982-1985

Short-Term Digital Communications Systems (Digital front-end to a voice PABX)

Text Management Systems (Disc-based text processing for document access and preparation)

Enhanced Voice Systems and Integrated Info Work Stations (Problem of standardization for interface).

Document Distribution Systems (Facsimile copies)

High-Resolution Displays (Improved information resolution)

High-Resolution Addressable Terminal Printers (Graphic information capability)

Teleconferencing (Three-screen video)

Videodisc Storage/Multimode Storage Systems (Writing capability/combined digital, voice, image)

Communications and Transmission Systems

1986-?

Corporationwide Communication by Satellite Transmissions

Decentralized Control in Broad, Shared Information Environments

Corporate Satellite Ownership

Space Industrialization/Communications

There are many dazzling choices open to corporate communications planners. At one end, one might consider paging systems

---

Integrated Electronic Information Network uses office automation that includes word processing, electronic filing, electronic mailing, message switching, and similar capabilities in a coordinated way. The equipment is standardized and compatible with each unit. It is integrated into larger electronic data processing capabilities that are centralized. The whole may form a communications network of national or international scope.

like Sky-Tel, which permits an executive to dial the office from commercial airplanes by using an air-to-ground radio; the signals are relayed over telephone lines. On the other hand, there is information dispatching by optic fibers, thin strands of glass used in place of copper wires—instead of electricity, laser light is transmitted. This will not only cost less and take up less space; it will improve the quality of communication processing. Of the vast array of technology options available in the 1980s, we will concentrate here on just three to indicate the potential for organizations: satellite communications, video projection technology, and information work stations. The purpose of all these endeavors is to increase productivity by integrating varied information technologies that improve performance at all levels and supposedly at lower costs.

○ *Satellite communications.* Twenty-two thousand three hundred miles above the equator, AT&T satellites catch microwaves beamed from the earth's surface and transmit back video and television images, facsimile, and other graphic materials, such as computer data and audio messages. IBM and other corporate giants around the world have moved into the new business of transmission by satellite. Two decades after the first Soviet Sputnik and the U.S. Early Bird Space Shots, Western Europe is joining in the global telecommunications market, hoping to win orders of $300 million a year. Arianespace, the satellite program of the eleven-nation European Space Agency, is producing and marketing its own satellite launchers, having broken the U.S./Soviet space rocket monopoly. Intelsat has ordered four Arianes satellites, while Western Union and RCA have booked space on their launchings. Arabsat, serving Arab Middle East countries, has also signed for three ESA satellites. With a prime location for telecommunications satellites, ESA plans 10 to 12 launchings a year for clients as close as Latin America and as far away as China.

In the near future, international competition for space communications will be fierce. The potential market for the next 15 years is $10 billion to transmit business information, telephone calls, and telexes; ground stations and ancillary equipment will add another $20 billion to this growth market. The Japanese are also entering this field with one-meter satellite dishes that are 25 percent more efficient than previous models. National governments are concerned about the way these transmissions breach their frontiers and about how to regulate such communications.

○ *Video projection technology.* This technology permits the projection of images and other relevant data in one central place for large audiences and/or in several locations for scattered participants. Colored, refractive, or direct image systems currently preclude optimal image and character resolution. GE's Light Valve improves graphic resolution on display screens, but it is expensive. Such video displays have been used to support management presentations and work groups both locally and for teleconferencing. AT&T uses a projector in combination with an IBM 370 for trend analysis application and projection. Mellon Bank uses the process for management and training support, as do Polaroid, J. C. Penney, and ARCO. There is a variety of video teleconferencing possibilities for medical, business, education, and government applications. Many foreign governments are experimenting with the technology, and the French government will use it for continuing education in conjunction with a 1983 satellite launching.

For meeting planners, it is a revolutionary tool, and rentals are possible through Bell System's Picture Phone Meeting Service. The Florida State Senate in Tallahassee has a GE PJ7000 large-screen video projector to display legislative amendments and to welcome notable guests and constituents in galleries in place of verbal-message interruptions. Many corporations are linking a far-flung sales force together in video teleconferencing by satellite, bringing a regional group together in a hotel to view transmissions that are beamed nationally or internationally. Some multinationals are already setting up a network of receiving sites to expand this new means for improving organizational communications. Certain hotels now offer teleconferencing (for example, Holiday Inn's Video Network (HI-NET) for 250 people at a cost of approximately $100 per person, with the cost going down as the numbers involved go up ($5 a head for 15,000 people).

○ *Information work stations.* The highlights of the impact of office automation on the organization were reviewed earlier. Here we will simply focus on some of the available integrated systems, a subject addressed by The Diebold Automated Office Program. A summary of its fourth plenary meeting on this theme is also available. Xerox's Office Information Systems Group offers an electronic work station or desk that includes word processing and text editing, text/graphics composition, file control, print-copy control, electronic mail, terminal emulation, and user-to-user communication. In addition to connecting other stations in one establishment, it offers intraoffice capability at high speed and low cost, with the possibility for modular expansion. In addition to intelligent machines, it has the Ethernet communication system, which does not require an expensive central processor to supervise message traffic. These self-regulating machines can send and receive at will and convey data at the rate of 500 pages per second. Soon a market analyst using this system will be able to summon files from different electronic memory banks, assemble a report on a video terminal, and circulate an electronic draft for fellow workers to consider and offer feedback on—all without ever moving from a work cubicle. These machines now have coaxial cables, which do not permit voice conversation. The next step in this technology will be optical-fiber transmission. Available for national transfers now, Xerox is acquiring Western Union International to expand the system on a global basis.

Wang Laboratories, Inc., operates on the assumption that today's primary office concerns and functions will continue to exist amid increasing complexity and decreasing resources. Gradually, managers will realize the full potential of automation for comprehensive storage, retrieval, conversion, and sharing of information. To meet the first phase of such needs, Wang's system features electronic tickler files, calendar management, people location systems, and intersystem exchange networks. Wang's plans call for pursuing development of image and digital voice storage, self-teaching and adaptive communications systems, and the marketing of work stations for use by middle management.

Interactive Systems Corporation focuses on user-oriented, minicomputer-based systems with a synergy of functional modules. ISC work-station design allows for a text editor, document formatter, data processor, and message systems and communications link. The user customizes an "island of information."

Tymshare's AUGUMENT is designed to improve clerical and professional information handling, especially by personnel with no data processing or technological training. It also features text processing, electronic messages, document production, photo and graphics composition, and information storage, management, and retrieval. In addition to its multiple-display capability, it structures information statements and has a storage file, which is helpful to beginners at work stations in structuring concepts and data manipulation.

Spatial Data Management Systems (SDMS), created by Interactive Television Corporation, is our last example of the new communications technology. SDMS does not use the conventional access to information systems; it gains access through findings on maps of information spaces, which contain data stored in a variety of media. This system can be used with moderately large management support data bases, including financial, education and training, and decision-support systems. The managers can use a modified "joystick" to fly around the monitor screen and zoom in on the desired information. SDMS also contains a microfiche reader, a keyboard, optical videodisc units, a microprocessor, and remote computer processing, as well as a teleconferencing application. SDMS's electronic desk emphasizes integration of multiple communication functions, multipurpose display, and other embedded hardware.

FUTURE MANAGERIAL CONCERNS

The transformation under way in organizational communications offers many challenges to managers. Information is not only power; it also means money in the metaindustrial work culture. The company that can stay ahead of competitors and government regulations has an advantage. Thus, *issues management* has emerged as a new profession, and a new Issues Management Association has been formed. The new field attempts early identification of issues that affect organizational operations, and develops long-range strategies to cope with them. It involves forecasting techniques and information gathering on a wide variety of topics covering such diverse subjects as telecommunications, economics, government regulations, and scientific discoveries. It includes identification of emerging issues, polling, monitoring, evaluation by experts, and even computer-based demographic modeling. For many corporations, the new development means having recourse to external consultants in the area of futures studies: The Institute of the Future in Menlo Park, The Center for Futures Research at the University of Southern California, TrendTRACK in Boulder, Colorado, the Hudson Institute in Hudson, New York, are some now at work.

Another concern is future microcomputer applications within organizations. These are some unfolding possibilities for computing: budget systems, personnel systems including human resources, statistical tracking systems, data transfer systems from the mainframe computers, storage systems, and documentation systems. The greatest need for managers will be obtaining the software to accompany all these technical applications that will revolutionize the manager's role. Finally, there is the human resources development challenge. Training people on a large scale to use the new communications technology effectively may well be the ultimate challenge!

CAPSULE CONCLUSIONS

Our odyssey through the impact of technology on organizational communications began with a review of the emerging information society. In the next two decades of transition, knowledge workers will cope with turmoil in the organizational environment as we seek to eliminate the obsolete, keep what is relevant in both equipment and information, and introduce the new technical inventions. The communications revolution will force us to further revise our images of self, role, organization, nation, and species. As we increasingly take a systems approach to institutional interactions, we will make greater use of informal and technological communications within offices and work spaces. To humanize the interchanges at business, we should begin by improving interpersonal and small-group communication skills. Then we might seek to improve other nontechnical aspects of business communications, such as personnel's foreign language skills, organizational interfaces during mergers and acquisitions, and networks of resources specialists for improved problem solving. Finally, we examined the new horizons for management information systems and the future technologies that will alter organizational communications, from space satellites to electronic work stations.

A central factor in why the metaindustrial work culture will differ so drastically from the industrial work culture will be the astronomical changes in communications capabilities. In the eighties and nineties, senior and middle management will struggle with the output of the microelectronics revolution, especially for information processing and exchange. As a result, at all levels of operations, both corporations and government agencies will never be the same. However, the technology continues to outpace management's ability to use it. Thus David Conrath, professor of management at the University of Waterloo, wisely warns us:

> Nobody seems to be concerned with how companies are going to have to organize or reorganize to take full advantage of this technology.... When such a system is introduced, it must involve the workflow, the authority hierarchy, the basis of centralization and decentralization, who makes decisions and how.... Previously management brought equipment for somebody else to use. Now they are going to buy equipment for themselves; they are going to be more wary of the effects on their own way of doing things.

CHAPTER 8   Changing Career Development Patterns

Education and training are primary means for perpetuating a culture. In a cultural analysis, it is necessary to examine how a group learns—how its members transmit knowledge, information, and folk wisdom to succeeding generations. The educational practices of a group, whether formal or informal, are culture-specific. They reflect the customs, traditions, beliefs, and attitudes of both the macroculture and the microcultures. For managers to better understand an organization's culture, they must examine the human resources development (HRD) system of a corporation, agency, or association. The enterprise reflects the culture of the society in which it is located. A company's philosophy, scope, and methods for career development also reflect a country's culture. HRD programs in the Orient would have different content, emphasis, and techniques from Western programs. Yet synergy in education and training today might lead to borrowing from the HRD practices of other cultures. Thus a Western corporation might introduce the teaching of Zen meditation to its executives to improve their stress management.

LEARNING AS A CULTURAL DIMENSION
Corporate culture affects the organization's commitment to the development of its human resources. The quality and appearance of new recruits, the care and methods used in their placement and promotion, the ways that performance is assessed and rewarded, the procedures for terminating association—all such organizational activities reflect the institution's culture. The organizational HRD system does more than transfer attitudes, information, and skills to employees, customers, and suppliers. It does more than enable personnel to earn a living, to supplement previous formal schooling, to socialize, and even to exercise power. It

is *the* mechanism for inculcating the organization's wisdom, history, and culture in its members. Corporate ideas and ideals, values and priorities, norms and expectations, are all passed on through orientation and training courses, management and executive development, and conferences and conventions. Thus organizational behavior is conditioned, consciously and unconsciously.

Some organizational cultures promote the raising of member consciousness and self-actualization. The American Red Cross, for instance, has this personnel objective: "to improve the quality of life and enhance self-reliance." According to its training department, this translates into training people to help themselves. The organization is thus supportive of training. Education in many organizations is a major activity that involves considerable financial investment.

The magnitude can be appreciated by examining one industry—the telephone utilities. In 1980, it was reported that the Bell System offered 12,000 courses in 1,300 training locations for 20,000 to 30,000 employees per day; such educational services involved a training support staff of 13,000 to 15,000 at a cost of $1.7 billion. Note, however, that the effectiveness of this training can be aided or undermined by corporate culture, as Donald Caplin reminds us:

> In 1961, AT&T set up a training program to teach managers how to coordinate customized sales. But when managers returned to the job, they proved unable—or unwilling—to implement what they had learned. In fact, 85 percent quit the company and the program was disbanded.
> Poor training—or something else? An analysis of the experience showed that the AT&T Program was the victim of "corporate culture." Organizational culture is a mysterious entity that has claimed a number of training efforts—but it also can help a human resource program....
> In the AT&T case, for example, the problem was that the culture valued volume; making as many sales as possible meant mass production. Although they learned a new set of behaviors, managers—in effect—were not rewarded for serving individual requests.

Yet corporate cultures can change, for it was this very industrial giant, AT&T, that pioneered a complete redesign of roles through a systemwide job enrichment program and a project to reward high performers.

Today, AT&T estimates that over 50 percent of all its costs are so-called people expenses. Alfred J. Walker, their manager of Human Resource Data Systems in Morristown, N.J., reports that this corporation has the largest personnel computerized data record in the world: 1.4 million employees. The system is used for human resources planning and utilization, government compliance, salary administration, management movement, decision information, data standardization, and upgrading personnel skills. With the divestiture of the Bell System, it is uncertain what will become of the HRM data bank, but one proposal is to create a separate company that would contract these centralized HR computer services to all the independent telephone companies. Organizational change at AT&T has brought the utility from an engineering-based to a marketing-based company, from telephone services to a computer/home communication corporation in the metaindustrial period. It is a classic example of why managers need to plan and manage change in an organization.

When transnational enterprises offer training and development on a global scale, their educational endeavors also become powerful mechanisms for local change. But their efforts may be culture-bound and need to be adapted to the host culture to be effective. Technology transfer, when it is sensitive and appropriate, can make a significant contribution to the host culture. Whether the corporation abroad is engaged in literacy or skills training, management or community development, its representatives should be aware of the influences of their own national and organizational cultures upon themselves. Then they will not use the learning process as the means for cultural imposition or for inappropriate and unrealistic teaching or instruction. For example, one does not expect management trainees in a culture dominated by rote learning to suddenly abstract and conceptualize. Vern Terpstra provides some guidelines for multinational corporations engaged in worldwide worker training:

- The general level of education locally affects the quality of people available for employment and training. Learning must be adapted to such realities.
- Managers should be rewarded in proportion to their success overseas in training of the locals. Their management control systems should take into account the local culture and its values.
- Every country, regardless of its stages of development, has its educational elites who are at the top of the local educational superstructure. The foreign manager should establish contact with this network of individuals and the institutions from whence they came.

GLOBAL HUMAN RESOURCES MANAGEMENT

The personnel process from entry to exit has been popularly designated the *human resources development system*. Leonard Nadler has defined HRD as "a series of organized activities, conducted within a specified time and designed to produce behavioral change." Nadler, a George Washington University professor, maintains that training equals job-related learning experiences, education equals individual-related learning experiences, and development equals organization-related learning experiences. He believes that HRD within organizations is moving toward greater use of media and learning modules for instructional purposes.

Devanna, Fombrun, and Tichy propose that organizations have human resources management strategies that deal with policy formulations, goal setting, and long-term positioning of the corporation in its environment. Table 2 presents their view of human resources functions on the strategic, the managerial, and the operational levels. It provides an interesting overview of what HRD involves within an organizational culture.

Organizational human resources development leads to the capitalization of human assets, the enlargement of human potential. In an information society, the corporation plays an increased role in the education of its own personnel and of the citizenry at large. *Fortune* 500 companies have founded learning corporations, and an expanding number of other firms are getting into the business of education. They provide educational hardware, software, and instruction. Westinghouse Learning Corporation, for instance, was involved in the Peace Corps, VISTA, and police training. In the United States, the education business within the private sector is a billion-dollar-plus enterprise.

And what of the future for organizational career development? Let's use our imaginations based on contemporary trends and project ahead to the turn of the century.

HRD Scenario 2000
Jack Armstrong is a satellite technician with Tel Com Tech, WC. Originally, this company was incorporated in the United States, until regional supranational economic authorities were established to charter "world corporations" and supervise their planetary business activities. Back in 1995 Tel Com received its WC designation from the Pacific Basin Regional Authority, a quasi-governmental entity, because the bulk of its enterprises were centered in the Pacific Rim area. Although Jack works out of cor-

TABLE 2. Human resources functions.

Level	Employee Selection/Placement	Rewards (Pay and Benefits)	Appraisal	Development	Career Planning
Strategic (long-term)	1. Specify the characteristics of people needed to run business over long term. 2. Alter internal and external systems to reflect future.	1. Determine how workforce will be rewarded over the long term based on potential world conditions. 2. Link to long-term business strategy.	1. Determine what should be valued in long term. 2. Develop means to appraise future dimensions. 3. Make early identification of potential.	1. Plan developmental experiences for people running future business. 2. Set up systems with flexibility necessary to adjust to change.	1. Develop long-term system to manage individual and organizational needs for both flexibility and stability. 2. Link to business strategy.
Managerial (medium-term)	1. Make longitudinal validation of selection criteria. 2. Develop recruitment marketing plan. 3. Develop new markets.	1. Set up five-year compensation plans for individuals. 2. Set up cafeteria benefits packages.	1. Set up validated systems that relate current conditions and future potential. 2. Set up assessment centers for development.	1. Establish general management development program. 2. Provide for organizational development. 3. Foster self-development.	1. Identify career paths. 2. Provide career development services. 3. Match individual with organization.
Operational (short-term)	1. Make staffing plans. 2. Make recruitment plans. 3. Set up daily monitoring systems.	1. Administer wage and salary program. 2. Administer benefits packages.	1. Set up annual or less frequent appraisal system. 2. Set up day-to-day control systems.	1. Provide for specific job skill training. 2. Provide on-the-job training.	1. Fit individuals to specific jobs. 2. Plan next career move.

"Human Resources Management: A Strategic Perspective," by Mary Anne Devanna, Charles Fombrun, and Noel Tichy, from *Organizational Dynamics*, Winter 1981.

porate headquarters in San Diego, he reports in this matrix organization to Paula Dittmar, a European executive also located at HDQ, as well as to Milton Robertson in Vancouver, Canada, and Harry Wu in Singapore, Malaysia. Tel Com's main operational subsidiaries are in those cities.

On the morning of January 4, 2000, Jack had an interview in the Career Development Center to review his semiannual career growth plan. There he was to meet first with Monroe Linton, the company's HRD executive consultant, who heads the center and is also responsible for career development throughout Tel Com's global network of knowledge workers. The corporation is committed to actualizing the potential of all its human assets. Since all personnel own shares in the corporation, they share in both its profits and its losses (which rarely occur), so their development is a high priority in the enterprise's culture. Linton, a black former football star and scholar from USC, carries the letters CHRS after his name on the center door. (He is a Certified Human Resources Specialist, a title earned through the International Society for Human Resources Development. The organization resulted from a merger of the American Society of Training and Development and like national societies with the then International Federation of Training and Development Organizations. In 1990, the formation of this HRD conglomerate dropped the words "training" and "trainers" from professional vocabularies.)

Prior to meeting with Armstrong, Linton reviewed the man's career history and forecasts on the computerized video display. The office microprocessor can instantly recall personal, educational, vocational, and social information on every Tel Com affiliate (the word *employee* had long ago been dropped). The coded information provides not only Armstrong's performance record since joining Tel Com five years ago, but results from sophisticated career testings and simulations at the center, along with predictions. This was all part of Tel Com's Talent Bank, a worldwide registry called HAR (for Human Assets Registry).

Through Linton, all managers in their far-reaching enterprise can get a printout on personnel who might fit their unit's annual needs assessment. At the end of each fiscal year, Tel Com expects managers to forecast resources needs for their operations. With regard to workers, this included two competency components—humans and robots. Linton's staff was to assist management in developing a synthesis between organization and human career needs and development. Their counterparts at the Robotics Research Center were engineering specialists who coordinated all the mechanical "workers" and conducted experiments on their performance improvement.

On this particular sunny Monday morning in their Torrey Pines Industrial Park facilities, Linton had arranged for a teleconference involving Jack Armstrong and Paula Dittmar in California, Milton Robertson in Canada, and Harry Wu in Malaysia. Together they would discuss Armstrong's career plan for the year 2000 in terms of his professional needs and corporate needs. Within the context of an information processing firm's culture, the conversation went like this:

Linton: Greetings, all! By now you have reviewed our HRD records and forecast on your bright young technician, Jack Armstrong. We hope to arrive through this conference at some mutual consensus on a career development focus for him over the next 6 to 12 months. Let's begin with Jack himself. If wishes were to come true, and you had no constraints upon you, Jack, what would you wish to do?

Armstrong: Well, I've had five years of documented achievement with Tel Com, and I think that I'm due for an educational sabbatical. I'd like to take a year off to go East to MIT for some technical communications studies. It's about time that I got exposed to some of that Eastern culture after being brought up in the West!

Wu: While I'd miss you on our project team, Jack, I can appreciate the wisdom and humor of your last remark about exposure to Eastern culture. I think I could live with your temporary absence from our activities *if* you could include some Vietnamese language and culture studies on your agenda for the next year. As you know, Tel Com has a major expansion under way in Indochina, and I was anticipating that you might join our Hanoi operations in 2001.

Linton: Thanks for that input, Harry. If we agree that Vietnam's in Jack's near future, there would be no problem in arranging some videotapes and holographics to upgrade Jack's proficiencies in the Vietnamese language and business protocol while he is proceeding with advanced information sciences.

Robertson: OK, all. But don't forget our down-range plan to set up a Tel Com industrial station on the moon in 2005 and beyond. Jack is a prime candidate for that mission. If we concur that this is the right time for extended studies, it certainly should include some long-range career preparation for that potential assignment. A Far Eastern stint for three years is feasible for Jack, but by 2004 he would have to devote himself primarily to specialized orientation for that moon launch. Since

I have principal space project responsibility, I naturally want to ensure that our best personnel for that interplanetary team will be ready. My staff and I envision Armstrong as a unit leader for a mission team of five human specialists and fifteen robots.

Dittmar: Well, fellows, since I have everyday interface and supervisory relations with our colleague, may I propose some compromises? Here in San Diego, we cannot spare Jack to be away for twelve months. We could release him part time for some local studies over the next six months, and then give him full time off for the following six months. Further, if he enrolled in our nearby UCSD, he could take advantage of their unique program in lunar studies. To meet Milt Robertson's concerns, Jack might do two things: (1) finish his doctorate in telecommunications with his dissertation research focused on problems related to establishing our "moon factory," and (2) set up an on-line computer interaction with the folks up north at Edwards Air Force Base. By staying on the West Coast, he also can pop up regularly to the nearby NASA facilities. After that, I have no objections to a short-term Vietnam task force assignment. That intercultural experience might even sharpen his coping skills for dealing with an alien culture in outer space.

Linton: Should Jack stay in this locale, we could take care of Harry's concerns through the nearby Indochinese Studies Center, and also expose him to the large Vietnamese community in Vista, California. Paula, your proposals are sound, but I think I can get you a substitute for Jack, so that he could be released for a full year of concentrated studies and research. We have an exchange program with the faculty at UCSD. I think I can arrange for one of their staff to join Tel Com for a year to cover Jack's professional responsibilities with us. On the other hand, Jack might have to agree to give some lectures or teach a course while also at the university studying. Well, sharpen the images on your video pictures and tell me what you think of these alternatives. Jack, why don't you start off?

Implications of the Scenario
Back in the present, what do we learn about future prospects for organizational culture and its HRD system? The scenario contains more facts and likelihoods than fantasy. Consider, then, these possibilities for the decades immediately ahead as revealed in this case:

- The corporate focus is on information/communications technology.

- There is a regional economic emphasis, and emergence of a supranational authority that charters world corporations.
- In this matrix organization, one operates globally and reports to people in other parts of the world.
- A multinational workforce operates on the authority of competence, not on nationality, race, sex, or other such obsolete employment criteria. (EEO is long since dead, along with unions of diminished influence.)
- A central corporate theme is meaningful career development and review in terms of larger organizational strategies.
- The presence of women and minorities in executive positions is an organizational norm, along with the premise of personnel involvement and ownership.
- The inclusion of HRD data in the total management information system for international application.
- The utilization of technological and personnel forecasting in comprehensive planning by HRD professionals who are more facilitators than personnel mechanics.
- The expansion of American professional societies beyond national borders, and their certification of professional competency. The internationalization of professional associations, both formally and informally, will be evident, especially through networking.
- The computerization of all worldwide personnel records and the use of a talent bank for full-time, part-time, and contract knowledge workers.
- The establishment of a new "personnel" entity for robotics management to counterbalance the Career Development Center for humans (fewer in number and of high-quality abilities).
- The common use of teleconferencing and other means of telecommunications, as well as of educational technology.
- The collaborative nature and approach of the management team, though separated by distance and macrocultures.
- The acceptance of sabbaticals for continuing professional growth.
- The cooperative relations and personnel exchanges between the corporation and the university.
- The use of other educational resources in the community for language and culture learning, especially by use of one's home communication center.

- The market focus on the Pacific Rim, and the international corporate headquarters in Western North America.
- The planning for expansion into outer space commercial operations.
- The sophisticated, cosmopolitan managerial approach, with its concern for the well-being of both the individual and the institution.

Since technology and its growth will soon dominate organizational life, it is important that technical and engineering personnel be continuously updated on new developments and that their educational experiences be broadening. Only then will we ensure their personal and professional development and counteract overly narrow specialization. Only then can we ensure that such persons are prepared to make more significant contributions to society and their organizations. A recent study by HRD researchers Rymell and Newsom recommends more self-directed learning projects in highly technical industries so that a wider variety of learning topics and educational resources will be used.

EDUCATING FOR CHANGING ROLES

General Electric had a slogan, "People are our most important product." Any firm that believed in such an ideal would devote a major portion of its budget to investment in its human assets. With the spread of robotics and computerization, there will obviously be fewer people at work in organizations, but these individuals will have higher qualifications and competencies. Such knowledge workers will not only be responsible for a wider scope of mechanized operations, they will require extensive support services. The high costs in obtaining and maintaining such personnel already demand that corporations provide creative environments to retain these valued employees. More important, company budgets will be extended to offer continuous reeducation of them to ensure high performance.

Even traditional industrial-age giants spend heavily today on personnel development. Westinghouse Electric, for example, has worldwide in-service training for hourly workers and spends millions on in-house management development. Most companies also send key persons off-site for workshops, seminars, and courses to keep them abreast of innovations in their fields and to permit them to acquire the latest technical or managerial techniques. A few statistics may underscore the scope of this current HRD investment in people. The American Management Associations, one of the largest adult education systems in the United States and abroad, reported that in 1980, 81,092 managers and executives took their short courses, which numbered 3,407. Through a subsidiary organization, such management education is offered by The President's Association from the CEO to the upper levels of management either in relaxing resorts or in-house. Furthermore, the AMA's management philosophy and services are available overseas through affiliated management centers, as well as through their International Management Association. Another piece of information may make the point: In 1981, 1 million influential North American executives attended some type of seminar, workshop, or conference at a total cost of $500 million.* The billion-dollar-plus business of education in industry and government experienced a 15 percent growth rate in the decade of the 70s. Why?

Numerous reasons could be cited as to why so many adults are going "back to school," or in fact never really leave the "classroom." The last half of the twentieth century has been marked by an acceleration in the rate of change, an explosion of knowledge in all fields of human endeavor, and a major shift from an industrial to a postindustrial way of life. The Metaindustrial Revolution is not only forcing the demise of many jobs and occupations; it is eliminating whole functional areas within traditional industries. This has been referred to as conventional technology obsolescence.

As this is being written, two newspaper reports come forth that underscore the problem and the challenge. Sony has announced a discovery of a new approach to photography that will "revolutionize" the industry and make present processes archaic. What will this do to the photography industry and positions as now constituted? Similarly, TRW in Hawthorne, California, reveals that it has had a team of scientists and technicians working for four years under NASA contract on the possibilities for establishing factories in outer space. Within the decade, materials processing platforms may be launched with a view to developing stronger alloys, more uniform crystals, and purer chemicals and serums. The expansion of research and manufacturing facilities

* D. M. Schrello, *The Seminar Market*. Long Beach, Calif.: Schrello Enterprises, 1981.

into space is likely before the turn of this century; it is but another catalyst for change in the way in which we work and form organizations.

We are already well aware of the implications of the spread of office automation and its impact on managers and secretarial staffs. But what will happen to traditional careers and vocational activities brought on by the expanded linkage of telecommunications and computer technologies? The French have a new word for it—*telematics,* which refers to the transmission of information by a blend of pictures, sounds, and memories that will transform our culture. These developments will have a profound effect on both society and organizational culture.

New technologies are transforming international trade and manufacturing; they are changing the very way in which we do business and design people's roles in organizations. Not only is human society in transition, but our traditional career roles are disappearing. First, analyze what is happening to the functions of corporate personnel and training. Daily more of such activities are being computerized in one form or another. The electronic data processing departments began by taking over their own HRD tasks because computer professionals were so "different." Now the EDP personnel are designing completely computerized human resources management systems not only for their own specialists, but eventually for all employees. A case in point is New York's Manufacturers Hanover Trust Company, whose HR functions in the DP area service 6,000 employees, including 1,500 computer professionals. Charles D. LaBelle, vice president for human resources in the Operations Division, described the company's six major activities in the information technology environment: to organize, acquire, utilize, evaluate, develop, and reward personnel. The computerized program is facilitated by HR advisers who act as a bridge between the DP and HR fields, as well as between their specialists. The approach is based on upward mobility for deserving performers, a skills data bank that matches personnel profiles with unit employee needs, coordinated use of external consultants, recruitment beyond local job markets, and monthly measurement of preset personnel goals. It is not improbable that the DP/HR management system may eventually be adopted by the whole banking enterprise. What then is the role of those specialists in personnel and training with corporate headquarters?

Second, consider how many jobs have disappeared since

computer programmers came into being less than 40 years ago. Now consider the number of corporations that have created the function of information resources manager. With the emergence of a watershed technology like microcomputers, that role is already becoming a key management position. Somebody has to coordinate the input and output of these smart machines within organizations. If the impact of the microprocessor on society may be greater than that of the automobile or the electric light, what will be its influence on organizations and their cultures? The influence can be seen in contemporary organization training. The introduction of "micros" into businesses has meant a proliferation of courses in "authoring systems for managers" or "word processing for executives."

Furthermore, communications technologies are altering the *way we learn.* As with programmed instruction, computer-based learning forces one to master one part of a lesson before going on to the next knowledge component. Still another illustration of drastic changes in the way we learn is teleconferencing, another spinoff of the Space Age. It is now being used for medical education programming of innovative healing techniques, for less expensive sales training in new product lines, for rapidly updating financial officers on the effects of newly passed bankruptcy laws.

In these turbulent times, what approaches can farsighted managers adopt in their human resources development efforts? Four proposals follow. It is my hope that they stimulate readers to come up with other approaches to capitalizing on human assets.

1. *Reeducation of industrial-age workers* for the realities of postindustrial society. To limit future shock and counteract the dislocations in the workforce caused by increased automation, business will have to cooperate with unions, government, universities, and other social institutions in massive "enlightenment" programs about the profound transitions under way in both macro and micro cultures. For example, instead of major, sudden layoffs of blue-collar workers, a socially responsible company might conduct orientation sessions on why the discharge is necessary, how to prepare for alternative careers, and how to seek retraining in the new technologies. Personnel departments might use organizational communications and training on how to make the most of increased leisure for greater development of one's potential. Advertising departments might devote part of their budgets to public service messages about social change. Champion International Corporation has demonstrated in its advertise-

ment series "Seeds for the Future" that a forest-product company can successfully use advertising for disseminating futuristic information.

Few major corporations, however, have sponsored mass media programming to raise public awareness about the future and how we can influence it. What organizations like the World Future Society and its publication, *The Futurist,* do for intellectual elites, corporations have the means of doing for their publics, from employees to customers. One healthy trend has been the emerging-issues groups or tasks forces that are arising within company planning departments. What is really helpful is when they make their reports available both inside and outside the corporation, as AT&T does. Increasingly, companies are establishing futures studies or technological forecasting units and departments. When their findings are offered to personnel, customers, and the interested public, they become a medium of education, as well as of public relations. This is the case with the useful newsletters *FutureScan* and *Trends* distributed by Futures Research Division of Security Pacific National Bank in Los Angeles. Each newsletter deals with a different issue affecting our future. Finally, some industries are sponsoring forecasting studies of their fields in conjunction with university futurists. When their results get beyond privileged information reports and into monographs and books for general use, a public service is performed. This happened when nine big corporations joined the state of California in investing in a futures research project with scholars at the University of Southern California. The outcomes included the remarkable volume *The Emerging Network Marketplace.**

2. *Training in coping skills* to enable personnel to deal more effectively with dramatic shifts in work or lifestyle. A variety of programs are currently under way from management-of-change workshops to stress-management seminars. I have been involved in conducting programs and developing learning systems on the change management theme for over 15 years with a wide variety of human systems. I have long maintained that when a company relocates an employee at home or abroad, productivity and profitability can be increased through training him or her how to deal with regional and international cultural differences. Many corporations are discovering that human resources development

---
* Norwood, N.J.: Ablex Publishing Corp., 1981.

training in stress management can pay big dividends in cutting down sick leaves and mental breakdowns. (To assess one's own ability to cope with change, see Appendix C.)

The health-care industry can offer both physical and mental preventive health programs. They are particularly effective when they are undertaken in conjunction with business and industry. Scripps Memorial Hospital in La Jolla, California, for example, has a successful project for coping with the transition toward leadership. Entitled "Easing the Trauma of Transition: Managing Your Upward Move," this innovative two-day workshop deals with the challenge of promotion, especially when a person may not feel quite ready for it. Consultant Lorrie McGrath reports that the focus is on the problems of personnel who are new to supervisory roles and self-assessment and who need to acquire managerial skills.

Employees and managers require assistance in managing the crises in life. People can be taught to be less rigid, closed, and fearful in dealing with rapid change. They can be helped to learn how to meet the challenge of the transitional experience, the turning points in life or career, the crises everyone must face from time to time. Such a crisis may be caused by death or loss of a loved one, by serious illness or surgery, by promotion or demotion, by job relocation or layoff, by corporate acquisition or merger, by divorce, or drug or alcohol addiction. Such crises become an opportunity for growth or regression, depending on how the person copes with the experience. People can change their attitudes and life and work styles; they can acquire more effective coping skills to manage the trauma of transition. In this period of increasing changes, individuals and institutions must develop mechanisms and strategies to promote ultrastability. Simply put, "When everything nailed down is coming loose, we have the capacity to keep our cool!"

3. *Developing skills in synergy.* This is vital in a world that is becoming ever more complex and interdependent. Organizations can do much to replace the obsolete industrial norm of rugged individualism and unlimited competition. Now is the time for corporations and agencies to teach collaborative skills among personnel, divisions, and subsidiaries. Now is the time to foster cooperation between companies within an industry, between public and private sectors, between labor and management. But it requires retraining and skills development to get people to work together so as to achieve results greater than they can accomplish

alone. People can be helped* to use their perceptual differences to create something by combined action which is better in quantity or quality.

Synergy brings about a synthesis between divergent cultures, groups, and views so that the resulting whole is greater than the sum of the parts. It is a metaindustrial concept that can ensure human survival and development. Synergy can become the bridge between the industrial and superindustrial way of life. It can facilitate human systems renewal, and help in the reintegration of traditional and new forms or technologies. It can become the means to increased national, regional, and international cooperation in economics and ecology, food production and distribution, scientific and technological development. It is already happening on an ever-increasing scale in management and executive development by team building and skills training.

4. *Learning to be strategists.* The real leaders of this world must be true strategists. A strategist takes a holistic approach in the planning and directing of large-scale movements or operations. A strategist can project beyond the moment for later effective utilization of combined resources. In other words, a strategist is a futurist who can grasp the big picture and synthesize the means for realistic solutions with the greatest impact. A strategist is a generalist capable of systems thinking and integration of parts into an overall plan; a manager is able to plan moves that capitalize on weakness in other situations, and able to create an environment that maximizes human performance. In contrast, a tactician specializes in the use and deployment of elements in an overall strategy. Within the metaindustrial organization, the strategist is the conceptualizer who provides the models and paradigms that bring together diverse disciplines and innovations so that they fit together. Such a person can move beyond conventional methods of problem solving by designing new roles, new rules, and new models.

The Western Behavioral Science Institute in La Jolla, California, recently opened a School of Management and Strategic Studies. In its announcement, it defined a strategy as

the ability to anticipate future developments for more effective planning; to realize the limitations and possibilities of future forecasting.

* Ways to accomplish this are examined in *Managing Cultural Synergy* by R. T. Moran and P. R. Harris.

This institute maintains that today's senior executives not only face situations of enormous complexity involving unprecedented constraints, but must operate with a sense of the larger social and business context and an understanding of highly interdependent social, economic, and environmental systems. Part of the strategic learning is done by computer linkage between WBSI and the executive participant's office.

Naumes and Paine cite eight characteristics that should be developed in HR programs for strategic thinkers:

1. Conceputalizing the policy formation process....
2. Developing comprehension, skill, and knowledge for diagnosing and dealing with specific and unique policy and strategy situations.
3. Gaining understanding of the complex realities, challenging questions and conflicting policy making.
4. Analyzing the organization's environment and its policy-generating structure.
5. Designing and proposing approaches that will help to prevent organizational stagnation.
6. Developing administrative and communication skills in presenting and developing solutions to policy problems....
7. Integrating or tying together concepts, principles, and skills learned separately in other more specialized situations.
8. Being cautious in accepting the many prescriptions that exist in the literature....

Career development efforts should aim at producing creative strategists who will influence the organizational culture in such a way that members will show more meaningful, productive behavior.

INNOVATIONS IN MANAGEMENT AND CAREER DEVELOPMENT

Today, both the community and government expect corporate managers to be vehicles for economic and social change. The expectations of the managers of multinational corporations are even higher. Great hopes are pinned on the contribution these transnational enterprises are capable of making in the developing countries and in the still developing segments of advanced technological societies. Some insight into the management education response to this broadened role for corporate leaders can be ascertained from the McNulty report on *Management Development*. It contained a summary of a joint conference between the American Assembly of Collegiate Schools of Business and the European Foundation for Management Development (held in Paris in 1981). The topic for the 600 management educators was: "Managers for the 21st Century." The managers agreed that management's field of vision is too narrow and that today's career planning is obsolete. (And as a management consultant, I would add that the vision of the management professors is too narrow and their business teaching often unrelated to the outside world.) In any event, these European and American scholars did arrive at these conclusions:

- Management curriculi will shift in orientation from functional to behavioral, and will include new teaching methods, such as "hands on" project work.
- Management schools, now mostly structured for big business, will have to include the teaching of entrepreneurship for managers of small, capital-venture businesses. (Here I would add that this instruction should not be directed only to business operations in developed societies with all types of sophisticated support services, but also to business operations in less developed societies without the infrastructure to support multinational business.)
- Noncognitive skills will become more important for business students than cognitive ones, and negotiating skills will have to be enhanced.
- There will be more emphasis on ethics, morals, and the process of learning, as well as on the quality of the output.
- There will be greater allowance in management education for the exercise of creativity, flexibility, and democracy.

Since the focus of the concluding section of this chapter will be on innovation in leadership preparation within higher education, let us concentrate here on creative possibilities within the traditional career development framework. The focus will be on recruitment, selection, training, monitoring, counseling, and evaluation, especially with reference to management personnel.

Recruitment. Among the varied prospects in this electronic age for identifying, interesting, and enticing qualified new applicants, these are a sample of what lies ahead:

- The transmission of computerized personnel records from universities or former employees for evaluation purposes.
- The exchange of data in organizational talent banks, facilitated by new types of employment service to match candidates with employers.
- The submission of videotapes or discs by employers to individuals or groups of candidates about the advantages of working in a particular company or agency, and vice versa, the submission of similar video data about the capabilities of the candidate.
- The early identification on an industrywide and international basis of future talent, the kind of people who fit the organizational profile as right for advancement within this corporate culture, and a tracking system to follow these future employees' accomplishments. Current personnel would be rewarded for submitting to the organization's computer bank these potential high performers and for assisting in their recruitment.
- The use of managers returning from abroad and recently retired executives as talent scouts and counselors, especially with local nationals overseas and in-country foreign students.
- Managerial and executive search programs seeking experienced management will be part of an overall, global humanpower plan based on performance criteria without discrimination based on gender, nationality, ethnic origins, or physical handicaps.

Selection. The selection process would emphasize choosing persons who are compatible with the organization's culture and current members. It would also be concerned with these prospective members' present and potential professional accomplishments and skills. However, greater diversity and latitude for people's uniqueness would be a principle of the selection process, which might employ:

- Video documents for preliminary interviews of candidates, and live satellite television interviews of prospects from all over the world; in the analysis of these recorded interviews,

attention would be paid to nonverbal communication and behavior.
- Increased use of simulation techniques, both computer and gaming procedures, through more sophisticated assessment centers for both new hires and promotion of existing personnel; these and other experiential observation methods will focus on intercultural communication abilities, abstract thinking capability, synthesis and synergy competencies, and technological abilities.
- Use of sophisticated, computerized instrumentation as part of a human resources inventory of the person's intelligence, aptitudes, interests, assets, personality, and needs for development.
- Employment and evaluation of situational, group-oriented problem-solving methods in the form of videotapes, case studies, dramatized critical incidents, and technological forecasts, all administered in customized scenarios to fit the corporation, association, or agency.
- Concentration throughout the career development process on people who excel in their present positions.

Training. This traditional management term will be broadened in the context of human resources development, and the opportunities for this will be manifold both within and without the organization. Some of the previous electronic and experiential methods used in recruitment and selection will be employed as part of the actualization of human potential. Other methods might include:

- Organizational learning centers that are electronically connected with the employee's home communication system or with university educational services.
- Special simulated preparations for unusual relocations or untraditional careers, similar to the type of orientation and training given to the astronauts for their space activities and moon work.
- Content that is based on futures studies and technological forecasting, as well as global and interplanetary data collection.
- Executive development that involves giving a young management intern a senior or retired executive as a counselor,

that provides a combination of line and staff experiences in the international marketplace, that is team-management-oriented and provides reporting responsibilities early in one's career, that offers opportunity to develop skills in coordination, consulting, negotiating, and intercultural representation, that gives priority to development of human relations skills and technical and financial competencies, that cultivates strategic skills and systems proficiency, that teaches about stress and life crises management for oneself, one's subordinates, and one's family, and that encourages creativity, calculated risk taking, and diversified life and business experiences.

Monitoring. Although individuals will be encouraged in the metaindustrial organizational culture to be more self-regulating, the company or agency will still need some type of tracking system to keep abreast of personnel development. The traditional personnel department function will be mechanized and revolutionized as it converges into a broader human resources management system. It will then involve:

- Comprehensive, meaningful, and current computerized personnel records.
- Standardized human resources accounting, which becomes part of the balance sheet and annual report on the capitalization of human assets.
- Search and support strategies for top-performing, nonconforming, and exceptional workers, who are then used as problem solvers, behavior models, and trainers with other employees.
- Integration of total HRD systems of subsidiaries and overseas operations, with emphasis on international HRD specialist teams.
- Systemwide human factor data gathering and analysis for improving organizational culture, as well as employee/customer relations and performance (i.e., more HRD research).
- Integration and utilization of people differences whether in terms of their capabilities or handicaps, culture or education, experience or aspirations, so that this is reflected in the design of facilities, provisions for career development, or accommodations of job requirements.
- Variety of provisions for personal and professional growth

from career exchanges and educational sabbaticals to new compensation benefits and personnel services (e.g., personality enhancement, use of drugs for improved health, dependent assistance, creative volunteerism, and constructive leisure guidance).

Counseling. Since there will be fewer employees in the metaindustrial organization, time can be spent with them in a variety of HRD activities, including coaching and counseling. This might include dimensions that were atypical in the disappearing industrial company or bureaucratic agency.

- Such corporation-sponsored guidance might be for an alternative career, or a second career, or retirement vocational activity.
- For employees returning from long service outside the home culture, it might involve reentry counseling or even outplacement services that would not be available to all personnel.
- When reduction in the force is necessary in a high-technology business, this counseling might be for outplacement in another corporation or industry, or for temporary educational leave, or to assist in the establishment of some entrepreneurial enterprise by the laid-off employee.
- Relocation assignments for the organization might involve a comprehensive counseling service for the employee's whole family, not just in relation to housing and other resources in the new community but on how all members of the family could grow as a result in this change.
- Counseling could be provided to executives to help them cope with the inevitable uncertainties and ambiguities of the unforeseen both in personal and professional life (this might take the form of group sessions with other executives and behavioral scientists within the organization, and more probably with peers in other companies or industries).

Evaluation. The assessment process begins before entry into the organization and ends after exiting from it. In the metaindustrial organization, it will be a continuing process that is both computerized and humanized. It might include such facets as:

- Review of human-machine relations or the human and robot interface.

- Changes needed in personal, role, and organizational images.
- Quality of performance in external community service and professional societies as a factor in career development.
- Degree of innovation demonstrated and contribution to the maintenance of a high-performing company.
- Individual contribution to policy formation and setting of new strategic objectives.
- Performance review of past job behavior, with a view toward increased productive behavior in the organization.
- Examination of the changes that are needed in the organization's culture or systems to improve performance.

The entire gamut of HRD efforts will be affected by electronic information technology, especially microprocessors and video equipment. The process of interviewing, for instance, is already being improved by video training tapes and learning materials that go from selection to termination. Knowledge workers may be full-time workers not just in-house but also at home, in and out of the organization for varying periods, sharing a job with a fellow employee or their spouse and with contract people. Certainly, knowledge workers wil be different in their aspirations and expectations of the organization.

Perhaps the following type of executive development programs offered by global corporations like IBM should be extended to the entire workforce:

Internal
- Three-week Advanced Management School for high-potential managers, focused on business process and environment.
- One-week Executive Seminar covering strategic issues plus external economic, social, and political developments.
- Two-week International Executive Program for senior executives worldwide, concentrating on strategic international issues.

External
- Participation in management programs of major university graduate schools.
- Participation in executive-level leadership programs that emphasize interpersonal effectiveness.
- Participation in Public Affairs programs dealing with federal operations or national policy issues.
- Participation in Humanities programs that provide courses of study on people, society, and values.

ELECTRONIC SUPERVISION

Elsewhere in this book, the issue has been made of managing workers who operate largely out of their homes with electronic technology. They may come to the office weekly or on occasion. The process of moving brains instead of bodies to workplaces opens many challenges for management and many opportunities for employees who prefer improved lifestyle over higher compensation. If a professional can work out of home or office in a Sunbelt site that is pleasant and uncongested, why put up with the inconvenience of mass urban centers and transportation problems, even for a slightly higher income? Electronic communication makes all this feasible even across nations. New communication technologies permit jobs to be performed virtually anywhere. Workers can be imported and jobs exported without the movement of anyone across national borders! The Satellite Data Corporation in New York City is now offering such services to clients. Experienced data and word processing personnel in Barbados are available for project assignments. The clients transmit handwritten reports, dictated tapes, or other documents via satellite with the help of facsimile machines, and these are reproduced almost instantaneously in the West Indies. The information is transferred into computers, and the keyed data is returned by satellite to a source in a printout or computer format.

The implications are highly significant for both management and career planning. We are only at the beginning of managing from earth projects that are both manned and unmanned in outer space. The same procedures used for transmission from the West Indies can be used from a space station.

COOPERATION FOR LEADERSHIP DEVELOPMENT

There is little doubt that a leadership crisis exists today in all spheres of human activity, be it university, corporation, or government. One reason is that many top administrators and executives are unable to understand or cope with the profound and fast-paced changes currently under way. They are playing in the old ballpark, by the traditional rules, and they think they have the same players. "Business as usual" is their motto, as deterioration and decline set into their enterprises and organization shock becomes prevalent. The crisis can be resolved, the new leaders can be developed, *if* the principals in the drama will share and cooperate.

In the Middle Ages, universities and monasteries were the great centers of learning. Monasteries were gradually replaced in this role by government agencies and trading companies. Today, more of the action in education and training seems to be shifting to industries and associations. Consider the postindustrial situation in high technology. University research, which pioneered in nuclear and space science, bioengineering, and other technological breakthroughs, is now falling behind in the information society. Adam Osborne put his finger on one aspect of the problem in his comments on the field of microelectronics:

Frequently the advances that occur in two or three years can be so stunning that users no longer have sufficient education to understand the new product. An electronics engineer who got his degree ten years ago would understand little or nothing of what is being taught in the classroom. Moreover, the faculties in university electric engineering departments are years behind the industry. No significant developments, either in semiconductor technology or the use of microelectronic products, have come out of universities, and this bleak situation does not look as though it will change in the foreseeable future....

Universities will have to reorganize their curricula to increase the output of engineers, while simultaneously preparing to cope with lifelong learning.

Now if this can be substantiated in a facet of engineering, what about the other academic disciplines and departments? There is common realization that many colleges and universities are offering majors and courses that are totally out of line with the world job market. Computer and space scientists are in short supply, while higher education produces an abundance of lawyers and historians. Even for the academic programs in business and the professions, the course content is often out of touch with the external needs of practitioners. The very administration of higher education, from a business management perspective, is frequently archaic. The continuing education programs, especially in management and executive development, are too theoretical, too fanciful, or too faddish, so that the leadership in this area has been lost to private corporations and educations. Universities and colleges, like so many other social institutions, have their own crises of survival, relevance, and development in the metaindustrial age. A very serious aspect of their problem is that industry is syphoning off the best instructors in science and technology.

Some of the challenges in leadership development for both

universities and government might be resolved if they entered into realistic collaboration on this HRD issue with major corporations. Such synergy among the three groups already exists in Japan. Big business can enter into profitable partnership with higher education. Government could not only encourage and subsidize such endeavors but participate in it. Here are some examples of the synergistic possibilities:

1. *Personnel exchanges* in which business leaders and researchers spend a year on university staffs or in government service, while faculty and public officials take temporary positions in industry.

2. *Joint ventures* of mutual benefit to all parties involved, such as corporate executives consulting on the design of university or government administrative systems; professors consulting on corporate renewal, educational systems in business and government; government officials consulting on improved regulatory procedures and grant programs; all three institutional systems sharing their innovations in management development, market and personnel needs, research discoveries and inventions that will affect the economy; designing public service volunteer projects in which all three systems participate for the benefit of the citizenry.

3. *Sharing information* on innovative educational technology, which may range from the use of electronic study carrels and holography in training to advances in computer-assisted instruction, voice-activated computers, and interactive television.

4. *Collaborative research* on human problems of management that affect both the public and the private sectors—such as the burnout syndrome, stress regulation, robot-human interface, job displacement through automation, design of new cybernated systems to reduce costs and increase productivity, creative use of increased leisure, expansion of high achievement, counteracting of underemployment, provision of meaningful living situations for the retarded and handicapped, two-career couples and job sharing, team management skills acquisition, and production of necessary educational software.

The cities of the metaindustrial age will be built around knowledge centers, just as cities in the industrial age centered around factories. These knowledge centers will be research facilities, information industries, and educational institutions. The latter have begun to change to meet the challenge of cyberculture. A Carnegie Endowment report on alternative forms of higher education told of many innovations in existing colleges and universities, as well as of the establishment of nontraditional university programs. To make career development programs more suitable to the needs of metaindustrial organizations, let us examine a few models that show promise.

○ *The USC/NIS Model.* Recognizing that the information industry may become the largest industry in the world (the United States already has 30 to 50 percent of the workforce employed in the information sector), the University of Southern California School of Communication and Center for Futures Research in the Graduate School of Business engaged in joint research with one state government and nine major corporations. To study the emerging network information services (NIS) they focused on its many applications and prospects as well as its implications for interactive training and education. The findings were shared among all participants and the public at large.

○ *Control Data/PLATO Model.* This is an educational data base system pioneered by Control Data Corporation. It is now being applied to industrial training. It can counteract teacher obsolescence and permit professional educators to interact with students or trainees in distant places, no matter how remote. It is a forerunner of the computer-aided education and training systems that can be distributed around the world by television or video cartridges to raise the educational levels of underdeveloped local people or managers.

○ *The SRI Model.* This resulted from Stanford University's establishment of a research institute, which is now an autonomous corporation called SRI International. It channels university-sponsored research to business and industry and undertakes research investigations for clients in the private and public sectors. It is one of many university-generated corporations that are engaged in the production of everything from genetic products to cancer cures.

○ *The In-Plant College Model.* Originally pioneered by National University in San Diego, California, and General Dynamics Corporation, it featured (1) a group of managers going through a program of business or professional studies together until graduation, (2) a single registration that provided a computerized projection of required courses until the degree was granted, (3) the use of plant conference and training facilities for university studies from 5 to 10 P.M.

○ *The Teletuition Model.* From the University of South Africa, this model is designed for executives who operate in widely dispersed geographic areas. It is essentially correspondence "tuition," or instruction, which includes in addition to written materials, TV, computers, radio, telephone, and tapes. Regional groups of managers meet to discuss course materials once a week for four to six hours, over 12 months, and one day a month at the university with faculty.

- *The WBSI Model.* The Western Behavior Science Institute provides postgraduate studies for executives by means of two eight-day intensive seminars every six months in La Jolla, California, that continue electronically by means of advanced computer technology supplied to the participant's office or home. Computer keyboards, video display, recording equipment, and printout units provide the communications links to the faculty, administration, and electronic library.
- *The INSEAD/CEDEP Model.* This is a 20-week "sandwich" program for managers to create change throughout a group of organizations, while engaged in multidisciplinary study, including the workings of member companies. Through the Centre Européen d'Education Permanente in Fontainebleau, France, representatives from 19 companies in four European countries participate in study teams of 10 to 20 managers of mixed age and gender.
- *The Oxford Centre Model.* This British model utilizes top professors in the Oxford Strategy Unit to advise key management in Britain and Western Europe. These consultants concentrate on management and trade unions with emphasis on banking, insurance, and public administration.
- *The Teknowledge Model.* This is representative of the new consultancies and management seminars in tune with metaindustrial realities. Founded in Palo Alto, California, by two distinguished Stanford University and Rand Corporation scientists, Dr. Edward Feigenbaum and Dr. Frederick Hayes-Roth, it provides Expert Systems Executive Briefings and conducts Knowledge Engineering projects for major corporations. They develop computer software for artificial intelligence applications and knowledge data bases.

These are but a sample of the innovative paradigms for cooperation between universities, corporations, and government that exist and need to be expanded in the process of leadership development. The walls of separation between and among these three key human systems need to be replaced by synergistic interface if scholars, executives, and administrators are to stay on the cutting edge of metaindustrial advances.

CAPSULE CONCLUSIONS

The metaindustrial organization will be increasingly involved in the business of learning, either for its own employees or as a profitable service to externals. However, this education and training will be more culturally responsive and sensitive. An enlightened organizational culture supports and encourages the capitalization of human assets. Postindustrial corporations and agencies take a systems approach to personnel development. This should be futuristic, international, and multicultural in scope. Continuing education will be directed increasingly to helping people cope more effectively with life crises and transitional experiences. It will include a wide range of skills from planning change to promoting cooperation. It will be comprehensive in terms of participants, excluding no group and focusing on synergistic interaction between young managers and senior or retired executives. Its importance has been recognized by our government, which now has tax provisions for corporate investment in HRD, and which is showing increasing concern for older workers. With 22 percent of the American population likely to be over 65 years of age by 2025, it is no wonder that alternatives to retirement are being studied.

Today's innovations in recruiting, selecting, training, developing, counseling, and evaluating personnel will become tomorrow's norms. The metaindustrial work culture will force government, universities, and corporations to collaborate in more synergistic ventures, especially with regard to human resources management. With a postliterate generation of workers, information in education and training will be transferred primarily through media technology. Increasingly, organizational cultures will invest in the enhancement of human competencies for performance improvement.

CHAPTER 9 Transforming Organizational Relationships

Among the many dimensions through which a culture can be analyzed is the way relationships are defined in that society, whether at home, work, or play. Cultures fix human and organizational relationships on the basis of age, sex, status, class, kindred, wealth, power, wisdom, and so on. In some cultures, family relations are especially important: extended families, including aunts, uncles, and cousins, live together; patriarchs or matriarchs have the principal authority; monogamy, polygamy, or polyandry is either permitted or forbidden. Macrocultures may also provide guidance on treatment of the elderly; on certain professional roles, such as teacher or judge; on the role of women; or on male-female relations. In Japanese culture, lawyers are not held in high regard because it is a sign of weakness when people cannot live in harmony and work out differences themselves, but must resort to legal advice. Just the opposite is true in American culture where legalisms, lawyers, and court suits abound. The local culture also provides counsel on business relationships—that is, the proper protocol with younger or older personnel, agreements and contracts, tips or commissions. Dr. Robert Moran of the American Graduate School of International Management is currently researching and writing about international business protocol for multinational managers. His work includes the issue of "bribery," which is a relative matter depending on what culture one is doing business in, what culture one comes from, and growing global practice in the world marketplace regarding "commissions."

By taking a systems approach to studying culture, it is possible to examine the *kinship system* that deals with all aspects of family relations, including inheritance. For example, in some cultures a successful person is responsible for an extended family. Thus, if one were a manager and needed to hire someone, family relations might take precedence over competence in the selection of a recruit or awarding of a contract. There is also the *association system*, the area of which social relations—the network of groupings, professional/trade/fraternal—are permitted or expected or tolerated in a particular culture. Basically, as we engage in international business, there are three fundamental orientations to be observed in social and work relations: The *integrated approach* is pluralistic, so friendships are made easily across social lines and barriers, and there are few distinctions between and among social and work activities and relationships. In the *associated approach*, there is covert awareness of distinctions and taboos in social and work relations but little overt concern is demonstrated when mixing takes place. And in the *separated approach*, there is great concern for maintaining certain relationships in society or at work, and rigid custom enforces the separation expected within the group. Job performance can be undermined when there is a conflict of such interests. This conceptual model may be helpful as multinational managers attempt to become more sensitive to local customs related to gender, color, class or caste, occupation, and so forth.

In microcultures, relationships may be defined formally or informally. Military systems differentiate commissioned and noncommissioned officers, as well as enlisted personnel, by a system of ranks, emblems, medals, and unit affiliation. Organization charts, work divisions, and personnel manuals help to formalize relationships in business, industry, and even government. Marketing, manufacturing, and research personnel have differing relations within their groups and among such units. Civil service has classification systems based on competence levels, years of experience, and education that separate people into work groups and affect relationships.

The industrial work culture also conditioned our thinking concerning white and blue collar workers and their respective places in the organization. We have stereotyped ideas toward the organization man and toward employee loyalty. Labor-management relations have usually been adversarial.

Organizational cultures differ in their approach to vocational activity, job titles, sex, and race. Equal Employment Opportunity legislation and affirmative action programs in the United States and elsewhere have altered relationships in organizations. There is more freedom and mobility for minority employees to enter any organization and to rise to the highest levels. Women are no longer restricted to certain tasks and careers. As a result, women are now moving into professions traditionally restricted to men, as well as into management and executive positions.

In 1981, even Pope John Paul II issued an encyclical on working, *Laborem Exercens*, in which he observed that women have the right to "fulfill their tasks in accordance with their own nature, without being discriminated against and without being excluded from jobs for which they are capable." It is an example of the type of documents and pronouncements that are occasionally issued within a culture by representatives of distinguished bodies to remind us of ideals and principles of human relationships. A charter on human or civil rights issued by nations or organizations is another illustration of a new consensus in this critical issue of relationships.

VALUE OF BUSINESS/PROFESSIONAL RELATIONS
Humans confirm and express themselves in relation to others. Career development depends on organizational relations. Such relations may be formed in terms of a *dyad* with peers, superiors, or subordinates—that is, interpersonal relations. Beyond this two-person interaction, people may expand their associations to a *triad* or *small-group* relationship, wherein intragroup relations occur as members of this unit exchange ideas, information, and insights. This sharing affects that group's member satisfaction, morale, and even productivity. Finally, such entities interface with similar units within the same *subsystem*. Now the emphasis is on intergroup relations, in the form of exchanges between and among departments, divisions, task forces, project teams, subsidiaries, and agencies. Thus a complex of interlocking relationships within a human *system* has an impact on organizational accomplishments and achievements.

Organizational theorists remind us that because of such relationships, each group develops a unique life space* and history as it seeks to satisfy member needs by the establishment of group goals, norms, values, and structures. As subunits interface with other entities within a system and its external environment, roles and relationships must be continuously reviewed and possibly al-

* One's *life space* or "private world" is usually conceived of as an invisible phenomenon, a psychological space. Groups and organizations also develop a particular life space. Within these spaces, human behavior is influenced, and human resources are utilized in a positive or negative way.

tered. Group dynamics* also involve the sharing of power, leadership, and responsibility, as well as the establishment of procedures for functioning and mechanisms for decision making and problem solving. In the industrial work culture, such organizational relations were fairly stable and long term; personnel had some feel for the expectations of others. The groups were more homogeneous, sharing more permanent cultural assumptions, ideals, and aspirations, as well as similar perceptions, prejudices, and biases.

Many businesses and professional relations have a significant impact on one's career, and on the work atmosphere—employee rapport, loyalty, morale, and motivation. Managers must understand the implications of these relations and use them to further organizational, as well as individual, effectiveness. Such relationships are the fabric of the social environment, the informal organization. They can facilitate or undermine the formal organizational objectives. These organizational relations contribute to the informal network of communication, the "grapevine," and often provide status, recognition, and reward not offered within the hierarchies. Inside these groups, an employee may have a leadership role that is not confirmed by job title or established role but that gives that member ego satisfaction and support. Apart from the production of goods and services, much of the internal activity of an organization is devoted to the maintenance of individual and group relationships. It is the lubrication that permits the formal organization to accomplish its mission. No manager can afford to ignore the dynamics of these institutional relationships, for often it is in the informal organization that the real action is taking place. It is the human side of enterprise at its best, the personal

---

Group dynamics/culture: When two or more organization members or employees interact, formally or informally, for a purpose, their behavior or performance influences one another and others. The process of their interaction, such as in a team situation, can be studied in terms of its communications, interrelationships, intrarelationships with other groups, cohesiveness, and effectiveness. *Group cohesiveness* refers to the attractiveness of the group to its members, their ability to work together. Group effectiveness refers to the optimal relationships that contribute to the unit's productivity, efficiency, satisfaction, adaptiveness, and development. The group culture is the unique customs, traditions, norms, values, and habits that are created in the course of the members' history together. The group techniques that may be employed to facilitate group growth are role playing, confrontation or leveling, observation and feedback, decision making and participation, sharing and communication, and various forms of team building. The group is usually interdependent within a larger organization or system, so that it may be thought of as a subsystem or subculture.

Transforming Organizational Relationships

dimension of business and work. (Appendix A has a section for assessing such organizational relations.)

To improve work relations and to facilitate their becoming more cooperative, we propose an experiment. Take a relatively unknown or aloof colleague to lunch or dinner and challenge him or her to join you in this procedure: It is an exploration in organizational relations and requires that each of you take turns responding to the following series of open-ended questions:

1. Basically my job is . . .
2. My career ambitions are . . .
3. Usually, I am the kind of person who . . .
4. When things aren't going well, I . . .
5. When I think of your responsibilities, I feel that . . .
6. Off the job, I like such things as . . .
7. I want to become the kind of person who . . .
8. My reaction to your observations is . . .

Today, with the emphasis on team and project management, there is a need to develop such mechanisms for creating rapid, intense work relations. It requires application of listening skills, so that one can quickly enter the other person's life space or frame of reference. To expand on this experiment, subsequent meetings might be held in which the process is built upon by consideration of these issues:

9. Ten years from now I . . .
10. What I hear you saying is . . .
11. My impression of you is changing, and now I feel that you are . . .
12. On the job I'm best at . . .
13. I feel underutilized in relation to . . .
14. Your job seems to be . . .
15. In conflict situations at work, I usually . . .
16. When I am supervising others, I prefer . . .
17. What I like about my co-workers is . . .
18. When I am approaching a deadline, I . . .
19. What I would hope to happen with regard to us is . . .
20. What I like about you is . . .

With imagination, one can extend or limit this conversational approach to suit the situation and the other person. The effort can have a payoff in improved vocational relations. It can counteract the effects of increased mechanization of the workplace. With increased emphasis on improving the quality of worklife, this approach may enhance work relations and contribute to the humanization of organizational culture.

METAINDUSTRIAL WORK RELATIONS
In 1973, Harvey Shapiro did a prophetic piece for *The New York Times* about IBM. He thought the computer giant was a model for corporations of the future—high-technology organizations whose main problem is motivating whole regiments of highly educated employees. In retrospect, this quotation shows rare insight into the metaindustrial organizational culture:

> IBM's production workers seem relatively contented, and the firm has had few labor problems.... Its products are made in relatively small work areas rather than impersonal assembly lines. Instead of breaking jobs into monotonous little tasks IBM keeps enlarging them, so a worker usually has something he (or she) can say he (or she) made. Since technology has produced a new generation of computers every half-dozen years, the worker has less opportunity to become bored because one is always adding new skills and learning new jobs. However, the same technology ... is "proletarianizing" the work of college-educated managers and engineers who constitute the majority at IBM. The complexity of the computer technology requires massive working groups in which each member has only a small role.

Shapiro was worried about the frustration and alienation that might result under these new work conditions. It is the small-group or team relationships that can prevent or counteract those problems and lead to the innovations that will make the vocational activity more challenging. What then are the changes to be observed in metaindustrial work culture with reference to interpersonal, intragroup, and intergroup relations?

Fundamentally, human relations in metaindustrial organizations are more open, informal, and flexible. They are also more intense, of shorter duration, and experimental. Leaders in team management or matrix organizations are more like coordinators, facilitators, and linking pins within and among the various groups that comprise the social system. They seek to shape the group or organization to the people, so they use both informal and formal communication channels and structures. They are willing to try out new organizational arrangements and relationships in order to promote synergy. In concluding this section, we will examine six categories of changes in organizational relations that are becoming more evident in this superindustrial period of human development:

1. *Knowledge/information sharing.* Among young, technically oriented knowledge workers, the relationships often center around sharing data and information, exchanging new ways for using the technology, and experimenting together with unusual techniques and processes. It is the shared excitement of explorers going into unknown territories, of sticking together because the unknown is so vast and complex. It is interdisciplinary and does not respect the traditional boundaries that separated knowledge areas and the professions. It is a sense of interdependence, a holistic relationship that seeks input and insight wherever they may be found, regardless of education, experience, nationality, age, race, or gender. It is the problem-solving task that energizes such people, and the teamwork required to find solutions with the collaboration of colleagues. An example of such attitudes is found in Elscint, an Israeli producer of medical diagnostic equipment with a 20 percent annual growth rate. Elscint is run by scientific innovators who created a system of senior scientists who act as "gurus" to inspire and direct young staffers, as well as to provide project guidance and product standardization.

2. *Performance competence.* Metaindustrial personnel are less impressed by job titles, seniority, and even advanced degrees held by fellow workers. They seek out individuals with a track record for high performance. In this technological work culture, achievement is respected, and the performers become behavior models for others. They are sought out in the office, at professional meetings, through computer networks and other forms of communication. Knowledge workers form relationships, especially in small groups, with people who are competent; they are intolerant of incompetents, even when they have impressive positions within the organization.

Capable and proficient managers thus gain adherents and support. Related to this is the concept of accountability. Metaindustrial personnel believe in the management of responsibility, so they do not mind being held accountable for their own or their group's performance, and they expect others to be similarly accountable. Polls today confirm that such people welcome challenges to their creative abilities. In the metaindustrial work culture, both management and employees refuse to tolerate mediocrity. Productivity, quality, cost control, and pride of workmanship are prime concerns.

Furthermore, they have new norms for measuring corporate performance. They expect greater corporate social accountability regarding the use of both human and natural resources. As John Biegler, senior partner of Price Waterhouse, has reminded us, the legitimate expectations of working people today call for systematic corporate accountability in many new arenas, such as improving both the living and working atmospheres, and setting performance standards for multinational corporations in the international business community.

3. *Impermanence.* Metaindustrial work cultures are often characterized by mobility, transcience, and fast-paced, brief ups and downs. This means that organizational relations are often of short duration. One therefore needs to be able to affiliate quickly and intensely in work situations that are frequently ad hoc. Teams and task forces may be set up quickly to accomplish a specific mission, function effectively for a few months or a few years, and then be disassembled. The individuals are dispersed to new assignments. Matrix organizations require ad hoc relationships that are both adaptive and responsive to fast-paced market and technological changes.

Although Theory Z management encourages organizations to have more permanent, long-term relations with employees and to provide greater job security, the vicissitudes of the marketplace in the high-technology fields may dictate otherwise. Economic sluggishness and recession, for example, have forced layoffs in the semiconductor industry. In 1981, innovative firms like Texas Instruments, Mostek Corporation, and Signetics Corporation had to discharge or furlough chip production workers. During periods of economic transition, many such metaindustrial manufacturers have had to resort to such tactics as layoffs and forced vacations until the next boom began. High-level managers and technicians do not have company loyalties in this industry, so they will pack up and leave for the minicomputer maker or new hardware or software producer that offers the most opportunity or challenge. Their relationships are with other professionals within the industry, not necessarily with a particular company, so many will move to "where the action is." Thus high turnover has become somewhat the norm among computer professionals. On the other hand, companies that have introduced human resources systems have adapted to the needs of such information specialists and have succeeded in cutting that turnover rate quite substantially.

4. *High speed/fast track.* "Third Wave Whiz Kids" involved in the computer revolution are often electronic entrepreneurs whose relationships change with the speed of their industry's changes. Such metaindustrial personnel work in the fast lane when their companies are on an upswing and experiencing record-breaking growth rates. To maintain such a pace during inflationary times means more productivity by hiring additional staff, increasing automation, or acquiring more contract workers. Under these circumstances, unless there is a strategy for maintaining some interpersonal balance, organizational relationships can be strained and unmanaged conflict increased. Life on the fast track can become intolerable if the human system is overloaded with input or meetings or tasks.

In these stressful times of transition, some personnel complain of "burnout." The syndrome is evident when formerly energetic people begin to show continuous exhaustion, feeling a great need to unwind or break out of their work culture. When excessive demands are made on an employee's time, talent, and energy, occupational stress sets in, performance quality drops, and relationships with co-workers and family deteriorate. The symptoms may be physical—headaches, stomach knots, insomnia, irritability, chronic muscular pain, and so forth. Or they may be psychological, manifested in increased disenchantment and cynicism on the job, forgetfulness, disappointment with colleagues, disorientation, or withdrawal from work relationships.

Managers can counteract such negative developments in metaindustrial work cultures and can reduce the personal costs of high achievement for themselves and subordinates. One strategy is to provide authority commensurate with the responsibility on the job. Other solutions include wellness programs, relation therapy, proper nutrition and diet, positive reinforcement techniques, learning new coping and communication skills, acquiring time management methods. Seeking out meaningful and stimulating relationships both on and off the job, while reducing what is meaningless in human relationships, can also contribute to an integrated lifestyle that is more in harmony with the demands of the postindustrial reality.

5. *Pluralistic/multicultural.* To have positive relationships in metaindustrial organizations, one will need to cope effectively with differences in people and to be able to create synergy

through them. Domestically, we will be concerned with cross-cultural skills in a more heterogeneous workforce. Since competence is a principal criterion, and not sex, religion, race, or heritage, one must be capable of dealing effectively with minorities in all facets of business operations. Since what is important is brainpower, not brawn, organizations will have more employees with physical handicaps and will seek to remove the barriers to their effective contribution. Similarly, male-female relationships on the job need to be continually reevaluated lest women be sexually harassed, or their potential contribution to organizational growth be delimited. On the other hand, feminist leaders such as Betty Friedan call for changed relationships so that women learn to work with men more effectively. The same might be said for black-white relations, rich-poor relations, white-collar/blue-collar relations, and similar industrial-age dichotomies that are increasingly inappropriate in a metaindustrial society. Diversity in the workforce and a more pluralistic society not only forbid discrimination on the basis of age, sexual orientation, ethnicity, and other such factors, but offer opportunities for a more interesting and varied work environment. Movements of migrants, refugees, and guest workers will continue to bring foreigners into the workforce. Metaindustrial organizations make meritocracy work and counteract racism, sexism, and ethnic biases.

The other phenomenon contributing to the "internationalization" of work relations is the global marketplace. Multinational business spreads beyond national borders, bringing in foreign managers, technicians, and even owners. Cross-cultural relations thus increase within and without one's native land and demand new skills that should become a regular part of all career development. Instead of trying to obliterate differences in human relationships, we need to become more aware of them and build on them to forge synergistic bonds with colleagues. As personal and professional barriers dissolve, we will not only discover new commonalities and strengths in one another, but we will prepare ourselves for future interterrestrial relations! Appendix D provides managers with an instrument for analyzing their intercultural relations.

 6. *Electronic connections/networking.* Vocational relations need not always be in person. Now we have the capacity for electronic relationships with one another for work purposes, as well as for professional and personal advancement. In addition, increasingly, by means of computers and word processors, we will be able to work at our home communications centers. Relations

with supervisors and managers, as well as with colleagues, will be drastically altered. Other business and professional relationships will be increasingly maintained through video or computer networks over vast distances in which the participants scarcely ever actually meet; yet they have meaningful electronic exchanges. They simply move their brains to one another's locations, instead of their bodies!

An interesting profile has emerged of people in the data industry who work at home. A 1981 study of the Gary Slaughter Corporation revealed that the salary of such personnel ranges from $18,000 for programmers to $35,000 for analysts. Of 13,000 persons surveyed, 760 were in the top manager category, while 469 were EDP managers and MIS directors. Obviously, the number and challenges of at-home workers and their management are likely to increase in the electronic cottages during the next two decades.

Many personnel in metaindustrial organizations form networks for a variety of purposes from advancing women in management to technological forecasting. In Southern California, for instance, 550 aerospace employees in 18 companies and agencies have formed a network to humanize the workplace. Called the Making a Difference Clubs,* this network was formed to assist both individual and corporate renewal and to strengthen cooperative relations between employees and management. Other networks have been formed electronically for computer exchanges between and among professionals in various fields. Apart from vocationally related interchanges, these networks have brought together interest groups of all sorts from lobbyists for a cleaner environment to those with a hobby of gourmet cooking. Such connections may be made informally, or through payment of a fee for a mailing list or to become a subscriber in a specialized information network.†

The ideals of metaindustrial work relations have been epitomized in the concept of androgyny—the male-female behavior balance in interpersonal relationships. Alice Sargent describes the men and women who exemplify this concept. In essence, they are:

Women managers who strive to become in business relations

- more entrepreneurial, and risk taking;
- more forceful and direct in task accomplishment;

* Box 337, Manhattan Beach, Calif. 92066.
† See Theme Packs.

- more clear and firm in self-expression;
- more self-confident in the development of one's potential;
- more balanced in the use of logic and feeling in problem solving and decision making;
- more supportive and reinforcing of others, especially women, by building networks and helpful community.

Male managers who endeavor in their business relations to become

- more authentic and open in communications, both verbally and nonverbally;
- more able to express feeling, even when it may involve exposing one's vulnerability and dependency;
- more supportive and cooperative in sharing competencies with others, especially men, and less competitive;
- more spontaneous and emotionally expressive;
- more able to value work for its self-fulfillment, as well as for career achievement.

It is the synergy of such male-female qualities in each person that will enable us to accomplish a true human emergence in this postindustrial age. Sargent believes a key issue of the 1980s is managing people better by being both tough and tender, compassionate and strong. An androgynous approach, she maintains, will not only counteract stress and morale but will build productivity in a more healthy work environment.

Metaindustrial organizations will offer new challenges to husband-wife relationships. First, one or both spouses will do more work for income in the home, which will alter their relations with each other as well as with other family members. Second, couples in which both spouses have a career find their relationship affected by this. In addition, the phenomenon of two-career couples affects corporate policies on recruitment, relocation, and career development, as well as employee morale, productivity, and even company profits. Whether the issue is the sharing of a single position, or the husband and wife working for two different employers, sometimes in two separate locations, it is a new dimension in human relations that can be successfully managed. In a recent survey of top corporations, two-career families, and directions for the future,* three-quarters of the couples studied reported:

* See B. Zeitz.

- Wives and husbands are satisfied with their marriages, but less satisfied with their careers and how to combine the two.
- Wives report more physiological and psychological stress than their husbands, and are more apt to be perfectionists.
- The healthiest people seem to be those who are satisfied with both their marriages and their careers.

In this investigation by the Career and Family Center of Catalyst, a New York-based research firm, 375 corporations were sampled. Responses indicated that 77 percent of the firms already provide flexible working hours to accommodate two-career couples, 95 percent offer maternity benefits, and 65 percent offer leaves without pay but with the position assured on return. The companies provide little support for what may yet become standard metaindustrial work practices—flexible workplaces, on-site or community child care, customized fringe benefit programs, sick leave for children's illness. Enlightened management seeks ways to ease strains and conflicts between home and job, especially for working couples and single parents, during this era of social and organizational transition.

RELATIONSHIPS WITH ROBOTS
In the metaindustrial organization's culture the human-machine interface takes on a new dimension because of the microelectronics revolution. The combination of machines and computer makes cybernation possible, providing a unique extension of human intelligence. Will the widespread introduction of robots into the workplace and home liberate us from drudgery and free us to concentrate on intrinsically human tasks? Much depends on the leadership provided to help employees with the job displacement caused by the new "steel collar" workers, to facilitate their introduction, and to train people in the most effective use of the artificial beings. It means maintaining a delicate balance between mechanization and humanization in the work environment.

Robots will eventually make a very significant difference in life. They will increase productivity because they can work 24 hour days. They are immune to safety hazards, unionization, and government regulations and obsolescence, and they do not make mistakes, get distracted, or demand coffee breaks.

For centuries mankind has conjured up images of automatic mechanical devices and tinkered with a variety of possibilities, as well as creating novels, plays, and movies on the subject. As a spinoff of our space technology, we now have a variety of such devices from mechanical arms, to a mechanical man, to sophisticated Viking crafts that probe the far reaches of the universe. The Viking crafts navigate, repair themselves, maneuver, and land on other planets to carry out tasks with a minimum of human interaction. Industrial robots, first manufactured in the sixties, are characterized by such performance parameters as range and scope of manipulation, quality of autonomic control, precision of reproducing movements, and reliability of functioning. The one-armed robots have six electric motors that control every movement for a limb with two joints, a rotating wrist, and a pair of pinchers. Add arms and wheels, and the robots become mobile. But what made them smart and inexpensive was electronic intelligence in micro forms. First, they could "see" quantified images; then "hear" by converting sound waves into number sequences; now they can "speak" by recorded word sounds that can generate messages. There are electronic hearing devices that can decode anyone's speech.

According to Dr. Adam Osborne of Osborne Computers, the robot of the future will be able to pick up and move objects, operate machines, insert, weld, and manipulate. It will be able to speak with an extensive vocabulary, generating almost any kind of sound. It will also respond to verbal and nonverbal sounds. In the next few decades, it is likely that robots will be capable of difficult mechanical tasks and will eliminate most of today's assembly-line jobs. Bank futurist Hank Koehn envisions automated plants with only a handful of human supervisors. In fact, you can see prototypes of such cybernated factories in such places as Deerfield, Illinois, where Sara Lee Bakery pioneered the concept. The rapid evolution of the robot will lead to the miniaturization of the control package, which will be used in work areas that are too boring, too dangerous, and too costly for human involvement.

Currently, robots with artificial intelligence are being used to shear sheep, sort fish, pack cosmetics and candy, sort and carry mail, sell products, search for radioactive damage, provide banking services, and play games. However, their principal application has been in the automobile industry. Toyota Motor Company has a plant that uses robots in all stages of production and 90 percent of its welding. Honda Motors' new paint factory at Sayama is almost totally automated and has few human workers. General Motors Corporation will spend more than $200 million by mid-1983 for the industry's most massive conversion to high-technology automation in 14 plants, using more than 800 robots. By 1990, GM expects to invest $1 billion in 14,000 robots. Richard Beecher, head of GM's machine perception and robotics department, commented that if GM does not use this technology, it will be driven off the market by competition and there will be no jobs for anyone. The United Auto Workers expects its workforce to be cut by 50 percent by the end of this decade. Only synergistic planning and programming by government, industry, and unions can alleviate the human misery and economic effects of this dislocation by coming up with innovative alternatives for displaced employees through retraining, educational and cultural opportunities, and counseling on new careers and markets.

Japan leads in the early eighties with 10,000 robotic devices, the United States is next with 3,000, followed by various European countries with fewer than 1,000 each. In Japan, at Fujitsu-Fanuc Co., robots are producing other robots and numerical control machines—an $8 million monthly production that involves few people. Automax Company of Tokyo has a robot that not only cleans but does the nightwatchman's job. Fujitsu Ltd. has secretary robots that do everything from stamping executive signatures to formulating schedules and providing time alerts. Nomura Research Institute has predicted that Japan's robot industry will record $1.2 billion in sales by 1985 and double that by 1990. Others forecast a 40 to 50 percent growth rate, especially as the industry expands into homes, hospitals, and offices.

American leaders in the field are Condec Corporation's Unimation, Cincinnati Milacron, Inc., Fairchild Camera and Instrument Corporation, and Texas Instruments. ITT, AT&T, IBM, and Xerox are vigorously pursuing both the robotics and electronic transmissions markets. West Germany, Italy, and Sweden seem to be the current European leaders. The Swedish ASEA and its new partner, Electrolux's Industrial Robot Division, expect to double their 1981 $100 million impact on the world market, especially by penetration of the United States. Future markets and applications for robots are limited only by human vision and by our ability to form innovative working relations with these human extensions. Polish futurist Jerzy Wesolowski foresees a European robot market of $640 million by 1985, and new generations of robots with multiple coordination of senses and appliances that have a range of manipulations greater than human capacity. The relationships between human beings and their machines are going through a profound transformation that will radically alter the work culture.

SYNERGISTIC ORGANIZATIONAL RELATIONS

Industrial work culture featured competitive, adversarial relationships. In the past, this seemed to be manifested not only between individuals and institutions but also within and among groups that were part of the same organization. Certainly, it has been evident in the whole arena of labor-management relations. Today, because of the magnitude of our economic problems and because of the complexity and increasing interdependence of our human systems, we cannot afford such relationships.

Thus a new type of industrial relations has been quietly emerging in this postindustrial period. The message of the past few decades from behavioral scientists—Elton Mayo, Douglas McGregor, Abraham Maslow, Rensis Likert, William Ouchi—is finally getting through to managers. That is, more attention must be paid to the dynamics of small work groups as a means of satisfying employee needs and improving organizational effectiveness. Likert stated it best when he advocated a corporationwide culture of cooperation. Some companies and industries are being forced in this direction by declining markets, productivity, and jobs. In the American steel industry, for example, both corporations and unions are emphasizing participative management and improved quality of worklife. Specifically, the United Steel Workers' 1980 contract calls for the development of participation teams, which Jones & Laughlin, Bethlehem, National, and other steel firms are now installing. The biggest obstacle to such problem-solving groups at the departmental level seems to be traditional supervisory style—listening, instead of giving orders, is difficult for managers conditioned by the industrial-age culture. The new trend was summarized in a special report in *Business Week:**

> Many companies, some in collaboration with once-hostile unions, are creating new mechanisms to gain worker involvement—self-managed work teams, labor-management steering committees, problem-solving groups, and redesign committees—that wed social and technical ideas in designing or rearranging plants.

Whether they are called quality circles or core groups, their principal purpose is the renewal of mature industries. Even in younger businesses, like Xerox's Reprographics Technology Group, councils of people at the same level from different departments are being used, along with vertical work-study groups from the same

* May 11, 1981.

department, to promote employee cooperation and increase effectiveness.

The metaindustrial work culture is characterized by collaboration, especially through ad hoc groups that foster synergistic relations throughout the organization and within the particular industry. Synergistic relations was the theme of William A. Kraus's *Collaboration in Organizations,* in which an alternative to hierarchy and a new value system are explored. Such relationships, according to Dr. Kraus, involve the sharing of competence, power, and authority, and the use of conflict-resolution methodologies. Metaindustrial organizations emphasize functions rather than roles; they are open systems that recognize the importance of process, as well as input and output; they use participative decision making. Collaborative institutions are flexible, adaptive, and feedback-oriented—that is, they have self-renewing mechanisms built into them. Employees recognize the realities of interdependence, the need for control over their immediate work environment, and the value of sharing a frame of reference. Kraus, a consultant for Organizational Development and New Technology Implementation at General Electric, proposes *collaborative behavior* that is directed toward achieving common goals; is open and innovative, with positive feelings emphasized; seeks coordination, consensus, and agreement; encourages authentic communication, trust, and helpfulness. When members behave in this way, group energies are mobilized in the creation of synergy, so that combined interaction produces something greater than the sum of the individual contributions.

Michael Doyle advocates the establishment within a corporation of an internal, collaborative, problem-solving group. It would serve a preventive, facilitative service for the purpose of solving problems and seizing opportunities. It may be outside the formal management structure, but collateral to it, and it would act on a continuing basis.

The cooperative approach is the only way to go in this information age, especially when dealing with knowledge workers. But the old ways disappear slowly, and personnel will have to be reeducated for greater team management. This section will examine three dimensions of organizational relations: the team itself, the managerial role of the facilitator, and the intercultural factor.

Team relations. A *team* is a number of associated persons performing jointly. *"Teamwork"* is cooperative or coordinated effort on the part of persons working together. In metaindustrial organizations, a team may be a temporary group formed to accomplish a specific task, or it may be an ongoing functional group. It may consist of hourly workers, technicians, professionals, or managers, or all four. Whatever the reason for bringing this collection of people together, they become a team when they collaborate to achieve a goal. When participants are able to share their perceptions, insights, knowledge, experience, intuitions, and creativity, synergy becomes possible. Each team forms its own microculture, which is manifested in *group* attitudes, ideals, customs, norms, expectations, objectives, practices, and results. For the team to be effective, its culture should foster coordinated efforts, productive activities, economical performance, and meaningful experiences. In metaindustrial corporations, there is a need to join technical specialists and information workers across disciplines, departments, and divisions. Intra- and inter-team relations are the key for accomplishing this, and there are strategies for doing this.

To promote maximum self-actualization for each member and for the group, there are behaviors recommended for effective team participation:

- *Sensitivity*—being able to express one's own and others' feelings; being able to reflect others' meaning and to respond empathetically.
- *Authenticity*—being a person of integrity who cares about others and levels with them in communicating, rather than playing games.
- *Tentativeness*—being relative, and not absolute, in input; being experimental and willing to learn by testing out new ideas and procedures.
- *Spontaneity*—being responsive to here-and-now data and experiences, in contrast to there-and-then matters; reacting creatively to people, rather than strategically or manipulatively.
- *Helpfulness*—being able to share oneself without imposing one's systems, values, opinions, and solutions; reflecting objectively the other's needs, thoughts, and capabilities for self-enlargement.
- *Openness*—being considerate of others' perceptions, viewpoints, and possibilities; not being locked into preconceptions and stereotypes.
- *Participativeness*—being able to share leadership, in both task accomplishments and group maintenance; being

group-centered as both initiator and follower, and encouraging others to contribute.
- *Awareness*—being conscious of time and economic constraints on the group, as well of the dynamics at work and the potential for synergy.
- *Tolerance* for ambiguity, uncertainty, diversity, lack of structure.
- *Congruence*—being nonthreatened and nondefensive because one is self-accepting and in harmony with oneself.
- *Trust*—in oneself and others; being able to foster the same quality within the group.

When members practice such behavior, group relations are healthy and facilitative. Team effectiveness requires that members pause occasionally from work on their task to review how they are relating to one another. Third-party observers, whether internal or external consultants to the organization, can be useful in this regard. Team development sessions are also useful for improving the way groups function. Increasingly, individual worker training is being done within the context of a group. Team job training is essential for metaindustrial organizations and matrix management.

Coaching/consulting relations. Modern managers must be skilled in creating and carrying out a helping relationship with subordinates and colleagues. Management consultant Ferdinand F. Fournies has done a book and a film on the concept of the helping relationship, and the title catches the essence of this point— *Coaching for Improved Work Performance.* The manager becomes a facilitator for the individual worker and the team. In a way, he or she looks on work groups as clients, and the manager engages in a consulting relationship with the group members. This involves skills such as these:

- *Genuineness.* The supervisor does not play games, but expresses reality, and levels with team members.
- *Acceptance.* The supervisor has unconditional positive regard for each individual in the group; respecting individual differences and competences, such managers communicate to the worker that they care and have regard for them.
- *Empathy.* The supervisor is able to get into the worker's and group's life space or perceptual field, can appreciate worker and group feelings and problems, and is sensitive to other people.

○ *Helpfulness.* The supervisor recognizes that the other must be ready and able to accept external assistance, and that unless the worker perceives the manager's efforts as helpful, then help has not been given.

Such a manager creates a team environment in which members are able to express themselves—including their fears and doubts—and in which the giving and seeking of constructive feedback are a norm. Verbal and nonverbal feedback help channel team energies toward goal achievement. They are also a way of helping another person change inadequate behavior. It endeavors to both minimize and utilize conflict.

Metaindustrial managers also make use of positive reinforcement. Dr. Yorham Zeira, a professor of business administration at Tel Aviv University, and Dr. Ehud Harari, a research associate at the University of California, recently surveyed employees of multinational corporations to determine what the best characteristics of a manager were. Out of ten possible leadership behaviors, giving *encouragement* to employees to upgrade their performance was rated as number 1 by those studied. The second-ranked item was the supervisor's ability to listen to subordinates, and the third-ranked item was the ability to foster mutual cooperation in the work group. People usually wish to develop their potential, to achieve with others, to produce synergy—the manager who practices coaching relations with colleagues helps this to happen for mutual benefit. Frequently, it helps if the supervisor acts toward the subordinate *as if* the person had attained the next level of performance to which he or she is capable of moving, and then the individual will work to achieve the level perceived by the manager as feasible for that person.

First-level supervisors need to be trained to be management advisers, not "overseers." That is the approach taken at Shaklee Corporation's plant in Norman, Oklahoma, where work teams manage themselves. An effective metaindustrial manager helps a work unit to become self-regulating, just like a cybernated system!

Intercultural relations. Most organizational relations today are intercultural. Therefore, we must learn to manage cultural differences if synergy is to occur. This is true for multinational managers and technicians who go abroad into a foreign organizational culture. It is also a reality for the managers of workers from minority cultures within a workforce in one's home culture. Intercultural relations are involved when one is transferred to another country, or even to another locality in one's own country. Such relations are also a growing factor in mergers and acquisitions when two or more organizational cultures interface. For employees caught in the merger squeeze, the culture shock can be as severe as relocating in a foreign land. In 1980, when Chicago-based Kraft Inc. merged with Los Angeles-based Dart Industries, it caused traumas, threats, and other negative reactions among employees of both organizations. Organizational psychologies realize that the workers, even at executive levels, often view such acquisitions as upheavals in their lives and that they need assistance with the transition process. These workers become suspicious of the new management, insecure about their positions, and anxious about how they will fit into the new corporate mold. This is especially true if a domestic company is acquired by a foreign corporation, which brings in a management team whose macrocultural and organizational backgrounds are quite different.

Organizational decision makers should be more sensitive to such cross-cultural differences, since they can undermine employee effectiveness both at home and in a host culture abroad. The very human side of enterprise requires sensitivity and skill in such intercultural relations. When people are transferred, relocation services provided by the corporation should be comprehensive, from providing job assistance to the spouse to coping with the new culture. It makes good business sense to have a foreign deployment system from recruitment to reentry that will cut down on premature returns from overseas assignments and facilitate international productivity and relations.

Stephen Rhinesmith, chief operating officer of New York's Moran, Stahl & Boyer, Inc., believes that relocation services should be comprehensive, whether a family is being moved or an entire plant. Rhinesmith maintains that employers can do more to facilitate community and company relations in the new site than the usual services of housing exchange and guidance in the new community. Whether it is moving a corporate headquarters or a factory, he urges a positive organization development program to create a new work culture in the new facility.

Cross-cultural management relations often occur when a firm borrows from abroad a good idea to improve business operations, or when a foreign firm buys into a domestic company or starts its own overseas operations. That is what happened when Kaxuo Inamori quit his engineering job and invested $40,000 in a high-technology organization that became Kyocera International. Then he brought this Japanese technology with its unique version of industrial relations to California.

Under the leadership of a Japanese Canadian, Arthur Jonishi, KI became a leader in supplying printed circuits, but its real innovation may be in American personnel relations. With a multicultural staff of 1,200 in its San Diego plant, there is a "work extra hard" philosophy. Each day begins with employee meetings—often outdoors—dealing with different groups and themes—executives, personnel and plant administrators, and hourly employees, on safety, sales, and production. The sessions start with key management observations about world economic conditions and how they affect the plant, or comments on various worker suggestions. After some group calisthenics, the personnel break into small groups for discussions of job-related issues. The management style includes consensus seeking, sharing a variety of work tasks as organizational need dictates, a "no layoff" policy, monthly bonuses and other recognitions of achievement, benefits ranging from annual bonuses, which can go up to 100 percent of monthly earnings, to stock options.

Among the Americans working with Japanese supervisors at Kyocera is George Woodsworth, personnel manager, who observed: "On the whole our workers are much more cooperative, much more responsible, much more efficient and productive than at any place I have ever seen." Even though managers admit that the hardest job is managing communications and cultural differences, it is obvious that new approaches to organizational relations can be successfully imported. A *Fortune* feature on how Japanese manage in the United States noted that a mixed American-Japanese style was employed to instill a sense of quality among American workers and to make them feel psychologically secure. Thus a synergy existed between efficiency and human-oriented management and between labor and management. The article included a word of encouragement from Hajime Nakai, president of Sanyo Electric Company's subsidiary in the United States: "I would advise American companies to regain self-confidence. Basically, we learned everything from the U.S."

CHANGING ORGANIZATIONAL INTERFACES
In this postindustrial age, external organizational relations are also being transformed. In complex human systems, there is great need for interdependence. Antitrust activities and regulations

were a part of the industrial culture when competition at any cost was the dominant norm. Today success and development depend—in the corporation, in the larger industry, and in the community—on collaboration and cooperation. Increasingly, a triangular relationship exists between business, government, and unions. Instead of viewing one another as antagonists, adversarial relations have to be replaced by synergistic relations in order for the economy to prosper and for human needs to be met effectively. Perhaps an examination of three interfaces of metaindustrial organizations will make the new approach in external relations more evident.

1. *Trade unions* were a product of the industrial age of development. They served a significant role in protecting worker rights and safety, as well as in obtaining just compensation and benefits for services rendered. Do they have any role in the metaindustrial culture? My answer to the leaders of a major union that is my client was: "No, unless trade unions radically change their purposes and strategies." Today, many businesses have successfully resisted unionization, and contracts negotiated by elected union leaders are often rejected by rank-and-file members. Many of the occupations on which the trade union movement was built are disappearing, and the new high-tech career people see no value in union membership.

Enlightened managers, who already take care of the "hygiene needs" of workers, are trying to provide a psychologically healthy work environment by involving employees more in everything from management to ownership. If a union is to survive, it must, therefore, develop a new relationship with both its members and the corporation or government agencies. If not it may end up like PATCO—out in nowhere and alienated from both employer and the public. Unions, if they are to survive, should help workers and corporations make the transition from the industrial to the metaindustrial work scene. They can assist mature industries to provide a more meaningful work environment and so switch to team management. Douglas A. Fraser, president of the United Auto Workers, epitomizes the new type of union leader. He is helping the automotive industry to make painful adjustments, and he advises worker concessions to save jobs in hard times. In his new role as a member of Chrysler's board of directors, Fraser has been able to bring about a profit-sharing plan for workers and a union voice in plant-closing decisions. As older industries struggle with change, union cooperation may result not only in the survival of some companies and trade unions, but also in a new relationship with management. Certainly, union and corporate leaders could do much together to humanize the workplace and lessen the impact of automation on traditional occupations and their skilled craftspeople. Joint ventures by unions and management might include counseling services and training programs for workers displaced by robots or forced into early retirement. With or without the institution of trade unions, metaindustrial organizations in the twenty-first century will maintain more synergistic relations between labor and management, until that archaic dichotomy disappears.

2. *Universities and schools* in the industrial age developed curricula to support the factory system and helped to make it work. Whether in preparing managers or mechanics, the formal system of education, both public and private, provided the trained personnel that industry needed. Now elementary, secondary, and university education suffer from overpopulation, severe economic squeeze, obsolete programs, equipment, and facilities, and a severe gap between the education provided and the occupational needs of the marketplace. It is not just a matter of inadequate teaching and skill level; it is often that people are being educated in obsolete content and skills. Colleges and universities, for example, often turn out majors in great quantities for which there is no employment prospect or vocational relevance. At the same time, they neglect to offer courses in the new scientific and technological developments.

The educational situation is so bizarre that some corporations are forced to begin their own degree studies for employees, such as Wang did in its master's program in computer sciences; or companies are contracting to take over school systems and programs, not only in developing nations but in their own country. Education has literally become big business—in industry and government and in the provision of the tools and technology for the new instruction, as well as in the companies' direct involvement in the learning process. Metaindustrial organizations are seeking more synergistic relations with formal systems of education, often through a corporate partnership with an educational institution in joint research, leased teaching equipment, sabbaticals for their personnel to teach there, and mutual involvement in community economic or cultural development. It is an exchange of knowledge workers in industry and universities, and a sharing of competence to improve the human condition. For a company, this can be *profitable* service, whether it joins with professors to establish a technological or learning corporation or co-sponsors a university's field expedition under the oceans, beneath the earth, or even out in space. Interinstitutional cooperative relations are a norm in the superindustrial age. If human assets are to be more fully utilized, there must be more collaboration between educators and business-people.

3. *Associations* in metaindustrial work culture will be renewed in purpose and services, or they will suffer organization shock, disappear, and be replaced by more relevant groupings. Professional, trade, and industrial or consumer associations exist to serve both member and customer. In a knowledge society, these associations have a real opportunity to share information rapidly by new means from computer networks to video teleconferencing. When synergy occurs between a corporation and the industrial or consumer association, both benefit. Both traditional and newly formed industrial associations can do much to promote self-regulation, consumer interests, and new research, especially when they cooperate with their counterparts in consumer organizations. Frequently, what new or small businesses cannot do on their own, they can accomplish through their trade or professional association—such as research, training, and marketing. Often, this association is in a better position to develop collaborative contracts or contacts with universities, trade groups, foreign governments, and other organizations. An association can become a focal point for companies and their employees to share joint educational, recreational, or health facilities and programs. In the metaindustrial situation, we can expect a proliferation of smaller, more informal networks of technicians with special interests.

CAPSULE CONCLUSIONS

Since relationships are a central component in making any culture distinctive, we have examined the transformation under way in organizational relations. As social beings, our associational systems and strategies have a powerful influence on behavior. Metaindustrial organizations are striving to enhance work relations in a new way. Both in interpersonal and group relations, they are searching for more meaning and helpfulness. In the technological age, with the increasing automation of the workplace, they are trying to upgrade the quality of professional relations among knowledge workers. With persons who value high performance and competence, such positive relations can help in stress management and the avoidance of occupational burnout. In the decades ahead of continuing change and transition, social relations will become more comprehensive and complex. They will be more intense, more temporary, and often based on electronic connections. In a world marketplace, these relations are more pluralistic and multicultural. Metaindustrial managers must, therefore, draw on both masculine and feminine qualities within themselves, becoming more androgynous in their work relations. Family relations, especially among two-career couples, can be strained in this new work culture unless those involved *share* their challenges and capabilities, as well as the home.

The spread of automation and robotics demands a new kind of man/machine relationship that expands human intelligence but that does not alienate the technical workers from themselves or others. The emerging personnel and organizational relations achieve their highest expression in synergy—combined action when differences and talents are shared. By collaboration and cooperation, organizations can become more effective through improved team relations and through managerial practices that are more facilitative and reinforcing. The same synergistic approach is necessary with regard to external relations, be it with the community, the consumer, the government, a university, a trade union, fellow citizens, or foreigners.

In conclusion, one might put these insights in the context of a metaindustrial organization's board of directors. In such a microculture as we have been sketching, board members would be chosen on the basis of competence, knowledge, and experience that can be blended together for wise counsel. Such a diverse board might include representatives of the workers themselves, as well as of consumers or customers, along with stockholders and technical specialists. Board relationships would be developed among members and top management that are in keeping with the type of team relations described in this chapter. In other words, the board would be looked on as a resource group to contribute to organizational self-regulation and development. No entity within a metaindustrial organization would be excluded from reevaluating and improving both its intra- and inter-group relations.

CHAPTER 10 Transforming Organizational Recognition and Rewards

Each cultural system satisfies basic human needs in unique ways. That is because each different way of life makes its own assumptions about ends and purposes of existence; what people can expect from each other, as well as from nature and the gods; what constitutes frustration or fulfillment. A people's perception of what is required for survival or development determines the institutions, programs, and procedures their society establishes to satisfy common needs. The time, the place, and the situation in which the people find themselves influence the patterns that emerge. An agricultural people may have a high regard and need for family relations, support, and unity. In contrast, those living in a technological society are less dependent on relatives and may not value the family in the same way.

Although the details differ from one cultural group to another and from one individual to another, humankind's basic needs are universal. Psychologist Abraham Maslow categorized human needs according to a hierarchy of five levels. At the first level are physiological needs, those things necessary to sustain life—from nourishment and exercise to sex and rest. Safety or security needs—both physical and psychological—come next. We seek to stabilize living arrangements and make life more predictable and less ambiguous. A person is motivated to protect valuables, accomplishments, and reputation; to promote order and discipline; and to avoid disaster, disruption, and danger. At the third level is a need to belong, to love and be loved. This is manifest in yearnings to be affiliated with someone or some group, to experience affection and to express it to others, to be a member and to be appreciated. At the fourth level are the needs to be esteemed and respected by oneself and others. Here people are concerned with experiencing feelings of adequacy, with feeling confirmed as people, and with achievement. The highest level of human needs is for self-fulfillment or self-actualization of one's potential. Here is where the needs of high achievers or top performers are realized in the form of self-confirmation, often apart from the accolades of others. Here is where the individual or group pursues excellence, perfection, ultimate values for self and society. It is an arena for the demonstration of creativity and the development of untapped human resources. In the metaindustrial work culture, the emphasis will be on satisfaction of employee ego and self-fulfillment needs.

Readers who would like to assess their own needs and motivations can use the Leadership Motivation Inventory in Appendix E, which is arranged according to Maslow's hierarchy of needs. In 1968, David S. Brown used a similar assessment instrument to survey 1,522 managers in government and private business. The percentage of responses in the top ten categories are shown in Table 3. The numbers in parentheses following each item refer to the comparable question in Appendix E. After completing that inventory, you might wish to compare your answers with those in the table and with a survey of your own subordinates.

TABLE 3. Summary of manager survey.

1. Feeling my job is important (21)	61%
2. Opportunity to do interesting work (27)	57%
3. Opportunity for self-development and improvement (28)	50%
4. Respect for me as a person (22)	44%
5. Chance for promotion (20)	43%
6. Good pay (5)	43%
7. Chance to turn out quality work (23)	32%
8. Knowing what is going on in the organization (13)	28%
9. Large amount of freedom on the job (26)	24%
10. Steady employment (1)	21%

Note that the top five responses in the table are in the two highest needs levels, where the emphasis is on psychological and developmental needs. In other words, as we move into the postindustrial period of human development, here is documentation of the emerging pattern of needs and motives among managers.

During the past 15 years, I have used the same leadership motivation inventory in my consulting practice with thousands of managers in more than 150 human systems throughout the world and have consistently obtained results comparable to the Brown findings. That is, managers' and professionals' top five responses are in the upper two needs levels: ego and self-actualization needs.

All knowledge workers in metaindustrial organizations are likely to have a pattern of needs that is comparable to that of today's managerial elite. Thus, if one were to administer the motivation inventory to supervisors and technicians in high-tech firms, it is likely that the top five responses of these knowledge workers would be in the same areas, that is, the upper two levels of the Maslow hierarchy.

Note that Dr. Maslow said there is a reverse side to his pyramid—that the opposite of needs is gripes or grumbles, and that as people become more educated and affluent, they move up to a higher level of complaints, such as concerns for ecology and social justice. For humans are never completely satisfied; their needs and complaints simply become more refined as lower-level ones are taken care of.

We should realize that people move up and down on the needs hierarchy, depending on circumstances. In a tight economy, there may be greater concern for security needs. Generally, in advanced technological or information societies, the trend is upward on the needs hierarchy. This is an important insight for executives who are designing recognition and rewards systems in metaindustrial organization cultures. It also relates to the research of Dr. Frederick Herzberg, who has long contended that industry responds only to the "hygiene needs" of workers—by providing adequate and safe working conditions, satisfactory pay and benefit programs—and that these no longer motivate employees, for such provisions are taken for granted. To develop positive work attitudes and productivity, Herzberg has counseled management to emphasize the "true motivators"—achievement, personal and professional growth, recognition, responsibility, and advancement. These are the real job satisfiers and are found primarily in the upper three levels of the Maslow hierarchy. They are also the key to energizing people in a metaindustrial work culture.

Obviously, there are cross-cultural differences in need levels to be considered in international business. The level of economic development will affect the level of general need. Thus, although we might expect that the masses in Third World countries might focus on survival needs, workers for multinationals in developing countries might form a microculture with needs quite distinct from the general public in the same nation. Furthermore, although a transnational enterprise may be operating in an Asian culture where the belief system of reincarnation dominates, personnel in a high-technology firm within that society might not fit the general pattern of fatalism, which generally causes locals to respond with patience and conformity to circumstances. Indeed, within their subculture, such knowledge workers might be more goal-oriented and dynamic in their behavior, as would comparable personnel in North America, Europe, or Japan.

It may be helpful to remind ourselves of the relationships between and among *needs, motives,* and *behavior.* As a humanistic psychologist, I prefer the following explanation: If people have a high need to be liked, they may be motivated to behave in such a way as to avoid conflict. Or if people are motivated to avoid trouble, they may play it safe in most situations. On the other hand, if people have a high need to achieve, they may consistently seek to excel. From this perspective, people set goals or objectives in order to satisfy their human needs. They then energize themselves or are motivated to accomplish these goals. This is the point of the management-by-objectives system in business and government. However, people sometimes meet obstacles in the way of achieving their goals; tension and stress may build up as frustration is experienced. Some people make adjustments to get around the barriers and accomplish their objectives. Others may react to continued frustration with hostility, rebellion, requests for transfer, withdrawal, inactivity, or apathy. Or the behavior may be defensive (projection, rationalization, or even sublimation) as people cope with unsatisfied needs.

THE WAY IT WAS
In the industrial work culture, which often focused on satisfaction of lower-level needs, some managers used a "carrot and stick" approach to worker motivation: Under the merit pay system, the more or better the work, the higher the pay or "carrot"; the lower the performance, the smaller the pay and no increases, or the "stick." Although this approach may seem logical, it is difficult for managers to set standardized performance levels for each individual, assess that performance objectively, and reward it fairly. This approach also puts all the control in the hands of the boss and causes the subordinates to become very competitive. It is a win/lose approach that is becoming inappropriate in the 80s.

Increasingly, Theory X assumptions—that the average employee dislikes work and will avoid it, avoids responsibility and has little ambition, wants security above all, and needs to be directed, controlled, or threatened with punishment in order to get adequate effort put forth—are proving inadequate. Douglas McGregor advocated a Theory Y management, more appropriate to the postindustrial age, which assumes that workers like to expend physical and mental energy and that they are capable of exercising *self*-control and direction and of seeking and accepting responsibility. He believed that the average human being has a high degree of imagination, ingenuity, and creativity, but that modern industrial life was only partially utilizing human capacity. That most of us are underemployed has been borne out by research indicating that the average person uses only 40 percent of his or her potential. Innovative, metaindustrial management may discover ways to tap into that 60 percent of undeveloped human ability. Another significant insight of McGregor's is that commitment to objectives on the part of personnel is associated with the *rewards* available for their achievement.

A recent Gallup poll report (May 18, 1982) confirmed that Americans take more pride in their work than Western Europeans and Japanese. The survey of 1,220 randomly selected participants in 15 national cultures was conducted for the Center for Applied Research in the Apostolate, Washington, D.C. Of the Americans polled, 85 percent said they took great pride in their work, as against 35 percent of the Europeans and 22 percent of the Japanese. Apparently the work ethic is still alive and well in the United States, and managers would do well to capitalize on this cultural motivation of Yankee workers. It also confirms what Japanese managers in the United States have been saying about the work efforts of their U.S. employees—namely, that they are comparable to or better than their Japanese counterparts.

Ten years before William Ouchi was writing on the subject, Stephen H. Rhinesmith published a cultural analysis of organizations, pointing out the advantages of Theory Z management to multinational corporations, especially in developing countries. He envisioned this as a mixture of both X and Y styles, in which we do not assume that all persons are self-motivated to work for organizational objectives because of variations in personalities and cultures. Therefore, leadership styles would vary in terms of controls and directiveness according to each individual's abilities, concerns, and level of development. Some people, especially in newly industrialized nations, may not be ready for Theory Y and need responsive management that prepares them to take advan-

FIGURE 10. Personnel motivation.

MOTIVATION*	SYSTEM I	SYSTEM II	SYSTEM III	SYSTEM IV
Predominant technique used: 1. Fear 2. Threats 3. Punishment 4. Rewards 5. Involvement	1, 2, 3; occasionally 4	4, some 3	4, some 3 and 5	5, 4, based on group-set goals
Where is responsibility felt for achieving organization goals?	Mostly at top	Top and middle	Fairly general	At all levels

*Based on research of Rensis Likert and his four-systems theory of organization.

tage of opportunities and to contribute to organizational objectives.

We referred earlier to Rensis Likert's analysis of a human organization. Essentially, Likert examined six critical factors of management—leadership, motivation, communication, decisions, goals, and control—in terms of four systems, which move from authoritative behavior by the manager to healthy participation by the worker group. Figure 10 illustrates the dimension appropriate here—motivation. Systems I and II are like Theory X management and emphasize the use of fear, threats, and punishment, and occasionally rewards. Systems III and IV are closer to Theory Y, with the focus on rewards and participation of employees at all levels in the achievement of organizational goals.

Young people in Europe are experiencing a wave of discontent because their needs are not being satisfied by their society or their government. Forty percent of the unemployed are under 25 years of age and their number is growing. In addition to housing shortages and social disparities, youth desperation and disillusionment mount as they experience a profound identity crisis in a world in transition. Many young people have expressed their anger and hostility in violence and are creating an alternative culture that escapes the understanding of their elders. It is a question of time before such behavior reaches American youth, especially among the unemployed and minorities. Workers, many of them relatively young, are already expressing dissatisfaction with the slow pace of change in the U.S. workplace as well as with the growing unemployment because of a stagnant economy and increased automation. Among blue-collar and unskilled employees, the disillusionment seems greatest and the alienation is expanding. Auren Uris and Jane Benshael summarized the situation in this way:

> That job dissatisfaction is no longer a function of only mechanical, repetitive work is most startlingly proven by recent strikes of a variety of highly skilled employees. From firefighters to doctors, baseball players to teachers ... the air traffic controllers seem to be part of a new pattern of dissatisfaction not with the work itself, but with a variety of issues related to it.

Uris and Benshael report that the complaints center on such stress factors as:

1. *Lack of control over the work.* People in technically sophisticated occupations get frustrated when they have little say about how the work is to get done.

2. *Lack of respect from management.* Skilled employees resent supervisors who question their commitment and think they are there mainly for a paycheck. They feel that they are treated with contempt and that good work does not get recognition. They are frustrated when constructive suggestions for improvement are discouraged or ignored and when they are not able to assume responsibility up to their capabilities.

3. *Lack of status.* Another source of frustration, this leads employees to seek tangible rewards, like increased pay or benefits, to make up for the lack of appreciation of the role they play as computer operators, technicians, secretaries, and so forth.

The problem seems to be with obsolete management approaches to employee motivation. Workers require more creative, relevant supervision, based on cooperation, and encouragement. Archaic means of recognition and reward can also fail to satisfy personnel needs or to motivate them. This can be manifested in such traditional and now questionable practices as giving a work group pins to mark improved productivity or attendance, or pens, watches, or retirement dinners to mark long periods of satisfactory service. This is the way it was, but these methods will be inadequate in a metaindustrial knowledge society.

Another problem is obsolete personnel administration. The metaindustrial work situation requires a computerized human resources planning and management *system* that is innovative and strategic. Some analysts have recommended that it include measurement of employee levels of satisfaction, job analysis and performance evaluation research, and continuous assessment of employee attitudes and needs.

THE WAY IT IS NOW

Enlightened management realizes that each generation, responding to the circumstances of its times, has different needs and motivations. In order to energize younger employees, one must seek out information on that generation's attitudes and outlooks. *Trends,* the Futures Research Division publication of Security Pacific National Bank, assisted its management in this regard by means of a report entitled "Late Teens, Early 20s."* The following summary will indicate the relevance of this source to our chapter topic:

A new generation of workers and potential managers in their early twenties is coming into the metaindustrial organization. They are achievement- and work-oriented, have lowered expectations, and are most interested in security and success. If they are the first-born in their families, they tend to be more leaders and achievers, while later-born offspring are less assertive and more likely to "coast" (*recruiters,* please note). This generation worries about being *disenfranchised* or locked out from opportunities and affluence. They are easily frustrated, unless encouraged. Some resent that life is no longer predictable, and follows a prescribed order, so they fall back into nostalgia. Others in their twenties welcome change and learn to cope more effectively with it. Highly refined in visual media, they expect information and knowledge to be presented visually, usually through TV or computers. They want to live simply but well, and have a strong consumer orientation, especially for products and services that are *individualized.* The generation of the Transitional Society, they enter the workforce that is oversupplied with middle managers and undersupplied with technical and entry-level unskilled workers. There is likely to be a decrease in emphasis on entitlements with this generation, and benefit packages may have to be adjusted accordingly. New types of performance rewards would be necessary to incorporate disparate levels of motivation within the group.

The Opinion Research Corporation has published a report on "Strategic Planning for Human Resources: 1980 and Beyond"

---

*Copies are available from Hank Koehn, Security Pacific National Bank, 333 So. Hope St., Los Angeles, Calif. 90071.

based on its research of employee attitudes. The findings confirm that even the needs of managers are not being met by many contemporary corporations and that motivational problems are not just with hourly laborers:

> The most consistent finding is that overall, middle managers' favorable attitudes are down.
>
> Over the years, they have found a "Hierarchy Gap" between attitudes of managers and clerical and hourly employees.
>
> Job satisfaction among all three employee groups recently declined to its lowest point ever.
>
> Job security among managers is lower than it ever has been.
>
> Managers' satisfaction with their advancement opportunity has, for the first time, dropped below the level where a majority is satisfied.
>
> Few managers, and even fewer clerical and hourly employees, currently feel that their companies are making promotions fairly.
>
> Managers' ratings or their companies' willingness to listen to their problems have most recently declined, with an even more dramatic decline in rating their companies' responding to their problems.
>
> All employee groups—particularly managers—have become more critical of the ability of top management.
>
> There is little relationship between education and employees' attitudes toward their work.
>
> Among clerical and hourly employees, there is a U-shaped relationship between age and satisfaction, with an array of employee relations concerns. Youngest and oldest are most satisfied. For managers, there is a linear relationship between age and satisfaction—younger managers are the least satisfied while older managers are most satisfied.
>
> Among managers, men have more favorable attitudes toward their jobs than women. Among hourly employees, the opposite is true. Among clerical employees, there is not a clear-cut pattern.

In multinational corporations, employee needs and motivation must be approached with differing strategies. Productive achievement is viewed differently from one region to another. Americans, for example, have a high regard for the work ethic, the will to achieve and succeed, but in many societies this is not the norm. Similarly, a non-Western culture may view authority and relations with subordinates in a manner very different from a Western manager who may be working in that culture. It may favor, as in Japan, paternalistic management, or it may frown on participative management, as in India or Saudi Arabia. Cross-cultural research reveals that in some cultures, commerce is looked down on; mercantile activity is for the lower classes, but the professions are esteemed. Some macrocultures have negative attitudes toward "foreign managers." Research has reported that in some countries the feeling is that managers are a corrupt, contemptible group whose main activities consist of scheming and systematic exploitation of people. This not only makes recruitment of competent people difficult, but increases operating costs when inflated salaries and benefits must be paid to attract qualified managers. When the local community has a positive image of enlightened management, greater cooperation, trust, and productivity are fostered between managers and employees or the public. The same may be said for executives who have positive images of changing worker roles and of their own function as managers.

During this transitional period in work cultures, the compensation and benefits plans of organizations are changing. The Conference Board released a study of 3,000 U.S. companies in 1981 that compared current benefits practices with those of the past decade. Under the leadership of its senior research associate, Michael Meyerson, the following trends were tracked:

- Employee preference for "more leisure sooner," such as through increased vacations (5 weeks per year now typical after 20 years of service) and holidays (10 paid holidays on the average).
- Expanded corporate health plans now covering mental illness and drug and alcohol dependency (typical coverage $100 deductible, payment of 80 percent of remaining bills).
- Transformation of pension benefits based on final average earnings with an offset for Social Security benefits (including inflation adjustments, vestment rights after 10 years of service, and 80 percent of benefits at age 60).
- Death benefits providing a lump sum to spouse plus early-retirement pension rights to survivor.

The Conference Board report also noted a tendency on the part of major corporations to reverse benefit trends during severe recessions in the economy, especially by seeking concessions from workers and their unions.

THE WAY IT IS BECOMING
Metaindustrial managers realize that the psychological contract between employee and organization may be more important than

any legal or union contract. Although a company has some authority to enforce its expectations of workers, workers can give or withhold participation to enforce their expectations of management. The system of recognition and rewards can increase job satisfaction and productivity. It is a vital dimension of organizational culture that should be better understood by modern managers.

When observing any culture, the manner and method in which it proffers praise for good behavior, brave deeds, length of service, or some other accomplishment is significant. In the business subculture, recognition is offered to executives by certain "perks" and privileges—special offices, dining rooms, parking places, and expense accounts—but these are changing or disappearing in the postindustrial period. In microcultures, such as the military or the police, these recognitions and rewards are quite formal—commendations, citations, medals, and a whole ranking system that is displayed on uniforms through stripes, bars, eagles, ribbons, and titles. Organizational cultures use a variety of means to recognize and reinforce accomplishment and high productivity, ranging from service pins and job titles to company cars and stock options. The size and location of one's work space and its decorations are part of this corporate reinforcement system, as are the compensation plans, incentive awards, and testimonial dinners.

Gibson, Ivancevich, and Donnelly provide some useful models and insights into the reward process in corporate culture. They maintain that management recognizes and rewards employees to attract people to join the firm, to keep them coming to work, and to motivate them to perform at high levels. They suggest that the employee is motivated to exert effort, to involve ability, skills, and experience, when performance results are objectively evaluated and rewarded. This results in job satisfaction. The rewards fall into two broad categories:

Intrinsic rewards. Such rewards originate and are felt *within* the person. They come from one's sense of achievement and accomplishment or from one's self-esteem. These rewards satisfy needs for being responsible, autonomous, or challenged. Such self-rewards are experienced by many lonely scholars and authors, and increasingly by metaindustrial personnel.

Extrinsic rewards. These are external to the job itself. They are given by the organization in the form of pay, promotion, benefits, praise, tenure, status symbols, improved work equipment and facilities, and opportunities to socialize with co-workers. Money, a major extrinsic reward in some cultures, modifies behavior at work and is a conditioned reinforcer of desired behavior on the job, as well as an anxiety reducer. Incentive pay or bonus plans have been used for individuals, groups, and organizations. The most effective plan seems to be with individuals, with the use of a bonus for outstanding performance. Other financial rewards in the form of fringe benefits can range from IBM's recreation program for employees to General Mills's picnic grounds. They also include pension plans, various forms of insurance, and vacations, but the approach to them is changing rapidly in metaindustrial organizations.

The difference in the metaindustrial work culture is the new developments in the recognition and reward process. Although extrinsic emoluments continue in altered forms, the focus is more on intrinsic reinforcers. For example, in order for management to provide a corporate environment that supports professional development, high performance, innovation, responsibility, and commitment to objectives, it might have a self-reward system in which a professional engineer would be involved in an entire project, from design to completion, rather than just in one phase. The job satisfaction comes from being involved in the whole process and from successful completion of the task. The system might include the creation of special work challenges for high-achieving employees, so that the reward is realized through goal attainment.

In customizing job satisfiers to individual needs, there are some personnel who respond best to greater autonomy. They need more independence and freedom on the job. Once they know the work objectives, they should be left alone to structure the job themselves. When a bright young knowledge worker is discovered, enlightened management will provide personal growth opportunities that maximize the worker's protential. The point here is that metaindustrial executives get to know their people and their needs, so they can individualize motivating factors. Since each employee is essentially self-directive and self-fulfilling, according to his or her own predictive system, management should endeavor to contribute to the maturation process of each person through a work culture that challenges the individual to excellence.

Better-informed and -educated workers are a driving force behind changing management styles, especially in the matters of recognition and remuneration. In the United States, it has been estimated that by 1985, 21 percent of the labor force will be college graduates, compared to 13.2 percent in 1970. An interesting report on the new look in the workplace has come from a nonprofit organization, the United Way. According to its long-range planning committee, the workplace may become the dominant social institution of the 1980s, affecting more people than family, church, or school. Therefore, it predicted, "Management credibility, authority, and legitimacy will be increasingly derived from the consent (and the cooperation) of the managed." Workers will expect a bigger say in how they do their jobs, the conditions under which they work, and the rewards they get. Project director Lynne Hall confirmed that the future work environment will be oriented toward information and service activities, as well as home entrepreneurship. The workforce will be more diverse, including parttimers and the handicapped, who expect flexible work schedules. Other benefit trends that Hall envisions are growth of employee services—such as drug and alcohol abuse and other counseling, day-care centers, and fitness and recreational programs and facilities. Some companies are already experimenting with lifetime employment guarantees, including "rental" of workers to other corporations during slack periods.*

REWARDING EXCEPTIONAL CONTRIBUTIONS
Perhaps the most meaningful way to recognize and reward employees, as well as to ensure their involvement and improved performance, is to provide either a profit-sharing plan or a share in the ownership of the organization. Metaindustrial firms are experimenting with a variety of strategies, including participation in stock plans, having the employees take over ownership and management, and formation of multinational cooperatives.

To increase productivity and profitability, many companies are "retreading" traditional approaches to recognition and rewards. In place of the old suggestion box method, metaindustrial organizations reward suggested improvements. But compare these cultural differences:

Japanese and American management demonstrate a marked contrast in the way they receive, reward, and implement suggestions for improving organizational effectiveness and productivity. Toyota is responsive to workers' needs and thus generates a half million such suggestions annually from its employees. It adopts 90 percent of them. General Motors, on the other hand, generates

* *Los Angeles Times*, November 1, 1981.

one suggestion per employee each year, in comparison to 17 per Toyota worker. GM adopts only about 30 percent of the suggestions received. There is a powerful message on reward systems in these data.

Y. S. Gypsum learned its lesson after it received only five to seven suggestions per year from 16,000 employees! It established a system and now generates 2,100 committee-approved suggestions in one operating month! The program pays for effort and encourages cost-saving idea submissions for cash awards. Suggestions are solicited through bulletin-board displays, paycheck stuffers, and a newsletter that recognizes people who have provided acceptable proposals. Each entry that is accepted, furthermore, becomes part of a companywide sweepstakes for larger prizes awarded every six months. The results are both money and energy savings, which lead to greater profitability. By publishing a scoreboard in the newsletter of results, a healthy competition is fostered between plants and their managers. The project needs to be continually promoted and communicated, but the biggest motivator has been not money and prizes but *recognition*. So old industrial techniques can be renewed and reused in new ways!

Since we are creating a knowledge society in which most of the labor force will be engaged in intellectual, not manual, pursuits, new motivators and satisfiers must be sought. Authoritarianism, threats, and penalties must be replaced with more positive and sophisticated ways to encourage a person to do innovative research, creative writing, or programming. Some trends in reward and recognition systems in advanced, technological societies are:

Encouragement of high-performing units and personnel. In this approach, the top-performing individuals and teams get priority on projects, support services, and recognition within the enterprise. They are asked to provide video feedback, to participate in group problem solving, and to serve as behavior models and trainers for average performers.

Positive reinforcement systems. Accenting what people do right in a systematic way is the basis of this approach, originating from the research of Harvard's B. F. Skinner. Desired behavior in job performance is rewarded. A system of positive reinforcers is designed and administered for improved behavior management.* Confirmation may be praise or pay, but it should be linked in a consistent manner to positive, improved performance.

Creative performance evaluation. Relevant, reliable, data-

---

* See L. M. Miller.

based performance feedback is provided to employees periodically. The manager does this in a helpful, consultative way, using intrinsic or extrinsic rewards appropriate to individual needs. In addition to the use of group evaluation of individual or team performance, this approach might also encourage self-assessment and goal setting.

Culture-based personnel practices. In providing rewards and recognition, what energizes knowledge workers in a metaindustrial operation might be quite inappropriate for aborigines in New Guinea who work in loin cloths as baggage handlers for Quantas. Stephen Rhinesmith maintains that there are three value orientations among peoples in various stages of development:

1. *Ascription.* Social and family backgrounds are important factors in management; rewards, then, are given to those related to persons in authority, either through family, caste, or tribal connections.
2. *Association.* Relationships and trust are foremost; rewards are given to those with whom one is associated, either directly or indirectly.
3. *Achievement.* Competence and accomplishment are highly regarded; rewards are given to those who perform best under competitive conditions.

Although the multinational manager in a high-technology firm may favor the last approach, local culture may dictate some allowance for the two traditional approaches, while teaching the local people to work more synergistically in a combination of association and achievement strategies.

Some special considerations in compensation and benefits programs have had to be extended to managers assigned to other countries, especially a manager from the First World assigned to a Third World post, or to a foreign assignment where foreign executives are targets for radical groups and terrorists. In the past, executives working abroad could expect a lifestyle that sometimes surpassed the amenities received at home, often returning quite affluent as a result of this international posting. Another Conference Board study by Burton Teague in 1982 involved 123 of the largest U.S. corporations with overseas operations. It found that a rising percentage of firms are providing foreign-service executives with special stipends, increased cash allowances for housing and other extra living expenses, and financial aid to offset tax liabilities. Reduced psychic compensations, as well as inflation and limited purchasing power, have made many executives reluctant to work abroad even when they are not in real physical danger. The survey showed that 69 percent of the companies provide overseas hardship allowances, and 11 percent offer mobility pay, the cash supplements varying with the foreign site of the transfer. However, with the emergence of a new generation of global managers and technicians who think and operate in terms of the world marketplace, there will be less emphasis in the future on such financial rewards for relocation abroad. Instead, offshore assignments will provide incentives that include more opportunity to travel or more temporary visits home; more overseas support services, especially to family members; and more electronic or satellite communications with home culture.

Energized models. The behavior of dynamic, energized managers is observed and learned by subordinates. In this "do-as-I-do" approach, supervisory or high-performing examples are offered instead of instructions and exhortations. Rewards are bestowed on selected pacesetters. The model may also be a work team, process, or product that demonstrates quality, and thus receives recognition.

Performance-contingent rewards are effective in management. Thus wage increases are increasingly tied to productivity increases. A manager can design the conditions in a work unit that will result in high performance and then use that group as a model for others. Since the work must be meaningful to the participants, there must be opportunities for exercising responsibility for the outcomes of the work. Further, continuing feedback on the results of member activities must be provided. To ensure a success model, the work team should experience variety in task activities and skills use, and be given relative autonomy in scheduling work and determining procedures. Management's role is to provide the conditions that facilitate achievement and then to confirm or reward those who perform well. For example, some companies guarantee job security to high performers, or offer to those who save time and money through increased productivity a percentage of the "savings," or provide financial and other incentives to outstanding employees.

Wellness strategies. These involve preventive maintenance programs, both physical and psychological. They increase productivity while cutting down on tardiness, absenteeism, and low morale. A corporate wellness approach can counteract the $25 billion that was lost to American industry in 1980 by premature death of employees, or the $700 million lost because of illness that kept people from work. As part of human resources management, a wellness approach fosters peak levels of mind and body performance. When metaindustrial managers care about employee well-being, employees learn to care about organizational profitability. Such an investment in human assets can have a big payoff. Already 500 U.S. corporations are putting money into personnel wellness programs, including cardiovascular fitness and stress and life-crises management. These programs are being promoted by Xerox, Kimberly-Clark, Merrill Lynch, Chase Manhattan, General Foods, and others. The underlying concept is that *staying* well gives one greater control over life and is less costly than *getting* well.

Control Data Corporation's Life Extension Institute has a Stay Well project that specializes in preventive medicine. It encourages diet and weight control along with exercise and lifestyle change. Gordon Shea, president of Prime Systems in Beltsville, Maryland, advocates wellness training in a systems approach to personal management of stress, unhealthy behavior, and skills development. Such a well-being regimen can be cost-effective as it results in healthier, more productive workers. It can be a way of coping with traumas, dependencies on drugs, alcohol, or smoking, as well as burnout. It correlates with company educational programs in life planning, whether for a second or a retirement career. Philip Randall, a Hay Training director in Philadelphia, suggests that now that people are living longer, smart management should enable personnel to enhance the quality of their lives. Such approaches develop a positive mental attitude in employees and increase their self-management effectiveness. Corporate wellness endeavors recognize the importance of the worker to the company—an enlightened reward system.

For six years the University of Wisconsin has been bringing together planners from industry with people from the health services organizations in workshops for Wellness Promotion Strategies. At their Stevens Point campus, they offer an exchange of ideas and information on the "wellness lifestyle." They define wellness as an active process in which the individual becomes aware of the possibilities for a more successful existence and makes choices that will lead to it. The choices are influenced by changes in self-concept as well as in one's culture and environment. The strategies are examined in terms of physical fitness and nutrition, intellectual and emotional health, spiritual values and ethics, and occupational and social factors. Family and community environments are of course considered as well.

Dr. James O'Toole, a futurist at the University of Southern California, maintains that American culture in general, and American values in particular, are changing. His research underscores the need for a new philosophy of organization and work that is responsive to these underlying shifts in social values and expectations. O'Toole cites, in addition to a demand for more leisure, another changing worker value in the United States—the demand for entitlements. To improve the quality of working life, Americans seek added economic rights (cost-of-living allowances, dental care, for example); constitutional rights (privacy of personnel files, protection of "whistle blowers"); organizational rights (voting on plant relocations, rejecting cross-country transfers or overseas postings); personal rights (relative to hairstyle, beards, clothes). Although economic downturns may temporarily curb such demands, such expectations will increase over the long run as workers in advanced, technological societies search for more self-actualization and psychological rights, especially with the introduction of labor-saving technology.

Sadami Wada, a vice president of Sony Corporation of America, was even more pointed when he noted that people-oriented management is the key to productivity, for corporations must earn dedication and motivation from their employees. Rejecting the adversarial approach to employee relations, Wada recommended the following to a recent Congressional Joint Economic Committee:

- Consider personnel expenses as a fixed rather than a variable cost.
- Educate employees at all levels, especially as generalists.
- Promote a sense of participation and quality in all workers.
- Increase the communication flow, particularly with reference to future company directions.

Meeting the needs of metaindustrial workers requires creativity. Innovative managers may have to "swim upstream" against the prevailing "wisdom" found in some business schools and executive suites. As Jerry Harvey, professor of management science at George Washington University, succinctly stated: "We've designed organizations that reward people who think narrowly and behave even more narrowly." The *Time** cover story in which

---
* May 4, 1981.

Harvey was quoted proposed that some business school solutions to U.S. economic and business woes may be part of the problem. The professional managerial caste, now being turned out at the rate of 500 M.B.A.s a year, seems to have flawed business concepts, techniques, priorities, and values. The median American M.B.A. graduate may be overpaid at a starting salary of $30,000. The indictment reads that such novice managers, though bright, are often too expensive, too aggressive, too restless, and lacking in loyalty and long-term effectiveness.

American professional managers seem to care less about what they produce and its quality and more about selling their product and increasing short-term profits. Geoffrey Hazard, dean of Yale's School of Organization and Management, is astonished that so many achievement- and success-oriented executives have so little sense of self-worth and confidence. President Bok of Harvard declared in 1979 that too many classroom discussions proceed on the unexamined assumption that growth and profits are the only corporate concerns. Such management education appears to neglect development of people skills in dealing with complex human challenges such as fractious minorities, imperious bureaucrats, angry environmentalists, and power manipulators. Metaindustrial managers, in contrast, need both technical and human relations skills; they should excel in thinking and judgment, as well as in understanding and stimulating the workforce.

REDESIGNING COMPENSATION PLANS

Organizational cultures in the West, especially in the United States, have overemphasized financial and material considerations in return for productive employment. In the metaindustrial period, a more balanced approach is being sought, blending financial factors with psychic and physical compensations. Information, and the latest computer to process it more quickly and meaningfully, can be very satisfying to a high-tech employee. But when the company permits that person to have such equipment and work with it at home, this can become a new form of compensation. The same is true when a corporation installs a computer link in a manager's house for more convenient communication with the office.

Reward systems today are characterized by greater innovation, flexibility, and customizing. In place of standardized fringe benefits for all, often inappropriate in two-career families, the "cafeteria style" is more in order. In this approach to compensation, employees are able to choose benefits to meet their individual needs. It provides them with the rewards and benefits that they prefer, instead of what an external person establishes for them. The computer system facilitates record keeping in such creative personnel strategies. With corporate counsel, workers design the medical or life insurance coverage and payments that are best for them and choose the manner in which they are to be remunerated. Within an agreed financial ceiling, the employee might increase or decrease weekly salary; in a two-income family, the workers may wish to divert more of one partner's funds into retirement or estate planning. Because of income-tax circumstances in a two-career family, the employee may indicate a preference for compensation in terms of subsidized education or travel or tuition payments for dependents.

The metaindustrial worker finds time off, whether paid or unpaid, an attractive feature. This form of reward can be in terms of part-time or contract work, which liberates the individual to care for dependents or to pursue personal or professional development. Such time credits might be contingent on productivity, years of service, or some other criterion. The opportunity and the means to do meaningful research will be increasingly valued in this postindustrial age.

Organizations of the future will seek to capitalize human assets, so employee education and training will be considered more an investment than an expense. Corporations and agencies will be more generous in their support of human resources development, both of their own personnel and of underdeveloped persons in the community. Sabbatical leaves for community service, university studies, contemplation, or recreation have already begun at the executive level, and it is just a matter of time before this privilege, with or without pay, is extended to others in the organization. A decade ago in the September–October 1973 issue, *Harvard Business Review* reported that in a survey of *Fortune* 500 companies, 24 percent had such sabbatical programs, and 41 percent thought they were a good idea. Author Eli Goldston proposed that different kinds of leaves be given at various times in an executive's career. Not only does this make good human and business sense, but it helps to reduce stress and burnout, and it spreads out managerial posts as automation decreases the number of workers required.

Edward Lawler has written on the role that reward systems play in organization development. He uses a systems perspective for specific pay approaches, such as gain sharing, skill-based pay, and flexible benefits. Then he analyzes their impact on productivity and quality of worklife, indicating their influence on both personal and organizational effectiveness.

Job redesign and enrichment have a corporate payoff, as was confirmed in a 1979 U.S. Chamber of Commerce survey. The overwhelming majority of workers surveyed indicated they would work harder and better if they were more involved in making decisions about their jobs. But there is a complementary message revealed in a 1981 international study of productivity by pollster Louis Harris and sociologist Amitai Etzioni. Three-quarters of the employees surveyed said they would be happy to have their salaries linked to higher productivity. Metaindustrial managers share the responsibility with their colleagues in devising plans to increase productivity and profitability, with suitable rewards to the employees for that extra effort and contribution.

Innovative incentive plans are one way in which companies have responded to this challenge. Sometimes they take the form of new perks, as in the case of Mitchel Energy & Development Co. of Houston, Texas. This firm finances homes for new workers through its own mortgage company at subsidized rates for up to six years; offers stock options worth up to $500,000 to executives marked for promotion, without employee investment; and tenders shares in a company-sponsored oil-well–drilling program. As a result, there is very little employee turnover at Mitchel. Yet, according to Deutsch, Shea & Evans, a New York executive search firm, most companies expect half of their new employees to leave within five years!

Increasingly, the new approach, then, is to give employees attractive financial incentives realizable in the future—if they stay with the organization. Hewlett-Packard's program, for instance, puts 10 percent of its pretax profits into a long-term profit-sharing plan that pays out fully only when workers have been with the corporation for 13 years. In that way, it counteracts the trend in the computer–genetic-engineering industries to successfully raid each other's workforce. California's Lawrence Livermore National Laboratories keeps its highly valued technical staff with such unusual practices as a combined package of a 10 percent pay raise, two extra weeks of vacation, a 12 percent loan for a new car from the credit union, which can be canceled if the employee leaves, gifts of company stock, and contributions to a company savings plan. It is no wonder this strategy has been referred to as "golden handcuffs" by industrialists! Recognition and rewards today can range from bonuses for high performance to incentive travel packages for reaching a sales or production goal. It is a manifestation of *expectancy theory,* which assumes employees will extend their efforts if the incentive is sufficient to challenge them. Naturally, it is equally important that the corporation live up to the workers' expectations and fulfill its promises.

For more than a decade, the Scanlon Incentive Plan has been operating in four De Soto, Inc., chemical coating operations. It has produced high levels of job satisfaction and a 41 percent productivity increase. Dr. Brian Moore reported on the experiment for the National Commission on Productivity and Work Quality, revealing these insights to metaindustrial managers:

- The basic philosophy of the Scanlon Plan is union-management cooperation that promotes teamwork because workers have valuable information to share with managers, and vice versa.
- The plan operates in a nonadversary atmosphere with management sharing relevant technical and financial information, and reserving concerns of wages, hours, and grievances for separate collective bargaining.
- The plan releases the productivity potential of a generation of better educated, more sophisticated management and labor, and often is the first step in a continuing series of innovations that improve employee relations and organizational effectiveness.
- The relationship between human resource cost and the value of production is the normal ratio of labor to productivity. Bonuses are paid out on the baseline measure related to total labor costs, and market value of goods and services produced as a result of worker effort. To improve base ratio, personnel are encouraged by this formula to learn more productive behavior.
- The bonus is paid monthly on a percentage of pay earned on an organization-wide basis and includes all employees. In the last ten years at the Desoto plants using the plan, this bonus has been 6%.

The Scanlon strategy involves a suggestion system, elected production committees, feedback mechanisms, and a participation process for employees. It increases knowledge of total plant operations, identifies workers with leadership potential, and educates personnel to the need to justify capital budget requests.

Guidebooks are available with ideas on the establishment and administration of a variety of compensation programs. However, there are many ways for meeting personnel needs and increasing productivity other than financial rewards.

CORPORATE ASSISTANCE FOR COPING

In this transitional society, wise corporations help their people to cope more effectively with change. Technological changes, for instance, may alter plant or equipment, process or method, and often diminish the need for qualified personnel. The right of management to displace employees when jobs become automated or computerized is now a matter for negotiations in the field of labor relations.

Reynolds Electrical and Engineering Co., Inc., is an example of a corporation that attempts to minimize upheavals and worker resentment through its contract with the Office and Professional Employees Union. It communicates the need for such changes and provides retraining or finds other suitable openings for displaced employees. Enlightened management also realizes that rapid social change may bring challenges and problems to a workforce. Increased leisure time may require programs that offer counseling to employees on constructive ways to use this extra time for development of their potential and that also provide new services so that workers can take advantage of opportunities for personal and professional growth. Such support can range from fitness and recreational programs at the corporate facilities to payment of membership or season tickets at community clubs, cultural events, and civic recreational offerings. Corporate investments of this type benefit both the worker and the community at large.

Metaindustrial management recognizes the impact that the stress and strain of the times have on employee behavior and productivity. Employee Assistance Programs (EAP) are growing in number. Michael Hurst of Hurst Associates, a Boston psychological counseling firm, estimates that already 5,000 American organizations have such programs. He believes that top management now realizes that instead of treating personnel as an expense, they must be viewed as human resources that affect productivity. From that perspective, EAP is a sound corporate investment, whether the company pays for all or part of the services rendered. Hurst also maintains that there are enormous potential corporate savings in this arena. He figures that U.S. companies and employees spend $63 billion on health insurance premiums, plus $20 billion in lost productivity due to physical or mental problems of workers. However, only $13 billion is spent on health care related to such difficulties. Yet most corporate HRD efforts, according to Richard Green, an OD specialist with Bell of Pennsylvania, focus on the 85 to 90 percent of the workforce capable of managing their own lives, often neglecting the 10 to 15 percent with personal problems that adversely affect both productivity and employee relations.

The President's Commission on Mental Health estimated in 1978 that 25 percent of the population had symptoms of anxiety, stress, and depression, and that mental disorders accounted for 12 percent of the nation's health costs. Since many of these citizens are at work, and future shock is not going to lessen, it stands to reason that enlightened management would develop a policy of employee assistance that is both caring and professional, preventive and rehabilitative.

Typical employee problems are related to alcohol or drug abuse (40 to 50 percent of the caseloads). The services, either on or off the work sites, include emergency hotlines and referrals to family counseling and therapy. Participation in the program is voluntary, but confrontation by supervisors of workers with a documented pattern of unacceptable behavior at the workplace is a critical feature of the program, and continuance on salary often hinges on involvement in treatment. A combination of information and education, skills training and/or therapy, and sensitivity about human performance problems can often result in the return of a more mature, happier, more productive employee.

The metaindustrial work culture creates its own unique pressures on people, whether it is the demand for high performance, the relationship with robots, or being forced to alter traditional roles by extended uses of the computer. One casualty of the computer revolution, according to Thomas McDonald, is "computer crazies." That is the way this psychologist describes the plopping down of a highly technological thing in the lives of people unprepared for it. He believes that computer-related stress and relationship problems are growing. Employees are disoriented by new terminology, procedures, or technical breakdowns of their terminals. When the latter happens, the blame is often placed upon the programmer or system analyst, not on the equipment or its manufacturer. Both families and bosses are beginning to complain that some personnel are "addicted" to their computer and are increasingly alienated from people. Instead of tolerating bizzare clothing or behavior in programmers and operators, management should act upon such signs that the worker may need some counseling. When everyone blames the data processors for computer breakdowns or foul-ups, it may be time for management to provide the computer operators with some means of releasing their frustration. Distress by passive computer personnel has already led to sabotage and violent outbursts that damaged equipment and people, even causing death. Dr. McDonald claims computer-related stress leads to absenteeism and high turnover rate (from 20 to 25 percent or more among data processors).

Wise management institutes preventive programs for this purpose. For those with inadequate training in computers and word processors, it may mean scheduling additional company classes to raise proficiency. It may demand greater attention to ergonomics—that is, redesigning the work station to improve the situation for the worker. It could involve encouragement of hobbies, clubs, and company teams among EDP personnel to foster human relationships. It might require counseling for computer specialists on coping skills, assertiveness, and relaxation techniques. Computer personnel have to appreciate that the machines cannot perform miracles, though they can give us opportunities to be more creative and to extend our minds. Responsible employers are aware of problems related to new technologies and inaugurate plans to benefit or assist workers in this regard.

When employees are relocated inside or outside their home culture, it can lead to trauma for both the workers and their families. To avoid culture shock and to facilitate performance at the new site, especially when it involves foreign deployment, enlightened management invests in systems that facilitate such transitional experiences. Research has demonstrated that certain factors are associated with success in an overseas assignment. In 1978, Paul Russell identified 80 traits that were related to improved performance abroad, including: (1) technical competence and resourcefulness, (2) emotional stability and adaptability, (3) acceptability of assignment to candidate and family, (4) ability to plan, organize, and use resources in a host culture, (5) interpersonal relationships, or ability to get along with the local people, (6) company growth potential, especially upon return, (7) host language proficiency, (8) cultural understanding and empathy, (9) physical attributes, particularly good health, and (10) such miscellaneous characteristics as leadership and character.

The point is that international personnel programs should do more than satisfy mechanical requirements—moving assistance, housing and schooling support for dependents, overseas pay and perks, and information on how to take advantage of the tax-relief regulations for Americans living and working abroad. These efforts take care of hygiene needs only and are expected compensations. Metaindustrial management relocating personnel around the globe must also invest company funds in (1) selection and recruitment of the right individual for the new assignment, (2) culture and language training and country orientation before departure, (3) on-site personnel support services overseas, which might even include recreational programs for teenagers or drug abuse counseling, and (4) reentry orientation and guidance. Employee assistance programs, whether domestic or international, are complex and diverse. They range from helping executives take advantage of tax options to counseling in second careers, retirement planning, and outplacement.

CAPSULE CONCLUSIONS

Metaindustrial personnel can be energized by improving the quality of their worklife and by satisfying the needs for self-development. They can be motivated to more effective performance through meaningful work and team experiences, intellectual challenges, opportunities to be responsible for their work and to be innovative. They are energized by participating in significant corporate projects.

Knowledge workers expect employers to take care of both their hygiene needs and their ego needs. When these needs are satisfied, an organization gets commitment and productivity as the employee's contribution to the psychological contract with the employer. In the decades ahead, there will be fewer people working for income as cybernation increases. Those who are employed will have both higher qualifications and higher needs to be satisfied through the job.

Furthermore, the new technical personnel will face unusual stresses and strains on the job requiring creative services by their companies. In this postindustrial age, compensation plans for employees will be far-ranging, often bewildering in their financial, vocational, and social options. Services that in previous generations were supplied by church and state will now be provided, directly or indirectly, by the corporation. Since the workplace, whether in office, plant, or home, will become such a dominant force in the lives of its participants, management is challenged to render recognition and rewards that contribute to the effective utilization of human energy, as well as to the development of human potential. As John Ingalls, a Boston management consultant, has observed, the enterprise should have an overall philosophy and comprehensive models and programs that contribute to personnel and to organizational and community development.

CHAPTER 11 Technological Work Culture of the Future

Is technology an artifact of culture or a driving force in culture's creation? Some argue that our culture began when primordial humans began to apply tool technology. Terpstra proposed that technology is shaped by humanity in accordance with prevailing values and social structures, so it is both "culture-using" and "culture-producing." Like culture, technology increases our capacity to cope with both our physical and our psychological environment. Currently, however, there is a lack of synergy between technology and the general culture. Progress in technology seems to have outstripped humans' capacity to absorb and manage it, so there appears to be a culture gap. In this book, we have been attempting to reduce this gap for managers. To further this aim, this chapter will summarize the main themes of the upcoming technological culture.

THE TECHNOLOGY/CULTURE CONNECTION

As the industrial work culture disappears slowly and painfully, the metaindustrial organization is emerging. This emergence is affected and accelerated by two new, interrelated technologies—microelectronics and information processing. Along with advances in genetic engineering, these technological revolutions are transforming society and organizations. Just as both technologies are contributing to the profound transition in global relations, so they are affecting corporate culture by the development of the knowledge business and the information industries. Hank Koehn summarized the contemporary situation:

> The planet has become a world market. The transnational product replaces the national product. The interlinked, interconnected communication systems are producing international consumers, as well as

demands for products and services.... Today our planet consists of countries that can be divided into four categories: pre-industrial; industrial; advanced-industrial, and early post-industrial.

To meet the challenge of the last two categories, *metaindustrial*, social systems are emerging, and with them a new organizational culture is in creation. As discussed in Chapter 1, the harbingers of tomorrow's corporations are referred to as high-tech, gen-tech, med-tech, and space-tech businesses. In 1980, two countries dominate these areas of business—the United States, the world leader in information industries, with sales in information equipment alone estimated at $30.5 billion (Japan is second-ranked at $8.6 billion), and Japan, sharing the leadership with the United States in the electronics industry, at $37 billion, with a 22.9 percent growth rate in integrated-circuit output at the start of this decade, which is double that of the United States. No wonder Japan has been referred to as the epicenter of the world's consumer electronics industry!

The next decades will see advances in space shuttle flights, commercial and private communications satellites, signal transmissions by glass fibers and lasers, and minicomputers and videophones in both office and home communications centers. Fueled by continued progress in miniaturization and the miracle chip, electronic wizards are reshaping our society worldwide and even causing some social dislocations. Yet microtechnology, with nearly infinite capacities and adaptability, also fosters individualization and permits people to design their lives more in line with their wishes, including working at home. While we thus create the macroculture of the twenty-first century, we are also experimenting with new forms of organizations. These transitional organizations will be originators of social norms and culture. In the process, we are also changing the role of manager and the art of management. We think more in terms of information resources manager and information management. The Bell scientists who are pioneering the new technologies suggest new terms:

- *Organization*, or the systematic gathering and structuring of information.
- *Processing*, or the storage, examination, assemblage, translation, and distribution of information, by people or machines.
- *Transmission*, or the transporting of relevant and timely information to the proper user.

In 1969, John Kenneth Galbraith defined *technology* as the systematic application of scientific or other organized knowledge to practical tasks. Developments in both hardware and software can be included under that broad umbrella. To close the managerial gap for nontechnical specialists, a new publication, *High Technology*,* was born. It describes the new fields—the ones that will influence metaindustrial organizations—as follows:

- Genetic engineering. The technology associated with putting biological knowledge to work. Applications in the chemical industry, pharmaceuticals, agriculture.
- The electronic office. Multifunction work stations. Word-speech recognizers and simplified programming that will humanize the interface between people and machines. The costs, and benefits, the potential savings.
- Automotive technology. Improvements in auto engines that will save money and reduce emissions. Research to overcome the limitations of potential competitors to the internal combustion engine.
- Communications. Interactive television: the technology and its likely impact on entertainment, education, business, banking, retailing. Electronic mail. High-speed facsimile. Microwave links between offices. Teleconferencing.
- Construction. Energy-efficient architecture. Cost-saving materials. Labor-saving methods.
- Space technology. The Space Shuttle: how it will boost our capability to orbit satellites and even build space stations. New uses for orbiters—including navigation, geophysical exploration, crop studies, weather prediction.
- Energy. Thin-film photovoltaic cells and the promise of low-cost solar-generated electricity. Improved batteries and storage systems. The technology of fusion power and the obstacles that must be overcome.
- Military/aerospace technology. Rapid strike force equipment. Stealth aircraft. Passive detection systems. Automatic target recognition systems. Laser weaponry.
- Transportation. Light-rail vehicles. Magnetic levitation for high-speed trains. Computer-tracked fast freight. Hydrofoils. Dual-mode personal rapid transit.
- Medical technology. Implantable replacement body organs, artificial limbs, diagnostic devices, information retrieval and medical data systems.
- Robotics. The move toward fully-automated assembly lines. New machining methods. Energy-efficient production methods.

* See B. A. Goldhirsh.

- New materials. Fiber-reinforced composites (carbon, boron, etc.) and "foamed" metals, which combine high strength with light weight. Inexpensive alloys that can substitute for more costly metals. Superconductors. New coatings, adhesives, and other materials.
- Measurements. New tools for measuring a wide range of phenomena. High-speed observations of dynamic processes, chemical reactions, subatomic particles. Cosmological observations.
- Personal computers. What's new and what's next. What they offer and how they can be used. Advances which will make them more useful, more popular.
- Artificial intelligence. Machines that think for themselves—or for you. (The question is not whether this will happen, but when.) And how we'll deal with the social dislocations as menial work is phased out.

The major catalysts in the development of metaindustrial society are the advances in computer and communications technologies, which are occurring at almost incomprehensible speed. Huyck and Kremenak urge a new technological paradigm in which humankind adopts a holistic relationship with the new technology: "We see our machines as part of that organic whole which includes all of us and all of them." Since computers, robots, and other forms of artificial intelligence are extensions of humans, Huyck and Kremanak call for a technology shaped by human values. Microelectronics technologies, for instance, represent a bright hope for improved service of human need, as well as for increased productivity. For this to happen, world leaders must engage in international planning to ensure a synergistic information society. Japan is the only nation currently engaged in this process!

Organizational culture is the communicable knowledge and mental programming of an organization, that human system's customs, traditions, norms, values, policies, and procedures—both explicit and implicit—that set its environment apart. Such organizational input and conditioning influence employee behavior and performance and also give them an institutional identity and an affiliation with the enterprise. Just as a macroculture develops a unique citizenry, so a microculture (such as a corporation or even a university) creates distinctive adherents. A human system expresses itself through its culture, which is manifested, in turn, in such elements as organizational climate, atmosphere, and environment.

In a prior volume, we provided a framework for understanding organizational culture. It has been amplified in Table 4 and may be helpful to executives and managers who wish to renew mature industries or who are already part of metaindustrial organizations. In the left-hand column are eight umbrella components of culture that can be applied to most organizations. In the middle column, these cultural components are broken down into some of their many characteristics as they would be manifested in the readers' own organizations. In the last column, examples of these characteristics are given as they would appear in metaindustrial organizations. A careful analysis of this representation will provide insight into organizations and indicate dimensions of the technological work culture.*

ALTERED ORGANIZATIONAL RELATIONS
One aspect of organizational change is the altering of relationships. With the introduction of computers and microprocessors, significant variations occur in corporate activities and relations. The spread of robotics in offices and plants will also change the organizational culture. A Westinghouse plant in Pittsburgh, for example, will now produce electric motors from 50 different parts at the rate of three motors a minute, and everything will be accomplished by six robots. This computer-controlled, mechanical process eliminates not only human mistakes, but human workers! Its operating cost is about $6 an hour, compared to an average of $18 an hour for an American assembler.

But the effect of robots is only one dimension of the impact of the metaindustrial revolution on labor-management relations and the corporate-union interface. As Paul Von Ward has reminded us, we are in the process of "dismantling the pyramid." He believes the cumbersome, pyramidal bureaucracy is the prime culprit in the destruction of human talent and waste of social resources. In the search for alternative organizational patterns, Von Ward recommends a synergy between Western and Eastern traditional thought patterns, so models are conceived that are less linear and more circular, curving back on themselves. To get a more multidimensional approach in our organizational models, he

---

* The author welcomes further research on and expansion of this preliminary formulation, which may be used in conjunction with the Organizational Culture Survey Instrument (refer to Chapter 2 and Appendix A), on which the author also welcomes additional research and validation.

TABLE 4. The metaindustrial work culture.

Components of Organizational culture	Organizational Manifestations	Metaindustrial Organizational Illustrations
Rationale and Identity	Reasons for existing Self-image Beliefs, attitudes Philosophy Space, boundaries Strategies, structures	Profitable, quality service; transnational system Energy exchange system Promote innovation, synergy, excellence Corporate social responsibility Business computer or conceptual modeling; futuristic, long-term planning; goal- and results-oriented.
Purposes and Standards	Mission, goals Objectives Corporate assumptions Norms Priorities, schedules Performance criteria Personnel rules Codes of ethics	Multinational operations, Pacific Rim focus MBO system to link levels, operations Use new technologies including robotics to facilitate mission Criteria of competence; creativity; tough-minded analysis High achievement, performance emphasis Rules customized, developed by implementers High standards, integrity; culturally sensitive behavior; commission, yes; bribery, no.
Look and Style	Corporate leadership style Policies, procedures Time sense Appearance, dress Food, fitness habits Corporate environment	Participative, consensus-oriented Manage responsibility, accountability 24-hour operations, long-term, futuristic Informal, casual, appropriate Healthful diet, wellness programs Dynamic, flexible, stimulating environment
Processes and Activities	Operational practices, projects Products, services Manufacturing, technology R&D Systems and program emphasis	Matrix, team management Knowledge, information processing Microelectronic technologies Technical, human factor research Interdisciplinary, software creation

Communications and Information Systems	Formal, informal systems External, internal systems Management info systems (MIS) Community, government relations Specialized languages, vocabularies, codes, signals	Functional, open, authentic, circular Mass media, closed circuit TV; feedback Centralized EDP, decentralized minicomputer Synergistic partnerships Computerized languages, security systems; nonverbal awareness, and multilevel communications and interactions
Human Resource and Personnel Patterns	Recruitment and selection Role and task assignments Career, professional development Education, training Skills acquisition, learning Performance regulation, control Human energy conservation, utilization	EEO, pluralistic; competency criteria Broad, flexible; self-designed Invest in, capitalize on, human assets Teleconferencing, teleprocessing CAI, self-learning AV systems Results- and achievement-oriented, monitoring by individual and team Emphasis on actualizing human potential
Interpersonal Relations	Organizational networks Personnel and contractor relations Client, customer relations Human-machine relations Intra-, inter-group, subsidiary relations Intercultural relations	Global electronic connections Integrated, helpful Consultative, facilitative Robotics interface Cooperative, collaborative Sensitive, skillful, interdependent
Recognition and Rewards	Quality of worklife and morale Personnel needs and motivations Employee status and respect Intrinsic, extrinsic rewards Compensation plans Incentives, ownership	Increase employee control over work space Ego, self-fulfillment emphasis to energize Democratization, participation opportunities More autonomy, professionalization Tailor to individual needs, choices Profit sharing, stock options, formation of multinational co-operatives

suggests use of the hologram, with its patterns of wave interference.

Most world and business leaders do not seem to anticipate the technological innovations and their prospects for improving the human condition. Too often people are not readied to use electronics and communications breakthroughs, and planned change in organizational culture is ignored. Two illustrations will underscore the issues involved: Advanced technological societies from Japan to France are exporting their technologies at increasing rates to preindustrial nations. Leaders in both home and host cultures do little to prepare inhabitants for the social and industrial changes brought about by this transfer. The new technological culture is covertly imposed on the traditional agricultural or industrial culture, causing significant disruption. And the advanced technology is not just new tools and equipment; it involves radically different theories, processes, controls, and systems. The transfer may extend from an R&D pilot project to licensing for production to a turn-key factory. If such cultural disruption is to be avoided and to be politically acceptable, all parties need to engage in synergistic planning of the economic and community goals of the technology transfer. A systems analysis is needed for the transfer of appropriate technology in realistic sequencing. Silvère Seurat, a French industrial consultant, has demonstrated that a system can be developed for conveying knowledge, skills, and experience from one people to another when they are at differing stages of human and economic development.

The transformation of the work culture, both at home and abroad, is best accomplished by cosmopolitan managers who take a global approach to management. This requires a new generation of business executives. Recent books indicate the role of executive leadership in the metaindustrial work culture. Cribbin of St. John's University proposes that leadership is the ability to gain consensus and commitment to common objectives in a win-win situation. The leader, he believes, has to give a lot to get support and loyalty from followers, and should espouse the key organizational values. Maccoby of Harvard University adds that new-style leaders will have to be caring, respectful, and flexible toward people, while adopting a participative management approach. Furthermore, he maintains, they do not lead by fear or domination, nor by condoning unethical practice or pandering to the worst in people. Instead, they demonstrate competence in renewing organizations, their structures, and their technologies.

They are able to respond to worker needs for a change in leadership style and for rewarding work.

Leaders are now required who take a holistic, systems approach to the management of complex systems, who understand what is happening in both the technological and international environments, who know how to use the computer effectively in both economic and public policy analysis, as well as in decision making, who appreciate the importance of team management and the criterion of competence. Such managers, even in slow-growth industries, learn to take advantage of the new technology and are not threatened by it. They encourage group entrepreneurial activities even within large, mature corporations. They are not afraid to support technological innovations. They seek return on investments from unlikely sources, and they foster a sense of excitement in the process.

Such business leaders are unorthodox by industrial-age standards. Donald Massaro, described by *Fortune* as the exuberant, audacious chief of Xerox's Office Products Division, is an example of the new breed of technologically oriented managers. An aeronautical engineer known for a fast mouth and an entrepreneur's impatience, Massaro rose to the presidency of Shugart, a leading flexible-disc maker, before it was acquired by Xerox. When he took over the Office Products Division, he did not fit the Xerox mold and demanded complete freedom from corporate headquarters. In 18 months, he put his division back in the black while operating as an almost independent subsidiary. He overcame the mismatch between Xerox's corporate culture and the unique culture of the office systems market. Massaro overcame Xerox's management style, which made it difficult to translate advanced research into marketable products. In the process, he made his division a power in creating the office of the future now. He provided a behavior model for subordinates, articulating "credibility." Massaro brought in fresh management, revamped the product line and marketing strategy, promoted open communications, reduced manufacturing costs, and came out with millions in pretax profits. Essentially, he built change into the division's management system and made ultrastability the norm. As a result, his people have become agents of change throughout the entire corporation.

Venture capitalists who found technologically innovative companies or divisions cannot afford to forget the principles and practices of professional management. Texas Instruments, once the shining star of American technology, is learning this lesson the hard way. In 1981, TI experienced a serious drop in profits, stock value, and employees because it is being squeezed out of markets or had entered unprofitable ones. Although still the leading producer of semiconductor chips, TI is faced with a dip in market demand and stiff competition from abroad while being unable to sell its products successfully to small businesses and home consumers. The company was so busy pushing its own innovations that it failed to listen to the echoes of the marketplace. In addition to marketing myopia, the corporation's style of management by fear was not only inappropriate for the metaindustrial work culture, but its rigidity hurt employee morale. To revive its leadership in the new technologies, TI is beginning to develop its marketing expertise. It will also have to learn that it has a new kind of worker who requires a new management style—the kind discussed throughout this volume.

EMERGING R&D EMPHASIS
In a 1981 address entitled "Human Resistance to the Technological Revolution," the Provost of Northwestern University reminded his listeners that new inventions and ideas alter the established order of things, making it necessary for people to learn new ways of responding to the new situation. But, Dr. Raymond W. Mack continued, most people want to avoid such stress and strain, so they oppose change. They find technological change somewhat easier to accept than social change. Mack reminds us that social change requires behavioral change.

The incidents at Xerox and Texas Instruments point up the ways in which the organizational culture can undermine or enhance technical progress and profitability. The reality is that even the best technological research has to function within the right atmosphere. Those in the West should learn the lesson of the Soviet Union: It is technologically backward not because it lacks technical talent, but because of the party's system of controls. Microcultures, like macrocultures, can have structural faults that inhibit their people from performing, that prevent them from maximizing opportunities.

A dominant theme in metaindustrial organizations is innovative research. Its primary efforts are directed toward technological advances, and the corporate attitudes and environment support such endeavors. The innovation process is conceived in three stages: (1) *input*, which is the contribution of research and development efforts, (2) *throughput*, which is the arena of manufacturing and production, and (3) *output*, which involves marketing and sales. David Gibson is completing a doctoral investigation at Stanford University on the impact of management on technological innovation. His review of the literature confirms his hypothesis that a Type Z management culture best fosters the innovation process; this culture is similar to what we have described as the metaindustrial work culture. Such corporate cultures are found often in Japanese technological companies, especially in their overseas operations. For example, when Hitachi Ltd. announced in early 1982 that it would be the first electronics firm in the world to manufacture the next generation of computer memory chips, the case was made for more synergistic innovation in Western companies. The new 256 K Ram high-intensity chip, incidentally, is expected to store 256,000 bits of information! That is innovative leadership supported by the right organizational environment.

The inquiring, research-oriented "mindset" will be prevalent in all metaindustrial organizations at all levels. But it will not be limited to product or marketing research. It will include human factor and future studies research. Skills in R&D management will be highly regarded. These strategies recommended by SRI International will be incorporated into organizational culture:

- Having a methodology for selecting R&D activities of high promise.
- Using a bottom-line mentality on R&D project undertakings and application.
- Determining the best criteria for evaluating research results in an uncertain economy and a turbulent social and political environment.
- Integrating user need and desires early in the R&D process.
- Evaluating the need for more information, the project itself, and its long-term payoffs.
- Using decision analysis to consider synergistic and nonsynergistic interactions among various R&D projects, as well as to enhance managerial judgment.
- Developing a system for assessing alternatives, probabilities, and team experiences.
- Creating a risk analysis and timing method for plotting research during business and social transitions.

Management by information, and less by ideology, will be the central feature of the new work culture. Such an approach encourages the formulation of hypotheses, the testing of possibilities, and the collection and analysis of data with a view to increasing organizational effectiveness. Thus organizational development surveys and studies of personnel attitudes and of customer/contractor reactions are standard and continuing practices. Through survey research, internal or external behavioral scientists are asked periodically to take the pulse of the organization and to diagnose corporate climate. Research skills are used to ascertain the validity of personnel practices, training programs, and instructional technology. More professional, scientific, mediawise market research is employed to weigh both the need and the impact of all products and services. Seeking and analyzing feedback are a way of life in metaindustrial organizations. Action and applied research balance theoretical research.

Technological forecasting and futures research are a vital factor in the future-oriented metaindustrial organization. One can only wonder how much better off the steel, banking, and insurance industries would be today if they had employed such a strategy. The new discipline of futures research provides managers with prospective scenarios, reasoned predictions, and early warnings. Mature industries, like General Electric, have already employed it in 30-year projection studies of the future of the business environment, so as to prepare for the changed situation in commerce and people. However, metaindustrial organizations incorporate an active and systematic study of the future on a continuing basis, so current decisions are made within the context of informed anticipation. Such strategies are not limited to corporate planning offices; it is used by all managers to spot trends and to adjust operations. Exxon USA uses the approach to see from 1 to 70 years ahead, which may indicate why this corporate giant has been so successful not only in energy production but also in office automation. Once such plans are formulated, they are continually reviewed and updated. Futures research is also related to contingency planning by companies with foresight. The metaindustrial organization seeks to shape its own future, to be more proactive in both the economy and society.

Futuristics helps management become more aware of options in problem solving, helps managers assess the effects of downline events and exercise broader vision in the interpretations of data. The corporate futurist uses a variety of computer techniques to extrapolate trends, thus avoiding reductionistic solutions and attempting to deal with nonquantifiable variables.

Burt Nanus, director of the Center for Futures Research at the University of Southern California, deplores executives who postpone action on problems until they escalate into crises. Metaindustrial managers are responsive to forecasts and are inclined to anticipate changes and their effects. To develop these new skills, Nanus teaches business leaders QUEST, a quick environmental scanning technique. It involves sharing understanding of possible directions in the business environment.

To minimize organizational risks in a transitional society, Sears, Roebuck & Company has a Monitoring and Forecasting System that attempts to make explicit the assumptions held about the future, to identify the alternatives, to estimate possible consequences, and to guide the corporation as a result of long-term analysis. The system monitors the businesses the company is in, the mix of what is sold, the customers and the way the company sells to them, and the markets and the geographic areas in which it sells. In assembling information for communication to management, the Sears forecasters use these eight major categories for analysis—demographics, public attitudes, values and lifestyles, technology, resources, government, international developments, and economics. The findings are then employed for goal setting, strategic planning, new ventures consideration, and establishing task forces for implementation. Such futures research will be an integral part of metaindustrial operations. Their managers will routinely read journals like *The Futurist* and newsletters such as *The Futures Survey* and those issued by The Tarrytown Group.

Smaller metaindustrial organizations supplement their research capabilities with external resources. This may be done through the use of contract workers or consultants. For instance, the organizations might draw on the R&D expertise of the Science and Technology Group from Gulf+Western Industries, Inc., which can provide technical assistance on everything from automated machinery to biomedical devices to optics. Or they might join a consortium of small companies to pool their research efforts, since metaindustrial firms tend to be more cooperative with one another in the same industry. Large or small, metaindustrial companies seek synergistic relations with universities and their research endeavors. In the fields of technology and medical research, this may mean the formulation of a joint-venture nonprofit corporation or a profit-making subsidiary enterprise. More of the metaindustrial budget is devoted to R&D for both internal and external investment. Models like the following can be expected to be replicated in ever-increasing numbers in the next several decades:

- Mallinckrodt, Inc., a St. Louis medical supply company, provided a $3.5 million grant to Washington University's School of Medicine to engage in basic research in hybridoma, cells that produce protein antibodies that attack viruses and bacteria. The corporation, in turn, will have exclusive license to market any product that may result.
- Westinghouse signed a contract with Carnegie-Mellon University in Pittsburgh to fund a $5 million Robotics Institute, with the corporation getting first patent rights on any research findings.
- Stanford University and the University of California at Berkeley faculty have created a nonprofit Center for Biotechnology Research and have already raised $2.4 million from six major corporations (including General Foods and Bendix) for research. Any profitable ventures from these investigations will come under the jurisdiction of a separate company, Eugenics, whose profits will be funneled back into further university research.

TECHNOLOGICAL INFLUENCE ON
METAINDUSTRIAL ORGANIZATIONS
The metaindustrial work culture will continue to produce new technologies that will cause change both in society and in the functioning of the sponsoring organizations. Whether the company exists as a spinoff of some corporate giant, by virtue of acquisition or merger, or merely from venture capital, there will be much industrial crossbreeding. Whereas in past decades, one industry could be neatly separated from another and a company's business could be easily determined, this will be more difficult in the postindustrial age. Convergences will be most evident in commerce, and fine lines of distinction between private enterprise and public institutions will erode. Profit-making corporations will increasingly contract with others to perform public services for them and government agencies and universities will establish quasi-public corporations that may even make a profit, as is done so well in France. The three most exciting areas for such

ventures will be microelectronics, information, and genetic technologies. These fields alone are capable of transforming the modern organization as we have known it. One can only speculate how long it will take university departments and schools to get the message, so that professors of science and engineering will converge in mutual instruction and research with their colleagues in business and the behavioral sciences. Certain trends are already evident in this regard:

1. *Internationalization* of metaindustrial organizations. The emergence of world corporations chartered by regional or international agencies is possible before the end of this century. Two developments are worthy of note here: In 1980, foreign investors spent $9.9 billion to gain control of U.S. firms, and foreign takeover activity increased in 1981. And multinational corporations from developing countries have not only had a rapid rise, but the focus is increasingly on high technology. Instead of continuing brain drain from Third World nations as was the practice in the industrial stage, the metaindustrial firm wishes to keep the local expertise in place in such countries. By forming joint ventures with the scientific and engineering talent in less developed lands, metaindustrial corporations help these peoples advance rapidly to the technological stage of development.

2. *Miniaturization* will be the key thrust of metaindustrial organizations. Thinking small led to microfabrication of the computer chip and to the microelectronics revolution. Going tiny will bring even smaller, faster, more energy-efficient machines. Under the leadership of Dr. Edward Wolf, the National Research and Resource Facility for Submicron Structures in Ithaca, New York, has pioneered such miniwonders as an etched line only six atoms wide, letters so small that the text of the *Encyclopaedia Britannica* could fit on a postage stamp, and transistors so tiny that 15 could fit across the width of a human hair. These Cornell University researchers are probing a new world that someday may change conventional laws of chemistry and physics. They have already produced extraordinarily tiny research tools. The outcomes of microfabrication research may offer metaindustrial corporations new capabilities for space industrialization. They are already changing the way we work on earth.

The outcomes are already evident in the field of microprocessors. It is in this arena that the prototypical metaindustrial organizations now operate—Hewlett-Packard, National Semiconductor, Intel, and Apple are the newcomers facing off with IBM, Xerox,

Wang Laboratories, Digital Equipment, Data General, and Exxon Office Systems. And they are only a few of the U.S. contenders, to say nothing of their foreign counterparts. In the search for related, but integrated, markets, Hewlett-Packard moved into laser printers because that is what their customers need and want. It seems that as competitors catch up with and even knock out of the market early technological innovators, the originators move on to a new technological frontier, coming up with new products that replace lost product lines and profits. This new way of doing business may prove characteristic of the metaindustrial age. That is, to continue being profitable, an organization must grow through continuing technological research and innovations that are quickly translated into income-producing products.

Metaindustrial managers are not given to conventional business thinking. They often demonstrate creative, zigzag strategies. One of these risk takers is National Semiconductor's CEO, Charles Sporck, who believes that his firm is catching up to the Japanese faster than any other U.S. company and that it responds more quickly to market forces than others in its industry. In contrast to this pattern of spectacular growth rates, there are smaller chip makers who customize to meet user needs. What Interdesign, for example, loses in volume, it makes up in pretax profit margins from tailor-made parts. In place of standardization, these mini-metaindustrial organizations prosper from the customization of their specialized products. Made-to-order chips has been Intel's secret strategy. The Silicon Valley pioneers have also been cloned in San Diego by such new enterprises as American Microsystems, Inc., and in south to central Florida by Harris Corporation and Burroughs Corporation. The microelectronics industry is expanding across the Sun Belt and across the Pacific Basin. Its biggest innovations may be in customer service and education. Assisting clients to integrate technological advances with minimum organizational disruption will be the real challenge.

METAINDUSTRIAL MARKET TARGETS
One way to gain insight into the new directions in the metaindustrial work culture is to examine the markets that attract its workers. We will take a brief look at two product markets—home communications centers and genetic engineering—and two geographic markets—the Pacific Rim and space industrialization. Each example will dramatically illustrate the interconnections between the new technologies and culture:

The home communications center. By the year 2000, many families in Western societies will have communications centers that will be used for household management, external exchanges, recreation, and business. A giant home information industry is already taking shape to supply and service the electronic cottage. These new marketing opportunities will include communications technology that will enable us to shop, bank, work, play, and interact without actually leaving our home base. Built on telephone networks and cable TV systems, these centers will go beyond conventional telephone, radio, and television to encompass personal computers, satellite connections, word and data processors, videotape and disc recorders, and videostereo and camera systems, all with a vast array of gadgetry. Home architecture and interior decoration are already changing, as affluent families establish media rooms to house the new equipment for entertainment or business purposes. Metaindustrial businesses are coming into being to supply the vast hardware and software needs in this emerging, profitable market. Perhaps the most exciting prospects are in video or teletext, a new industry that may link 8 million U.S. homes with computer data banks by 1990. These home information retrieval systems are breaking down old market boundaries and creating new competitors, such as AT&T with Times Mirror Videotext Services with Field Electronic Publishing with *Time* magazine and CBS. The videotext market is bringing together contenders from utilities, retail establishments, publishing houses, and financial institutions.

Beyond these *information and service providers* are the *systems operators,* which can include such strange bedfellows as Dow Jones for financial information and *Reader's Digest* for The Source, which offers its subscribers everything from financial planning and legislative monitoring to word processing and a postal system. The next level of the new business is the *transmitters,* which range from Ma Bell and the big broadcasters to a variety of cable companies. Finally, the *home terminal makers* include the small computer manufacturers like Apple, Atari, Western Electric, and Zenith Radio. Such creators of cyberculture will bring into households everything from electronic newspapers and mail to business, education, and game opportunities for personal and professional development.

Not only will these agents of change expand human potential by the use of artificial intelligence; their technology will cause a convergence of traditional bodies of knowledge and work—physics, chemistry, mathematics, and electronics. For the 1980s, the results of these technological advances will be a surge in the service industries, the real force for economic growth in the near term.

Biochemical technology/genetic engineering. Some of the trend indicators of the metaindustrial culture come into sharper focus with the commercialization of the natural sciences. Internationalization, industry/university collaboration, research emphasis, and industrial crossbreeding all seem to converge in the new applications of biology and chemistry and their synthesis with physics. It is a further illustration of the breakdown of the traditional academic disciplines and the lowering of the barriers between scientist and businessperson. The continuing education of scientists will require them to study business, and executive and management development will now include a reeducation in applied sciences. The innovative institutes of the University of Wisconsin's Extension offerings on "Business Opportunities in Genetics" are prototypes of things to come in professional development and adult education. Short, live seminars and videotaped courses will proliferate to update participants in molecular genetic technology and other revolutionary technical applications in industries: such as pharmaceuticals, organic chemicals, minerals, food and beverages, agriculture, forestry, and synthetics. Furthermore, financial and investment counselors will join in such learning experiences, for that is where the financial action of the future lies.

One dimension of the metaindustrial market centers on genetic engineering. A *Time* cover story, "Shaping Life in the Lab," described gene splicing as the most powerful and awesome skill acquired by humans since the splitting of the atom. Recombinant DNA, single cell reproduction, fusion/synthesis, and the creation of hybridomas (cells that produce pure antibodies) are the stuff of these emerging business enterprises.

This is the new alchemy that can produce new drugs and cures, as well as miracle products and food crops. It can bring together unlikely partners and knowledge workers in the production of fuels, plastics, and "green revolutions," as well as contribute to innovative processes for recycling wastes, mining, and refining. Even the usually conservative British *Economist* referred to biotechnology as one of the biggest industrial opportunities of the late twentieth century.

However, the market should be realistically appraised from near-term and long-term perspectives for its impact on metaindustrial work culture. Its rapid growth has been helped by the U.S. Supreme Court's confirmation of patent rights for new life forms, such as an oil-eating bacterium, and that ruling has been extended to gene splicing in general. The new industry has also been aided by the U.S. Office of Technology Assessment's conclusion that genetic technology may contribute to filling some of humankind's most fundamental needs, from health care to food and energy. As a result, 20 companies got into the business of biotechnology in 1980/81, and 60 corporations are now prospecting in this new field. *Bioengineering News* reports that established firms in the biotechnological supply business are beginning to invest in the industry's production companies. Stanford University is now licensing the patented process for gene splicing developed by Stanley Cohen and Herbert Boyer; it estimates that 200 companies are already using the process.

The near-term market is now producing insulin, growth hormones, and the potentially useful chemical interferon. Under a USDA contract, Genentech is working on a vaccine against hoof-and-mouth disease, a major killer of food-producing animals. Its workforce is a harbinger of the staff composition of future meta-industrial operations—40 Ph.D.s, 65 technicians, and executive leadership from Herb Boyer, the scientist-entrepreneur who is not only very informal in his manner and dress but also suddenly very wealthy. Also among the four major genetic engineering firms in the world is Cetus Corp., whose president, Peter Farley, graduated at the head of his classes in both medicine and business—a perfect example of the new blending of careers. Cetus's work on the anticancer drug interferon holds promise, and this California firm now produces 6,000 patient doses daily. Meanwhile, in Rockville, Maryland, Genex expects to double its $1 million business in gene splicing and is moving toward both the development of a bacterial organism that would convert biomass such as wood and grass into ethanol and the production of vitamin/amino acids for food enrichment.

The international dimension of bioengineering businesses is evident in Biogen, S.A., a Geneva-based firm that is opening U.S. operations and is involved in contracts for gene-spliced insulin and animal growth hormones. The business universality of molecular biology is revealed most clearly in the field of agriculture, where laboratories are discovering ways to produce more food with less energy. Advances in genetic engineering and plant chemistry bestir visions of growing plants created from the single cell of another plant and of separating and perpetuating healthy genetic characteristics.

The immediate applications have been demonstrated in the

greenhouses of Whittaker Corporation, Somis, California, in which 3 million heads of lettuce are grown where only 30,000 would have grown in a tilled field outdoors. All this is possible because of hydroponics—plants are grown in water and nutrients and a computer-controlled environment. One might not raise an eyebrow about General Mills being in the hydroponic growing business, but it may be a surprise that Whittaker and Control Data Corporation are. (These are examples of industrial crossbreeding.) It is the electronic control components that make this innovative approach possible. The metaindustrial technologies combine biology, chemistry, and computer sciences, and create new types of careers. Hydroponic farming is not subject to the vicissitudes of weather and seasons. Farmers and ranchers are now electronically tied by computer to universities for consultation on animal feeding and nutrients, selective breeding, high-protein diets, and artificial lighting methods. Prized stock are now multiplied through embryo transplants.

The giants of the ag-tech business are DEKALB AgResearch and Pioneer Hi-Bred International, both involved in the creation of hybrid seeds. Researchers at the University of California at Davis are engaged in improving photosynthesis to make plants grow faster, and in using genetics to "infect" plants with pure soybean protein to increase food quality and quantity. The big chemical and oil conglomerates—such as Dow, Monsanto, Allied Chemical, Du Pont, and Union Carbide—are backing such research and often are directly involved in it through their subsidiaries. The activities include gene transfers, cloning corn, and refining sorghum into sweet syrup. Shell, Atlantic Richfield, Occidental Petroleum, and ITT have entered this field by purchasing seed companies. According to *Forbes*, such firms have staffs of genetic and agricultural Ph.D.s as well as M.B.A.s for an intriguing mix of scientists and businesspeople. Among a growing number of young entrepreneurial companies coming into agriculture are Agrigenetics Corporation of Denver; Advanced Genetics Science Ltd. of Greenwich, Connecticut; International Plant Research Institute of San Carlos, California; and Collaborative Genetics of Waltham, Massachusetts.

The list of firms getting into these biochemical technologies grows daily. What are the long-term markets in these metaindustrial businesses? Geneticists hope to endow plant foods with the capacity to draw their own nitrogens from the air and to transfer nitrogen-fixing genes in bacteria to yeast, a slightly higher organism. Some researchers hope to create bacteria—a new form of genetic robot—that can collect scarce metals by leaching (or dissolving) them directly out of the earth, or force petroleum from the earth, or force gold from the oceans. Hoffmann-La Roche, Eli Lilly, and other drug companies, along with the oil corporations, are among the big funders of new ventures. Industry analysts believe the new businesses in bioengineering could be worth as much as $40 million by the end of the century.

In the process of such developments, the traditional barriers between researchers and producers, between academics and business, and between knowledge disciplines continue to crumble. Salk Institute, for instance, has established its Biotechnology Industrial Associates in La Jolla. SIBIA, as it is known, launched a wholly owned profit-making subsidiary, Timkin-Sturgis Research Laboratory. Among its corporate partners is Phillips Petroleum, which paid $10 million for 37.4 percent of the shares. Its neighbor, Scripps Clinic and Research Foundation, in Torrey Pines Industrial Park, has formed a joint venture in biotechnology with Eli Lilly and Miles Laboratories.

Biotechnology and microelectronics have been provocative stimulants to the formation of commercial ties between universities and business. Monsanto contributes $23 million for cancer research at Harvard. Exxon gives MIT $8 million for combustion research. Burroughs, CDC, and 3M donate up to $5 million for computer research at the University of Minnesota. And ten firms buy subscriptions to Stanford's Center for Integrated Circuits for $750,000 each. With it all comes issues of academic freedom, power, and integrity, as well as university policies on patents, licenses, and profit sharing for professors' research. And yet university-business relations can be promoted for mutual benefit. The possibilities for synergy are boundless, as was recently demonstrated by Ohio University and Denver's Genetic Engineering Inc., which are involved in the successful transfer of genes from one animal species to another! Medical, agricultural, and industrial applications of biotechnology truly boggle the mind as new frontiers are penetrated and human ignorance is pushed further back in the pursuit of profit.

Perhaps the implications of this burgeoning market and its prospects for innovation and synergy can best be understood in a case analysis of one small company that expects to survive the biotechnology shakeout now under way. Imagine being at the 1982 annual meeting of Hybritech, Inc. of San Diego, and listening to this report of its president, Ted Greene. These are extracts of his remarks to shareholders, which appeared in the public press:

- Sufficient capitalization this year of $12 million and a solid patent position give the firm an edge over the 200 other biotechnology companies started up the past two years.
- First on the market with the new Tandem series of diagnostic kits using monoclonal antibody technology that tests for anemia, pregnancy, prostate cancer, and allergies, a $1 billion market now that will grow to multibillions in the 1990s.
- Confirmation of agreements for research or production with Johnson & Johnson's Ortho pharmaceuticals division and with Johns Hopkins University medical school.
- New product research that brings scientific concepts into the marketplace, such as "antibody switch" that turns a cell's body switch on and off, or a "bifunctional" antibody molecule that binds two different antigens.
- Facility expansions of 50,000 square feet in nearby San Diego industrial parks.

Pacific Rim ventures. The new technologies will turn the Pacific Ocean into a lake of commercial exchange. Bounded by Canada, America, and Mexico on the east, and by Australia/New Zealand, Japan, China, Indonesia, and Malaysia on the west, the Pacific's key trading cities will be Hong Kong, Singapore, Tokyo, and possibly Sydney, Manila, Vancouver, Los Angeles, and San Diego.

Derek Davies, editor of the influential newsmagazine *Far Eastern Economic Review,* observed in a recent interview: "The 21st Century is the Pacific Century. I believe the United States has been blind to this. This place is growing and Europe isn't. This place is more important economically than Europe." According to Davies, Hong Kong is the financial center of the entire geographic area, more active than Tokyo and less regulated than Singapore. He believes that the world's center of economic gravity is shifting to the Trans-Pacific, and he expects a 600 percent expansion of trade, with the Peoples Republic of China to be the focal point. It certainly should be a central endeavor of the metaindustrial work culture, and will pull Micronesia and other Polynesian peoples into the twenty-first century.

The reality of all this is appreciated by the U.S. Department of Commerce whose assistant secretary, William Morris, recently told businesspeople that Los Angeles could not become a hub of Pacific trade unless they begin to meet foreign competition, which has cut the U.S. share of the Pacific market down to 33 percent in 1981. He lamented that Taiwan, South Korea, and Hong Kong have followed the Japanese lead into major consumer markets. Richard King, president of King International, reported that trade between Los Angeles and the Pacific Basin amounted to $44 billion in 1981 and should double in the next year. California traditionally has done well in the area by exporting products of aerospace, transportation, metals, chemicals, and instrumentation, but it is agribusiness development and expertise that will be most in demand in Southeast Asia. It is predicted that there will also be a big market for high-technology products and services.

In the 1980 International Management Seminar of the Pacific Basin Economic Council, futurist Herman Kahn confirmed, "The center of dynamism that used to be in the Mediterranean, and which then moved to northwest Europe and to the North Atlantic, is moving to the Pacific Basin." The full potential of the region can be realized only through cooperation. In the same year, William Kintner, former ambassador to Thailand and president of the Foreign Policy Research Institute, put it another way in a forum on the same theme: The spread of European Western civilization was due primarily to the development of modern science there and nowhere else. Its technology has become a prime mover, bringing peoples of the world into closer contact, as well as being a force for changing political arrangements in the international community. In turn, the United States became the chief instrument of Pacific Basin exchanges and a principal force in the creation of ASEAN. Now new actors, chiefly Japan and China, are promoting social heterogeneity. The spread of both American and Japanese technology could increase the interconnectedness of the region, especially in the area of communications. Trade, tourism, cultural and scientific exchanges, and government and institutional meetings should promote cooperation in the Pacific community.

The countries on the western rim of the Pacific Basin are coming alive to the potential of this unique area. Taiwan's economic planners, for instance, have already launched their own multibillion-dollar, high-technology version of Silicon Valley. They are shifting their economy from labor-intensive to high-technology production. In the Hsinchu Science-Based Industrial Park, 21 companies have put $21 million into development and production, and 12 of these are affiliated with American companies. Their aim by 1990 is 200 firms doing $1 billion in sales and that the endeavor will raise the technological level of all their industry. At the other end of the rim, Canon USA is broadening its push into the American camera market and is typical of the West-East flow of Asian technology. This producer of cameras and copiers uses electronics and optics technology, primarily through robots, and puts 6 percent of sales into R&D annually.

Asian-American business and technological synergy are demonstrated in the success story of H. P. Hwang. A Korean educated in the United States, he revolutionized one part of the American electronics industry and is now worth $100 million. Hwang's Televideo Systems, Inc., of Sunnyvale, California, surged to the forefront of cathode-ray terminal manufacturing. His CRTs for office or home are expected to reach $35 million in sales in fiscal 1981. Hwang has forged a successful business merger between his native and adopted lands. Information technology will link the far-flung Pacific peoples together in peace and prosperity.

Space industrialization. Despite a 9 percent cut in the 1981 budget of $6.5 billion for NASA, space endeavors prosper from Russia to France to Brazil, primarily because of advances in communications satellites. Greater international cooperation by governments and private industry is needed in the next 50 years if the business potential of outer space is to be realized. The commercial links between earth and other planets are being forged by Columbia shuttle orbits. The aerospace and communications industries are the first to benefit from this pioneering endeavor. Future shuttle crews may build and maintain satellite and solar power stations for transmission of communications and power to the earth. Before 2025, these crews may also be involved in highly automated factories in outer space, which benefit from the absence of gravity. Such a microgravity environment offers many advantages in the processing of metals, fluids, crystals, and cells. By the end of this decade, NASA predicts that pharmaceuticals and crystals made in space will be sold on earth, a new boon for the drug and microelectronics industries. Boeing marketing specialists Gilbert Keyes and John Bosman maintain that the major obstacles to the commercialization of outer space are not technological, but financial, organizational, and political. The chief of NASA's technical planning, Joseph Loftus, thinks that the space shuttles may have the same impact on the economic development of the United States as the advent of the transcontinental railroad had on the American West.

After telecommunications, the commercial emphasis of metaindustrial organizations will be on power and manufacturing opportunities in outer space, as well as on the search for materials not obtainable at competitive prices on earth. Lest one pass off the marketing prospects of such visionary efforts, consider what is happening now in some very pragmatic corporations. McDonnell Douglas is going to experiment with a materials processing system—continuous-flow electrophoresis—for separating biological materials in near-zero gravity. In conjunction with Ortho Pharmaceuticals, it expects to produce ultrapure serums, vaccines, and other drugs within the next few years. Separating enzymes in space is less costly and can lead to the prevention of numerous deaths due to blood diseases.

TRW in Hawthorne, California, hopes to establish plants in earth orbit before the end of this century. Project manager Neville Barter predicts that these factories will float in the vacuum outside the earth's atmosphere, where temperatures hover near absolute zero and gravity is virtually zero. These factories will produce new and improved products that cannot be manufactured on this planet, such as metals that float on water, ultrapure crystals that will enable computers to take quantum leaps into miniaturization, superstrength alloys, and frictionless bearings. Barter thinks that corporations that ignore the potential of vertical R&D expansion will be bypassed by other companies who take an early lead in space industrialization. TRW itself is interested in the prospects there for improving materials used in jet engine turbine blades, semiconductors, cutting tools, coatings, and bearings surfaces. Under NASA contract, the TRW project team is building three minifactories, which are scheduled for orbit by space shuttle in 1985.

The Futures Research Division of Security Pacific National Bank in Los Angeles, California, has already issued a report on this new commercial frontier, entitled *Trends: Capitalism Goes into Orbit*. Vice president and editor Hank Koehn observed, "We are starting to reap the material benefits of our original curiosity and dreams. The great adventure of mankind is being extended and all of humanity will benefit from the knowledge gained and the riches produced thereby."

Only metaindustrial organizations and their new work culture may have the vision, know-how, and energy to commercialize space. Only postindustrial thinking and competence will push beyond the initial phases of space communications and manufacturing to the generation of solar power, the mining of gases and minerals, and the colonization of the cosmos. The endeavor will first help solve some of the earth's problems, such as pollution, natural resources depletion, food shortages, and overpopulation. But the real value, as Koehn commented, may be to replace envy with incentive, conflict with international cooperation, and war with peaceful exploration.

Japan expects to have a $1.5 billion export-aggressive space industry by the mid 1990s. The European Space Agency is now selling space on Ariane, its three-stage expendable rocket system. Along with the United States and Canada, ESA is developing the Spacelab research module to be launched soon from the shuttle. As James Oberg has noted, "The immediate goal is to establish easy and economic access from earth to space and back, and to conduct frequent scientific sorties into orbit." Oberg believes that permanently occupied space stations of considerable size may be a reality by 1990. The Soviets, on the other hand, are concentrating on occupied outposts in low orbit just beyond the earth's atmosphere and may accomplish this even before 1990. In any event, launching Spacelab as a space station for 100 metaindustrial workers may take ten space shuttle trips to deliver the materials. NASA has contracted the University of Houston to design a space village large enough to house these workers in outer space. Larry Bell, director of the university's Environmental Center, claims the issue is which nation will lead the way in space industrialization. Although establishing major facilities in space will be enormously expensive, in terms of money and energy, Bell says the expenses can be justified if they protect and improve life in our world community and produce financial dividends.

Many people are skeptical about the realities of commercialization in space. This is understandable, because people are normally reluctant to make such grandiose leaps in their thinking, no less invest very large sums of money in activities that don't promise a quick, tangible return. But very practical steps are being taken to bridge the gap between two subcultures: engineers and scientists in aerospace, who are largely government-related and -dependent, and R&D executives from Fortune 500 companies in the private sector. Tom Harford heads up a project for the American Institute of Aeronautics and Astronautics (AIAA), a professional society for those in aerospace technology. By invitation only, AIAA conducts field trips to ten NASA installations for tours and briefings on the commercial implications of space-technology developments. Three hundred and fifty executives from 150 companies have already participated. Harford found from his experience that these two cultures do not yet know how to talk to one another. R&D executives are in awe of the briefing information they receive, and are wary of making decisions about involving their companies in probing new frontiers.

So far the field trips have resulted in much consciousness-raising but only a few joint ventures, such as that between Johnson & Johnson and McDonnell Douglas for a project on a future shuttle.

According to Harford,* government and industry must cooperate if the commercialization of outer space is to be feasible, but political decisions have yet to be made for funding a major national space industrialization effort. Harford cited one small San Diego company that has a leg up on its competitors—GTI Corporation, whose president, James K. LaFleur, has succeeded in contracting a joint endeavor with NASA to send a $2 million metallurgical device aboard the space shuttle. Experiments on the alloy in zero gravity will be conducted. Perhaps corporate leaders will take this new market seriously now that Prudential Insurance Company has announced that it is an investor in a venture to privately finance the fifth space shuttle. Of course, if the investors buy the shuttle, Prudential expects the marketing rights for commercial cargo space aboard all five orbiters!

Finally, skeptics might do well to read a report on "Space Industrialization" prepared by International Resources Development, Inc., a Norwalk, Connecticut, market research firm. It predicts that the commercialization of space could provide billions of dollars worth of products and services in the *next two decades!* The March 1982 journey of the shuttle Columbia proved the feasibility of business enterprises related to satellite communication services, pharmaceuticals, and materials processing, and semiconductor production in low or zero gravity conditions.

We have reviewed only four metaindustrial marketing opportunities. There are numerous others in the fields of health services, energy alternatives, and oceanography. The point is simple: The new worlds ahead for human development require new ways of thinking and functioning. Above all, they demand new management philosophies, concepts, processes, strategies, and skills. This is the essence of the emerging technological work culture and the successful metaindustrial organizations that will flourish as a result.

* Personal interview, May 21, 1982.

CAPSULE CONCLUSIONS

A decade ago the Club of Rome published a gloomy report on our future, entitled *Limits to Growth*. Its prime architect, Aurelio Peccei, is still pessimistic and warns that the 1980s may see dangerous collapses unless humankind starts a new period of cooperation and solidarity. Peccei cries out that our value systems have not kept pace with technological developments, and that we make poor use of democracy and planning. He thinks the world needs more social and political, rather than technological, innovation. But he is hopeful about young adults, who seem better equipped than their elders to see and select what should be mankind's future. Although I share some of Peccei's sentiments, I am more optimistic about our human emergence. Culture, a human creation, offers hope, for we are in the process of developing the new metaindustrial culture worldwide. The leadership in this process is coming from knowledge workers engaged in scientific, technological, and business research and development. These professionals and corporate executives are in the forefront of concurrent revolutions in communications and information processing, microelectronics and biotechnologies.

Metaindustrial technologies are transforming not only our daily lives but also the way in which we formulate our social institutions and do business. They are stimulating us to design more appropriate and relevant macro and micro cultures. Specifically, they energize us to provide a postindustrial work culture that is more attuned to human needs for the twenty-first century. A new kind of management is needed in terms of: *how* we work with automation and robotics, *when* we work within a 24-hour time frame and with increased leisure, *where* we work, globally or in outer space, at home or in a corporate facility, *whom* we work with in a more pluralistic and technical work environment, *what* we work with, as with new tools and materials, and *why* we work to obtain greater self-actualization.

To keep up with our advances in technology, we are forced to design new organizational paradigms and a new work culture. To survive and succeed under such circumstances, management must become more cosmopolitan, holistic, systems-oriented, risk taking, and entrepreneurial. Management and executive development must now provide continuing education in the sciences to businesspersons and in business administration to scientists. The merger of both sets of talents in metaindustrial corporations also requires skills in managing change, cultural differences, and research. Tomorrow's executives today must acquire the capacity not only to coordinate but to facilitate; not only to cope but to promote synergy; not only to plan but to forecast; not only to react but to be proactive. Such executives can be comfortable in a world marketplace; they anticipate space industrialization. Metaindustrial leaders seek out new markets for new products and services, such as home communications and biochemical technologies as well as new locales, such as the Pacific Rim and outer space.

The metaindustrial work culture is characterized by three basic norms of human behavior:

1. *Openness* to new ideas and possibilities, new peoples and processes. It espouses flexibility and relativity, rather than rigidity and detached objectivity; responsiveness to human needs and environmental concerns, rather than mechanistic approaches and a disregard for society's input and rights.

2. *Innovation* in solving problems, in meeting challenges and opportunities. Such creative approaches to management and research are the key to productivity, economic and social progress, and optimization of human capabilities.

3. *Synergy* in work, union, government, and community relations, in both national and international operations. The complexities of metaindustrial life and changes demand cooperation and collaboration. Metaindustrial managers move beyond traditional boundaries that separate labor from management, science from business, industry from industry, corporation from university, commerce from government, and nation from nation. Only through cultural sharing and integration can we begin to serve adequately human need on this planet and take advantage of the potential benefits of space industrialization, particularly with reference to new services, products, energies, metals, lifestyles, and human activities!

CHAPTER 12   Developing Organizational Potential

One of the themes woven throughout this volume is that key executives need vision if their organizations are to achieve their goals through people. Top managers should be future-oriented and capable of sharing their optimism about new directions with employees. Then they will excite and energize personnel to perform for their own and the organizations' benefit. To say that we are in transition from an industrial to a metaindustrial work culture is an abstraction. Executives should be able to translate reality into understandable challenges for co-workers.

Dr. Martin A. Apple, founder of Ean Technology, a company in the field of molecular genetic engineering, provided a useful analogy to make the point. In thinking about why it took the Israelites 40 years to wander through the desert in search of the promised land, Apple concluded that perhaps Moses knew his people had been conditioned by the experience of a slave culture under the pharaohs. So he used the passage period to prepare them for the culture of freedom, where they would be more autonomous and would also have to assume more responsibility for their own lives. Then Apple, this pioneer in new technologies, wondered whether many managers are still fighting "the last war" with their classical strategies and methods, and not facing up to the transformation under way in the conduct of business.

An outstanding leader of American industry, Don Mitchell, vice chairman of the Marriott Corporation, made these astute observations on management's challenges for the future:

... I discovered that business was something more than making money, although I won't deny the importance of remuneration. The process of establishing a goal, convincing others that it is reasonable and attainable, and then managing a team to achieve that goal, has been immensely gratifying and challenging. In short, it's been great fun.... The first challenge of management is to convey this sense of purpose—this fun—in business to a new generation.... To me, business has a definite social purpose. We've got to get our message across to young people so that we can get our fair share of the talent in the upcoming generation.

Now here is a leader with vision, capable of conveying to employees what is happening in society and business and the new directions corporations must explore. Thus personnel can be helped to cope more successfully with a vastly changed environment at home, work, or play.

The opinion polls of Daniel Yankelovich confirm that the present shifts in American culture mean a decisive break with the past. Yankelovich's surveys demonstrate a collapsing of norms within a single generation. Consider, for example, the tens of millions of women who no longer regard having babies as self-fulfilling, preferring to remain childless and pursue a career. The typical U.S. family now consists of a single person. Such rapid social changes affect both the market and the work culture. Yankelovich reports from his studies:

Vast shifts are taking place in the composition of the workplace. A generation ago, the typical worker was a man working full time to provide complete support for his wife and children. Today, fewer than one out of five people who work for pay conform to this standard.... By 1980, more than two out of five mothers of children age 6 or younger worked for pay. In families earning more than $25,000 a year the majority now depend on two incomes: the husband's and the wife's. Ironically, while women are clamoring to get in, men have been slowly edging out of the workforce.

Yankelovich describes many other work trends, and concludes that most jobs are organized as if these changes had *not* taken place. The implication is that current personnel practices, fringe benefits programs, and work schedules are often obstacles to the new lifestyles. Instead of helping employees into the postindustrial culture, many companies still adhere rigidly to traditional industrial relations that are increasingly inappropriate.

Yankelovich's findings indicate that growing affluence has stimulated the search for self-fulfillment, despite some setbacks in periods of a troubled economy. This need is a powerful unleashed force that irrevocably affects not only the macroculture but also the institutional microcultures. Yankelovich suggests that the search is for a new American identity and philosophy of life that are better adapted to the economic realities ahead. Self-worth is being gauged less by material acquisitions and more by less tangible, quality-of-life values. This may explain why more chief executives are quitting after only months in their posts, as happened with the last two presidents of GAF, a New York–based diversified manufacturer, and why 25 percent or more of the active men in their prime (ages 16 to 65) are dropping out of the workforce—because their work no longer has meaning!

Yet how many businesses, associations, and public agencies have seriously attempted to redesign and enrich jobs, and to create a work environment that energizes people? By developing a metaindustrial work culture, an organization can provide greater meaning and self-fulfillment on the job.

INNOVATIVE LEADERSHIP THINKING
It is the responsibility of leadership to ready members for successful coping in the changing environment. The eighties and nineties are the decades of transition for twentieth-century enterprises. The new Moseses in executive suites across the globe should assist their people to prepare for the twenty-first-century work culture and lifestyle. This text has tried to emphasize the impact of information and its technology, of automation and robots, and of science and genetic engineering on the transformation of human society and culture. As a result of these influences, some individuals will suffer severe future shock, as some institutions will experience organization shock. But the effects can be limited, and at times prevented, if corporate and government leaders will raise the consciousness, as well as the coping skills, of themselves, their families, and their colleagues.

As a good beginning, top managers can exercise innovative leadership by helping their employees and the community at large to become computer literate. Computers represent an enormous leap in humanity's ability to communicate. They can bridge the chasm between the liberal arts and sciences, between business and technology. But if the general population is to benefit from the new and exciting tool, corporations will have to contribute funds, equipment, and staff to the formal systems of education. Perhaps the place to start is with the managers themselves whose role has been changed so radically by microcomputers.

Another theme of this volume is that fast-growth companies in

Developing Organizational Potential

new technologies provide a look into tomorrow's metaindustrial organization and its culture. Many of these new ventures are the direct outgrowth of space technology applied to communications, national defense, medicine, transportation, business operations, and home conveniences. To contrast mature management in older industries with the emerging ways of doing business, and thus offer the reader some sense of the new commerce and managerial styles, we will focus briefly on one industry and one company. Such insights may curb organizational wanderings in this transitional period and contribute to the necessary bridge building into cyberculture.

One spinoff of space-related research has been the application of high technology to agriculture. The recent feature by P. Steinhart in *The New York Times Magazine* calls it "The Second Green Revolution" and describes such commercial breakthroughs as the following:

- Crossbreeding of unrelated plant species, such as the "sunbean" which results from a sunflower and a French bean, or the potato-tomato.
- Purified corn DNA cloned in bacteria on a glass rod for eventual reinsertion into other plants.
- Dwarfed peach trees that take less space and produce a better-quality fruit with a higher yield.
- Regenerated protoplasts, or the marriage of two cell nuclei to combine chromosomes and genetic information from two species that do not normally reproduce sexually, such as with corn, wheat, and barley.
- Growing food plants in salt water, hydroponically, or even in sand.
- Creating chemical products and drugs from plant cells on a mass-manufacturing basis, such as anticancer alkaloids, steroids, anticlotting agents, and insecticides.

Soon, this burgeoning biotechnical industry may be able to provide us with seeds so that everyone becomes a farmer in his or her home. Such scientific/business synergy may turn out to be the solution for the 20 percent of the world's people who are undernourished. U.S. advances in this arena may boost further the present American record of providing 55 percent of global food exports.

The ag-tech business market has been projected at from $50

billion to $100 billion in 20 years. But let us focus our microscope on one company, engaged in commercial plant tissue culturing. Its analysis is a miniature case study that contrasts the way it will be with the way it was.

The International Plant Research Institute is a profit-making corporation with *Institute* in the name to comfort the many academics who cross over from the university to the business world. This San Carlos, California, firm is only five years old, but it is the largest of its kind in the world. It is a veteran among the "big four" of the infant industry (including Cetus, Agrigenetics, and Genentech. In addition to working in fields, IPRI works on the cellular and molecular levels in its independent research laboratories, utilizing cell culture and gene splicing as its primary technical processes. In this way barriers that prevent different species from mating can be eliminated and variations of plants can be created that are, for example, disease-resistant.

To get some feel for the metaindustrial managerial style practiced at IPRI, we interviewed its founder, Dr. Martin Apple. The following synopsis will indicate departures from classical management approaches and new directions for developing organizational potential:

1. *Recruitment* is worldwide in the unending search for the best people. Thus a multicultural workforce has been created in which competence is the major norm, *not* sex, age, color, race, or even language. Professionals are sought who have a record for innovative achievement and who want recognition, not money, as a top reinforcer.

2. *Selection* involves innovative techniques such as taking candidates for hiring or promotion into situations requiring risk taking and problem solving to see how they handle stress and crises. Fast-growth companies involve high stress, total dedication, and fewer vacations, so personnel selection is a key factor.

3. *Management* of a cross-cultural team of knowledge workers requires elimination of national and disciplinary obstacles, so that people can work together more creatively and effectively. (See Appendix D.) This means that managers must hone their listening and facilitative skills. To promote synergy among such professionals, the focus is on conceptualization and task accomplishment. The interdisciplinary approach is extended outward by bringing together different communities of expertise and different industries. Executives learn to manage differences. The crossbreeding is not restricted to plants; it includes scholars and indus-

trialists as well. Executives are urged to view themselves as managers, not technicians—that is, organizers and coordinators, not doers. They are expected to practice both administrative and interpersonal skills.

4. *Leadership* is to be modeled by executives and extended to the whole work group. It is oriented toward measurable and significant results achieved in growth, high profitability, staff accomplishment, and company innovation. To attain such ends, corporate leaders are urged to anticipate rather than react; to refuse to tolerate mediocrity; to insist upon growth (personal and professional); to use power to make things happen; to be managers, not technicians; to reward in direct proportion to achievement; to seek solutions to problems rather than problems in solutions; to foster interdependent relationships; to strive not to avoid failure, but to achieve success, and then to share accomplishment with the team; to be occasionally surprised, but never overwhelmed; to be consistent in style, actions, and expectations.

5. *Communication* is circular, informing staff of what they want to know; of what is expected of them; of how they measure up to expectancy; of organizational structures and policies and how they relate to the individual; of outlook and prospects for both the corporation and the individual; of reasons for changes in procedures; of credit where and when it is justly due in proportion to real achievement; of why things are done or not done; of positive feedback and constructive criticism; of pride in group effort and progress toward measurable team goals.

6. *Motivation* is demonstrated by managers who prove they can do all the jobs they supervise, but not as well as the subordinate; by managers who are personally friendly, who emphasize the importance of a subordinate's work and praise achievement; by managers who provide first-class technical assistance to subordinates who run into problems; by increasing responsibility in proportion to demonstrated proficiency; by distributing unpleasant tasks equally; by striving to help the staff advance; by setting objectives *with* staff, not for them; by pay scales that are in line with competitors and fringe benefits that are top flight. Managers should seek to understand reasons behind deviant behavior, finding out why people are griping, and then resolving the matter.

7. *Development* of people who respect themselves, as well as the system, is a high priority. This involves enhancing their competence by informing, involving, respecting, and trusting them. Training is more than entry level, and is provided whenever per-

formance is less than standard. Helping subordinates develop is a managerial responsibility. Development requires that scientists learn business methods and that business specialists get training in technical terminology and concepts. One strategy is short staff meetings that may involve up to 50 people for broad input purposes. For example, frequent morning "brainstorming" sessions of 30 minutes are held in which all contribute ideas for new research and marketing possibilities, and all receive feedback on their offerings by the end of the workday. The recognition of being first is the reward. Personnel get exhilarated through these "high frequency" sessions with colleagues.

8. *Decision making* is participative in that these high performers provide input, but the final choice is made by key management. "The telescope is passed around" for everyone to see what is happening and to offer ideas and solutions, but final decisions are made by the executives with the responsibility for programs or projects.

As Dr. Apple noted, "If your company is growing at 50 to 100% a year, you don't resist change, you welcome it." His attitude is that he and his colleagues are creating the future together, so they should all share their visions. No wonder IPRI had a 445 percent gross growth in 1981! The challenge for such fast-growth businesses is to create the infrastructure for survival and development. In contrast to traditional industries, the $15 billion agribusiness in California is very dynamic, shifting constantly. Next will come seed research in outer space when the *Columbia* carries agribusiness experiments.

The startling difference in the metaindustrial work culture was brought into sharp focus by William Nelson, president of Nel-Tech Developments, Inc., a Portland, Oregon, electronics firm, when he commented to a group of chief executives: "Our key management could not care less about retirement pensions and exit planning. We are here-and-now oriented. As CEO, I am only 35 years old, and my management team is even younger!" No wonder the new form has been dubbed "the emerging adhocracy" by Alvin Toffler.

As beneficiaries of the "big picture" of what is happening today in business and society, top management has a responsibility to redesign a more appropriate work environment and to prepare personnel to function effectively under the changed circumstances.

As a conclusion to this book on new ways in management,

four steps for building bridges and facilitating the transformation into metaindustrial organizations are proposed.

STEP 1: IMPROVING MANAGEMENT PLANNING AND EFFECTIVENESS

In crossing the bridge to postindustrial business operations, it behooves managers *not* to throw the baby out with the bath water. Yes, we are in a new ball game, with new players, new rules, and a new game plan. But the art and science of management refined in the twentieth century has proven philosophies and practices that can be partially transformed and made relevant for a turbulent marketplace and a volatile economy. Management tools and techniques need to be updated, put in a new context, and adapted to our changing circumstances. Third Wave complexities require multiple methodologies, not necessarily abandonment of past managerial technologies. The effective manager should be able to adapt to the stage of the organization's development, and use the strategies appropriate to those unique circumstances.

Conservative and mature corporations may require new perspectives and applications of basic management procedures. Corporations that are in transition need *transformational management*. Corporations that probe the new frontiers of products and service need innovation and experimentation to discover new forms of management. Regardless of the current status of one's organization, we are all in transition to the twenty-first century. Therefore, managers have to alter their style to the organizational state of development, not only of their own company but also of those enterprises from which clients, contractors, suppliers, and other community representatives come. This implies that we operate on a behavioral continuum that challenges us to use differing approaches when dealing with an industrial-age conglomerate or with high-tech firms. Since the objective reality in which business must be conducted is fluid, the manager should be flexible in responding to changed conditions and proactive in planning.

The American Management Associations has long espoused the idea that management is an emerging profession and that managers should be more professional. Addressing AMA's Presidents Association, James F. Kingsley provided a definition of management that has proved viable for the last 40 years:

Management is guiding human and physical resources into dynamic organizational units which achieve their objectives to the satisfaction of those served, and with a high degree of morale and sense of attainment on the part of those providing the service.

To accomplish this, the AMA and other management educators have consistently urged managers to improve their understanding and skills in planning, climate setting, organizing, decision making, and leading. Essentially, if an organization hopes to be productive and profitable, the basics of management are to plan, control, and develop people. To accomplish this, Kingsley counsels top managers to plan consultatively, to delegate authority, to monitor performance, and to develop human resources. Thus managers can transform the strengths of personnel into social benefits and gain personal satisfaction in the process.

AMA's Management Course for Presidents reviews these fundamentals of management even with chief executives, for they are the keys to a successful enterprise. Special emphasis is given to the *strategic planning process,* which its catalogue defines as:

a team process that assists the chief executive officer and top management group in preparing their basic plan for future growth and development, by surfacing, identifying, and confronting issues which need resolution in order to achieve superior performance and profitability.

In earlier chapters, we reviewed these management dimensions from the perspective of metaindustrial organization culture. We advocated more management emphasis on systems, synergy, and strategies. Let us focus a moment on strategies with reference to planning, a central leadership function.

The strategic management planning process has these benefits: (1) organizationwide clarification of assumptions and terminology, (2) creation of a unified goal to which personnel energy can be directed, (3) dynamic procedures based on the idea that change is reality and strategies should be altered accordingly, and (4) results-oriented measures of performance and system of rewards.

Such a process involves people at all levels in the organization in mapping out where the group is, where it wants to go, and how it is going to get there, including the ways of assessing success in the journey. With so many organizations in passage today, strategic planning should be envisioned as an ongoing process for maximizing opportunities, allocating resources, evaluating future probabilities, and achieving objectives. In the seminars for The Presidents Association, Dr. Michael Karmi discusses "Strategic Planning: Assumptions for Managing the Future." Participants examine:

- Principal environmental assumptions—political, social, economic, international, and technological.
- Setting and communicating corporate objectives, and the role of top management.
- Coping with the new economics, including chronic inflation, the high cost of money, and slow growth.
- Productivity management by increasing human motivation, as well as through automation, cosmopolitan managerial styles, and techniques that synergize different cultural approaches.
- Forecasting techniques, environmental scanning, and external factors that affect business—such as global inflation and economic development, government regulations, and changing social and consumer patterns and values.
- Innovative planning in a creative corporate environment open to new ideas, risk taking and the unconventional, and group entrepreneurship.

The systems approach to strategic planning as employed by AMA Center for Planning & Implementation is outlined in Figure 11. Regardless of the method used in strategic planning, the process engaged in with employees or members is more important than the plan that results. Nevertheless, the plan should be written down, if possible, in fewer than 25 pages, and be actively used by management at all levels.

A key ingredient for success in this process was identified by Sun Yat-Sen when he wisely observed, "It is not the practical workers, but the idealists and planners that are difficult to find." Strategic planners project into the future to set long-term goals, but focus on short-term actions with operational, tactical, and contingency plans. Strategic planners share the "big picture" of global management in the context of both society and business. Strategic planning cracks rigid mindsets, counteracts stagnated thinking, and is a mechanism for planned change. It provides for major market downturns and wipe-outs. Daniel G. Hulett, director of Hulett Associates in Stamford, Connecticut, summarizes the process: It involves development of an action plan for planning,

FIGURE 11. Steps in the strategic planning process: a team approach.

I Orientation and Preparation	II Intensive Planning Session (5 days)	III Intersession	IV Intensive Planning Session (5 days)	V Follow-Up Visit
Developing the planning base • Team assigned • Process outlined • Previous plans and planning analyzed • Preliminary data assembled	**Internal Analysis** • Philosophy • Basic policies • Problems and opportunities • Resources • Personality • Structure **External Analysis** • Competitive factors • Environmental factors: political, social, economic, cultural and technological **Translating the Planning Base into Strategies with Tentative Objectives, Action Plans and Assignments** Develop list of tentative programs and projects Group and assign priorities Identify action plans and cost/benefit analysis Develop schedules and assign tasks for intersession	Three to four months to start work on action plans, cost/benefit analysis, and data assembly. Meet and confer with middle managers. **Intersession Visit** Team Director reconvenes team for review of action plan progress. Assists with problems and initiates preparation for next intensive planning session. After this review and evaluation, time is allowed for completion of assignments. **Completion of the Strategic Plan**	Review and summary of intersession assignments to finalize the plan. Establish priorities for all programs and action plans: • Rank and analyze • Evaluate resource requirements • Select options • Complete gap analysis • Develop resource schedule, control procedures and monitoring system • Write the overall plan • Prepare planning calendar • Schedule team director's follow-up visit	Assess performance against plan. Evaluate effectiveness of monitoring and control systems. Discuss/resolve problems Assure that planning system is operating effectively Arrange annual update session

Source: The Strategic Planning Process: A Team Approach. Center for Planning and Implementation,

defining the current situation, visualizing the future, producing a statement of general mission, setting goals, devising specific plans, specifying immediate action, taking action, and measuring progress and results.

Strategic management and planning demonstrates how some current managerial practice can be most appropriate in the meta-industrial work culture. It is a team approach that continually analyzes the internal and external forces that stabilize the organization and help it to cope more effectively with the only certainty in the future—change. The process enables us to build change into our organizational systems and styles. Figure 12 offers an overview of strategic management in the form of a matrix. It examines the macroculture in terms of technical, political, economic and cultural systems, and the organizational microculture in terms of mission, structure, strategies, and human resources management. The interplay of such factors can ensure the success or failure of the planning process. Strategic planning may help contemporary managers avoid what they accuse many academics of—searching for tomorrow's solutions to yesterday's problems. In doing this planning, it would be wise to confront the issues of vital concern for 1,508 CEOs in North American *Fortune* 1,000 corporations during 1980: (1) double-digit inflation, (2) government intervention and regulation, (3) high cost of money, (4) low productivity, (5) high energy costs, and (6) economic fluctuations.

STEP TWO: DEVELOPING COSMOPOLITAN AND TRANSFORMATIONAL STRATEGIES

The First Global Conference on the Future, held at the turn of the decade in Toronto, had an intriguing theme: "Through the '80s—Thinking Globally, Acting Locally."* That motto and the conference proceedings reinforce the notion that today's executives cannot afford to be too conservative, provincial, or enthnocentric in their thinking and planning. When modern managers are cosmopolitans, they create a better future for themselves and others through their actions. To improve the quality of life for all, such individuals move beyond cultural limitations in their perceptions and seek opportunities for cultural synergy. Such leaders conceptualize in terms of the world market and multinational or multicultural involvements, on this planet and beyond!

* See E. Cornish, ed.

FIGURE 12. Strategic management planning matrix.

MICROCULTURE

Considerations to reduce the gap between *now* and *future* goal accomplishment by analysis of interacting forces.

	Mission	Structure	Strategy	Human Resources Management
Technical Systems	*Definition of new technologies in light of prior history and current situation *Market identification of needs	*Integration of technology for internal operations *Sale of technology and services externally	*Operations task force for productivity studies *Environmental scan and market planning	*HRD–training for new roles and relations *Recruiting for technical and sales staff
Political Systems	*Statement on organizational relations to government and its regulations *Analysis of political situation within industry and the organization	*Establishment of Political Action Committee or Government Relations Department *Assign roles for balanced distribution of power (i.e., matrix management	*Community Action Plan to increase influence *Sharing management control through mechanisms for more participation	*Training for personnel in social and political change *Team building in power sharing
Economic Systems	*Clarifications of what organization does within a changing economy *Economic focus on metaindustrial growth factors	*Set up productivity measures and quality work teams *Seek venture capital for subsidiaries	*Profit sharing based on achieving production goals *Engage in economic forecasting for new products and services	*Inaugurate program in customer service training *Brainstorming sessions on potential innovations, inventions, and patents
Cultural Systems	*Mission alterations in response to internal/external forces *Evaluate policies and processes as to relevance in postindustrial culture	*Create corporate culture in tune with contemporary changes *Revise policies, personnel manuals, operational practices as a result	*Encourage high-performing behavior models *Emphasize every employee being a manager over his/her work space	*Recruit competent achievers who reinforce metaindustrial values *Management of accountability system introduced

MACROCULTURE

Evidence of this new metaindustrial outlook is present everywhere for those sensitive enough to see and hear, let alone grasp, what is really going on in the transformation of the human family. Such evidence helps to explain why such diverse groups as the World Business Council, the American Business Council of Life Insurance, IBM, and Digital Equipment Corporation are arranging lectures and seminars on the content of M. Ferguson's *Aquarian Conspiracy*. It makes more comprehensible efforts of private investors from the Space Transportation Company who are negotiating with NASA to finance new orbiters in return for exclusive agreement to market all nongovernment activity on the shuttles, as a positive step toward space industrialization. It explains the motivation of a Willy Brandt to promote the North-South Dialogue and report, or a Lopez Portillo to facilitate the Cancun economic conference of world leaders in the First and Third Worlds. It is also evident among the planners of the UN Conference on Trade and Development, who are concerned about the $46 billion in reverse foreign aid given since 1960 by the Third World to North America, Europe, and Australia in the form of their scarce resource—a quarter of a million university graduates. At a time when nations are spending $550 billion annually on weaponry, it is understandable that Robert S. McNamara, on retiring from the World Bank presidency, would speak out against the "disgraceful" government record in alleviating global poverty. We can appreciate his concern for the 1.3 billion people, a quarter of the world's population, whose per capita income does not exceed $200 a year, when we realize that the world's arms sales equal the total annual income of the poor half of the earth!

The new cosmopolitan attitude is manifest in the modern trading companies such as Philipp Brothers Division of Engelhard Minerals & Chemicals, Ulme-Renoci, Inc., of Pittsburgh, and the Carl H. Schmidt Company of Southfield, Michigan. The Japanese trading companies have been the masters at making the East-West twain meet, as in the case of Mitsubishi International Corporation, based in New York City. With a 1981 trading volume of $60 billion in commodities, these firms represent a broad range of goods exchanged between the United States and Japan, as well as in numerous multinational transactions. Today MIC handles such diverse transactions as purchase of Saudi Arabian oil for Japanese clientele, the import of Brazilian shoes for U.S. stores such as Sears and Thom McAn, and the export of American soybeans to Western European customers. Amid a kaleidoscope of global economic change, these companies promote international prosperity and peace through world trade. Such business activities are transforming the marketplace into a global entity, forcing domestic manufacturers and suppliers to project beyond their own borders.

The growing internationalization of business is another factor requiring all managers to be cosmopolitan, to realize that different cultures have different and appropriate approaches to the management process. It is no longer possible to contain the global marketplace within a single international division with specialists in foreign trade. Instead, all management development should include the missing ingredient of training in general cultural awareness and specific cultures in which the company does business. Education in comparative management and culture will enable managers, technicians, and sales representatives to be more effective in business both at home and abroad. The insights from cultural anthropology that have been pointed out in preceding chapters can help to reduce the rate of premature returns on foreign assignments and increase productivity while located in a foreign culture. This same body of knowledge is also useful in improving relations on the job with our own people from minority backgrounds and in better comprehending the influence of organizational culture on worker behavior both at home and abroad.

The attitudes and skills of the cosmopolitan manager have multiple applications. Let us review three areas suggested in this text:

○ *Technology transfer.* When a new technology—scientific, mechanical, or behavioral—is transplanted from a home to a host culture, cross-cultural sensitivity is needed. First, it will facilitate the integration of the foreign specialist and his or her family into the local culture. Second, it will improve customer relations overseas and ensure that the training and technology provided are appropriate to the local situation. When knowledge workers transfer their expertise to other peoples, especially when the locals may be less educated or less economically developed, it should be not an imposition but a helpful sharing that will contribute to the unleashing of the host culture's human potential. The person offering the technical assistance needs to be trained in patience, flexibility, and autonomy, as well as in coping with diversity and ambiguity.

The sponsoring organization should invest in a "foreign deployment system" that includes (1) careful recruitment and selection of overseas personnel, (2) predeparture orientation that will enhance skills transfer, (3) on-site personnel support services, and (4) reentry counseling, which may even involve outplacement on return to the home culture. The scope of this human resources development for international business goes beyond language, culture, and areas studies. It should encompass practical teaching in cross-cultural communications, supervision of people from a differing cultural background, the role of women in the foreign culture, and ways of limiting culture shock, facilitating adaptation, and dealing with foreign bureaucracies.

○ Cosmopolitan executives make sure their organizations provide comprehensive relocation services, both for overseas assignments and for transfers within their own country. As psychologists Ronald Raymond and Stephen Eliot remind us, uprooting is painful. Relocation can accelerate identity crisis, cause marriages to crack and careers to flounder. The whole process of adjustment can be expedited and made more humane through intelligent management of the transfer. In a 1981 Survey of Corporate Relocation Policies among *Fortune* 1,000 companies, Merrill Lynch Relocation Management's findings included these insights:

- ○ 96 percent provided relocated employees with assistance in disposing of their present homes, and about half used a relocation firm or bank to purchase the house.
- ○ 61 percent now offer mortgage differential allowance to compensate employees for differences in mortgage interest rates between new and old locations.
- ○ Despite a drastic decrease in foreign subsistence aid to employees, within the last two years, 23 percent of the companies were providing cost-of-living allowances, while 99 percent allowed at least one house-hunting trip to the new site.
- ○ 23 percent of the firms offered job-finding assistance for spouses, to deal with the growing phenomenon of two-career couples.

To promote synergy in the new cultural setting, enlightened companies offer relocation services that range from culture and language training to moving, housing, and educational assistance for dependents. When a large number of personnel are deployed to a new site, an opportunity exists to build a metaindustrial work culture. Stephen H. Rhinesmith believes that organization development technology can bring another dimension to corporate relocations. His New York firm of international relocation specialists now seeks to develop strategies to create a new organizational culture among transferred employees when a corporate headquarters is moved or a new plant established.

○ A final example of why cosmopolitan mindsets are integral to metaindustrial organizations can be found in the increasing trend of investment and purchase of local businesses in one country by another. In the United States alone, foreign investors spend more than $10 billion annually to buy or start American businesses. The trend of U.S. takeover of foreign companies, if not reversed, is at least being balanced. In 1980, for instance, there were 631 foreign acquisitions of existing American companies and 742 new businesses begun by other nationals here. This means that more than 261,000 American workers in these acquired operations may now have a "foreign" boss. Also in 1980, of the $37 billion in U.S. business assets acquired, $19.1 billion of them were in banking—of California's 20 largest banks, 9 are owned or controlled by foreign interests. But that is the free enterprise system, and it now operates globally. The reader might put this "foreign invasion" in context. Harvard professor Raymond Vernon reminds us that half of Canada's industry, a quarter of Mexico's industry, and a tenth of Europe's industry are made up of American subsidiaries. In 1981, U.S. investments abroad outweighed foreign investments in the United States—about $214 billion to $66 billion. Our point is made. Those operating in the world marketplace have to be more cosmopolitan; it simply makes good business sense! But it will not happen automatically. Personnel need training in global consciousness and intercultural skills!

STEP 3: ACTUALIZING EMPLOYEE POTENTIAL
"The organization of the future will base its control and effectiveness on the growth and accomplishments of persons within the organization." So spoke Gordon L. Lippitt when he lectured at Cornell University in 1977. This distinguished behavioral scientist predicted that tomorrow's management will act on three new concepts: of people with complex and changing needs, of power based on collaboration and reason, and of organizational values based on humanistic and democratic ideals.

The very organizational, management, and assembly processes of the industrial work culture at the very least often caused personnel to be underemployed, at the very worst caused them to be alienated on the job. The metaindustrial organization will have mainly knowledge workers with higher education and expectations. To challenge such persons, corporate environments must be more creative, and jobs must be more meaningful. People are looking for more responsibility and control over their own work space. They can be trained for effective team relations and productivity. Managers should first be behavioral models of energized, high-performing professionals. Then they will be in a position to create high-achieving teams that get excited by work and by working together. This volume has provided an overview of contemporary efforts under way to transform the workplace, resulting in improved productivity and profitability.

Kollmorgen Corporation in Stamford, Connecticut, is a good example of a high-tech company that points the way toward the emerging work culture. The major business is printed circuitry, direct-current motors, and electro-optical equipment, organized in 13 divisions in the United States and Europe. It has a decentralized structure reflecting its leaders' philosophy that people work best in small groups. When an operation grows so large that personnel can no longer identify with it, the units are split into smaller autonomous divisions or profit centers. Each team member in these mini companies is fully informed of finances and is made to feel like a partner in the enterprise, enjoying the risks and rewards of profit sharing. The corporate motto sums up this company's approach: "Freedom and respect for the individual are the best motivators, especially when innovation and growth are objectives." This is translated into practice by treating division managers like corporate presidents with direct access to the board, giving bonuses for team performance, minimizing overhead while maximizing involvement, social engineering to improve work environment, and risk management. The fact that the corporate staff comprises only 30 persons for $225 million in business tells the story.

Since the metaindustrial workforce will be more multicultural, new intercultural skills will be required for diverse personnel to share their insights and talents. With traditional barriers that constrain human contributions eroding, people will be able to serve in any level of the company or agency regardless of their race, sex, age, or vocational activity. The main criterion is competence: Can you do the job well? Are you willing and able to learn? Do you have the necessary knowledge and information? These are the issues for selection and promotion, not archaic standards of gender or color or education. Managers are learning not to sell people short. Human beings have tremendous untapped resources and capabilities—we need to provide opportunities for them to grow.

Both life and work are becoming more complex and stressful. Enlightened management can deal more effectively with this reality by involving their people more in corporate goal setting, planning, and decision making. Research indicates that most people use only 40 percent of their potential, so metaindustrial managers search for ways to release those unused, unactualized capacities. We should recognize that the industrial work culture inhibited us in many ways, and as we remove perceptual blinders and binders, people will become better able to draw on their hidden talents. Remember, for millions of years the human species was earthbound. Now that we have landed on the moon, we are revising our images of who and what we are and what we can become. Humans daily break physical records of endurance and athletic accomplishment, illustrating that we do not know the upper limits of our potential. Many physically or mentally disabled people have been rehabilitated and prepared for productive careers. With the women's liberation movement, many women have discovered new roles and capacities. But although women have moved ahead in a variety of vocational activities and at all levels of the organization, there is still much to be done to bring about true male and female equality in the workplace. In other words, the organizational culture has to be more supportive of women seeking to find themselves and to make greater corporate contributions.

Equal employment opportunity and retraining of male attitudes are not enough. Psychologist Matina Horner, president of Radcliffe College, has done extensive research on women's fear of success and their worry about the possible negative consequences of moving ahead in a career. Some women have anxiety about outperforming people they care about, especially males. Other areas that might require personal counseling or group training within the company concerned about tapping women's potential are fears about the impact of a career on personal relationships, the need to balance the various aspects of their lives, and the effects of discriminatory practices on women's self-images and expectations. The fact that women now represent 51 percent of U.S. college graduates indicates that society has a big investment in the proper utilization of this human resource.

In the case of male managers and their wives, the corporation would be wise to invest in the development of these women and to help eliminate the communication gap with their husbands. When the executive travels, it is wise to include the spouse. In a knowledge society, spouse programs should be relevant, meaningful, and informative. In 1981 in such a session for CEO wives sponsored by The Presidents Association in Carmel, California, the women provided 29 descriptions of their role, ranging from go-between and business entertainer to psychologist and counselor. Corporate funds would be well spent in meeting some of the needs of these women who have so great an impact on executive performance. Maxine Wineapple, director of New Options, Inc., provided this summary of the issues and concerns identified by these spouses: (1) being one's own person, (2) stress involved in frequent relocations, (3) being a responsible diplomat in terms of the executive's relationships with employees and business associates, (4) integrating and managing time pressures of the executive and the family, (5) resolving conflicts between the executive's needs and the spouse's or family's needs, (6) effective planning of leisure time together in a busy executive's schedule, (7) dealing with the impact of stress on the executive's health, and helping that person cope better with the pressure of tremendous responsibility, (8) developing and maintaining a personal and positive sense of identity and security, (9) improving interpersonal relations, timing, and diplomacy, and (10) creating synergy between company and family requirements, so the executive does not become a corporate bigamist!

There are many groups of unemployed or underemployed. Although lack of job opportunity, training, or motivation may be part of the problem, perceptual constraints often hold people back from making the kind of contribution that is possible for them. Their numbers include inner-city black youth, Hispanics, senior citizens, and other minorities. With American productivity falling at a rate of 0.6 percent and forecasters predicting a shortage of trained knowledge workers in the mid-eighties, we cannot afford to neglect any group in our efforts to capitalize on such precious assets. For the sake of illustration, let us focus on the aging employee and retirement programs.

Retirement at age 65 and Social Security programs are a product of the twentieth-century industrial work culture. The future metaindustrial trends were highlighted in 1981 at the White House Conference on the Aging. Forced retirement will be removed as we seek to retain competent and capable people until they are ready to disengage. In cyberculture, the average life span is likely to move up to 100 years from its current 74 years. So not only will we stay on the job longer, but the options available to us will be broader. Some senior personnel may be retrained in computer programming; many are already being brought back from retirement for this purpose. Companies will offer their respected senior workers more opportunities for part-time and at-home work. Exit planning will not be restricted to executives; it will be extended to all employees, to assist them in a planned transition from active full-time careers to meaningful, but less physically demanding, vocational activities. Corporations will set up resource networks of retired personnel, not just for social purposes, but as a human resources pool to draw on for special task forces and emergencies.

We have not been very creative in managing the aging process and its problems! We have lessons to learn from cultures that honor their elders and use retired executives as "gurus" for younger managers. Organizations cannot afford to neglect the wisdom of the experienced, for such people provide a valuable sense of history and hope.

Many people never get an opportunity to contribute to organizational growth because of stereotyping in recruitment interviews or the use of questionable standards for credentials. Because people lack certain experience or a diploma, they are often ignored by personnel departments who say, "They don't meet our standards." One wonders how many of today's personnel workers would have interviewed the two college dropouts who founded the successful Apple minicomputer company and what the traditional personnel administrator would have done with the twice-married housewife when she was divorced, had three kids, and was pregnant. This woman went back to college for a master's degree in health care. Now at the age of 47, Joy Sutherland is an executive with Northern California Research, a financial consulting, marketing analysis, placement, and headhunter service in the health care field. And suppose a young woman came West with her son and applied for a secretarial position at Copley Press in San Diego. Could one then have envisioned her becoming an executive secretary, wife of the CEO, and then, as a widow, running this string of 40 newspapers? Yet that is what happened to Helen Copley, the capable chairperson of the board for that press empire. To underscore the point of never selling people short, and of encouraging them to develop their potential, we end this discussion with an anecdotal case:

WOULD YOU HIRE THIS MAN? Born in Haskell, Texas, a little farm town. His father was a daring and pioneering oil field firefighter who deserted his wife and son. At 12 this lad worked in cotton fields and saved his money so that by 14, he owned 40 acres of land. At 19, he and a buddy owned a gas station and car dealership, which he sold to go to Texas Technological College. He switched from engineering to business administration, but dropped out in his junior year to go to Washington, D.C., to apply as a clerk for a $1,440 a year job with the Interior Department. *Would you hire this man?*

As a clerk he wrote a report on financing low-cost federal housing that was brought to the attention of a rising bureaucrat, Robert Lovett, because the report was a "minor miracle of clarity and vision." The fellow also went to night school and finished his degree. *Would you promote this man?* Well, Lovett, then assistant secretary of war, did encourage the lad to join the Army Air Corps prior to WWII. The ambitious young man was promoted to first lieutenant, put into establishing training programs and setting up management systems. By war's end, he was at 32 the nation's youngest full colonel. *Would you now hire him* as he left the military for civilian life?

From then on Charles B. Thornton's career was meteoric. He brought together a team of management specialists for the Ford Motor Company that were dubbed "The Whiz Kids" when they turned around operations from loss to profits in one year; then did the same for Hughes Aircraft by reorganization until he built it to $200 million in sales and a leader in advanced electronics. Then in the 50s he put together a group, bought a small microwave tube company as a base, and turned Litton Industries into the "General Motors of high technology."

Before his death in 1981, Tex Thornton, horseman and pilot, not only was the head of one of the nation's leading conglomerates and winner of the Presidential Medal of Freedom, but had found time to give himself to numerous civic and charitable works from Junior Achievement to the World Affairs Council.

The next time you hire a young hopeful, think of that story. One can never know just how far a person may go as a result of encouragement. A good management strategy is to treat employees at one level beyond where they now function—if their supervisors express such confidence in them, be assured such persons will strive to reach the higher level perceived for them.

My research on high achievers has convinced me that corporations have not fully utilized top-performing employees as problem solvers, trend setters, and behavior models, and for management. No wonder Peter Drucker bewails the leadership gap between what we need and what we do in our organizations. This elderly guru of management consultants advises us to reward *achievement* not just effort. Drucker suspects the 1980s and 1990s will require tough-minded managers who are willing to sacrifice 40 percent of the low-performing workforce, so the productivity of the performing 60 percent can turn the whole organization into 100 percent high performance.

Psychologist David McClelland's research on motivation confirms that any new information or skills required by an organization are best obtained by seeking those who can excel in their jobs already, which is an indication of their internal drive for achievement. If you cannot employ their actual services, at least use them as models and study their methods. McClelland's consulting firm, McBer and Company, has translated his research into a competency model for performance appraisal. The firm's approach focuses on the individual performer, not the job, seeking to identify the competencies or qualities the individual brings to the work to make that person effective. McBer researchers distinguish between the superstars and the others, average or below, to uncover the critical traits in behavior and personal attributes that discriminate between the two populations. This leads to a written competency description analyzing traits, skills, abilities, and motivational patterns. Once the data are analyzed, it is possible to train people to improve their productivity. The importance of high-performance leadership and companies has been recognized by the School of Business of San Jose University, which now offers seminars on personal and professional effectiveness.

Improved career development programs within human systems can be a useful strategy to actualize people potential. Dennis Briscoe, a professor of management at the University of San Diego, proposes this in his human resources management (HRM) checklist:

> The effective human resources manager in the 1980s will focus on the following activities:
> ○ Frequent interaction with the chief executive officer, board members, and the corporate planning committee.
> ○ Early and in-depth involvement with corporate strategic decisions on such matters as growth, diversification, mergers, new products or services, and new facilities.
> ○ Career planning for employees, including development of career paths, assessment of individual interests and goals, monitoring of job assignments for employee development, and career counseling.
> ○ Development of well-defined, visible, and enforced corporate policies on sexual harassment and employee privacy.
> ○ Development of a comprehensive (probably computerized) human resources information system for traditional functions such as

record keeping, payroll, and government reports, as well as for skills inventories, personnel development, and planning purposes.
- Development of win-win labor relations.
- Efforts to control costs of health care, pension, and other benefits through self-administration and self-funding.
- Validation of employee selection procedures, focusing on the use of the selection interview as a realistic job preview.
- Efforts to accommodate, integrate, and develop a diverse (age, sex, race, ethnic, religious, values) workforce.
- Development of an open, performance-based compensation system.
- Implementation of an employee communication program.
- Development of corporate programs for the retraining and development of employees.
- Comprehensive technical training and the use of practice-feedback techniques for supervisory training.
- Use of methods to listen to, use, and encourage employee input and participation, such as "quality circles" and the Scanlon plan.
- Development of a corporate plan for dealing with the issue of pay equity.
- Thorough job analysis for all jobs in the organization.

Briscoe agrees with top executives who think the HRM function is one of the most exciting areas for development in the business world, and that it is becoming the focus of the highest-level thinking and policy making. He predicts that by 1985, 450,000 people will be working in HRM jobs in the United States to improve work environments and technologies. He believes that human resources departments and development programs are critical for realization of personnel potential.

A recent report by S. Lusterman suggests that HRD efforts should place more emphasis on acquisition of skills in communications and negotiations to meet the growing social and political demands placed on managers. The study reported that companies are actively encouraging managers to participate in more after-work activities in political, social, and public affairs, to serve on corporate task forces to analyze public issues and help develop strategies to foster organizational interests, to utilize sabbatical opportunities to work full time on public affairs assignments outside the company, and to attend workshops that focus on the operations of the U.S. political systems.

There is growing evidence that people are using more productive energy off their jobs than on their jobs. In fact, studies indicate that many workers would prefer more free time, compensating vacations, short workdays or weeks, and alternative work schedules to pay increases. Unless corporations can provide a creative environment that energizes people, companies and government agencies may face a real challenge to retain the best personnel or to gain their real involvement. A new generation of workers is placing a higher priority on the quality of life, so that even "fast-trackers" are turning down high-powered, high-paying positions if they interfere with their personal growth and interests. The metamorphosis under way in the traditional work ethic has even hit the executive level where more managers think "the company does not own me" and are seeking greater self-actualization opportunities.

Marsha Sinetar, a California psychologist, says the "organization man" is dying and that "management by power, fear, or status will not work anymore." She adds that "a good manager in the new age asks his or her staff: 'How can we do this better? How can we achieve this goal?' " Participation, openness, explaining the rationale behind decisions, giving workers the full picture are her clues to better metaindustrial management. Since earning money is not enough, though its pursuit may motivate somewhat as a behavior reinforcement, Sinetar proposes that people also work (1) to relieve their own egocentricity, (2) to provide goods and services, and (3) to perfect themselves as human beings.* Corporations should, then, make more of that inner need that employees have to express their talents.

Group norms can become a means to foster productivity and achievement through peer pressure. An organization's potential can be realized when managers concentrate on facilitating positive, achievement-oriented group standards throughout the enterprise. For example, one of the most underutilized groups in a corporation is its board of directors. First, the CEO should not be seeking directors who will be merely "rubber stamps." Instead, the most competent community resources from a broad spectrum should be appointed and then developed into a team that will provide administration with insight, information, problem-solving skills, vision, and confrontation. The programs and services of the National Association of Corporate Directors[†] exist for such purposes.

Since the organization is an energy exchange system, it can achieve its potential only if it is adaptable and uses feedback ef-

---

* *Los Angeles Times*, January 18, 1981.
† 135 West 50th Street, New York, N.Y. 10020.

fectively. Dr. Kurt Motamedi of Oregon State University's School of Business considers *adaptability* to be a system's ability to sense and understand its external environment, in order to alter both its internal and external environments. *Copability* is a skill to be developed not only by individuals but also by institutions. It is the ability to conserve a sense of identity in the midst of stress and strain, while planning appropriate change in attitudes, constructs, skills, and processes. It requires integration of and balance between adapting and coping to prevent us from becoming too inward or too outward in focusing our energies.

Human capital is a precious resource to be channeled, conserved, and optimized; it must not be underused or misused. It is not an inexhaustible resource. It is the source of an organization's development and creativity. Therefore, capable personnel should be encouraged to ever greater contribution and responsibility and accomplishment. Only then will our species be able to explore the universe and industrialize space for the benefit of all.

STEP 4: BECOMING MORE PROFESSIONAL MANAGERS

Addressing an assembly of MIS executives from N.V. Philips in Eindhoven, The Netherlands, Dr. Dorothy L. Harris startled the audience. This associate dean at the School of Business and Management, United States International University, San Diego, stated simply: "You are the new priesthood, the new educators, the new creators of culture." Managers in multinational corporations have an enormous influence not only on the lives of their fellow employees, but in the worldwide communities in which their companies operate. Transnational leaders of this type function in the global marketplace. They are also deeply involved in community development and the process of human emergence.

At a time when many social institutions seem to be inadequate, people look increasingly to corporations not only to provide jobs but to exercise social responsibility and leadership. But business is people, coming together to voluntarily accomplish what they could not do alone. Business produces a unique synergy between and among investors, suppliers, employees, customers, and even neighbors to achieve something that is useful, productive, and profitable. Through the free enterprise system, we allocate human and material resources to meet human needs and serve a common good. But to succeed, business requires an informed, competent, and cosmopolitan management. Dr. Neill

Miller, a psychological consultant from Philadelphia, uses the concept of *omega leadership* to describe those persons who see themselves as managers, not technicians. To Miller this means professional managers who use power constructively, seek solutions to problems, insist on people growth, share success, reward achievement, strive for personal accomplishment, instill respect, and foster interdependence, not dependence. But what is professional management and how do we learn it?

An ideal is offered in this sage comment of James L. Hayes, former president of American Management Associations: "Management is the magic of combining individuals who are fulfilling their potential as human beings into groups that enjoy success in achievement." To do this well, Hayes believes that managers must first develop themselves and then develop others in the organization by inspiring, motivating, guiding, and even teaching. Robert Townsend, a successful CEO and the author of *Up the Organization*, adds this dimension to the concept: "We need human, broad-ranged, compassionate, but tough leaders, as well as managers." Townsend maintains that management could become a profession if there were a code of ethics and an agreed-upon body of principles. Dr. John S. Fielden, dean of the College of Commerce of the University of Alabama, contends that management is an art as much as a science, for its practice requires "so many capacities, like risk taking, one's own emotional stability, one's self-concept, one's will to manage, one's ability to communicate and interrelate with people."

Throughout this book, we have provided new perspectives on the functions of management. Peter Drucker, addressing the International Management Congress in Tokyo some years back, got the audience's attention by stating that the major assumptions on which both the theory and practice of management had been based for the last half century were rapidly becoming obsolete. Traditional organizations and management educators do not like to face that reality. To prevent further managerial obsolescence, Drucker proposed some new assumptions on which to construct a more relevant management system:

Management's task is to make knowledge more productive. The capital resource of a developed economy is the application of knowledge in concepts, ideas, and theories. To make knowledge productive, managers today should emphasize quality applications, encourage knowledge workers to plan for themselves, and be prepared to accept a variety of ways to "get the job done."

Management is both science and a human art in its concepts and principles, tools, and techniques, language and discipline. But management is also a culture and a system of values and beliefs. It is the means by which society makes productive its values and beliefs, its traditions and heritages. Management may well be considered the bridge between a civilization that is becoming worldwide, and a culture which expresses divergence.... Management must become the instrument through which cultural diversity can be made to serve the common purposes of mankind.

May these wise and profound "Druckerisms" inspire readers to the creation of the new metaindustrial assumptions of management that will lead to the new managerial theories and practices appropriate to the twenty-first century!

Today's businesses in new technologies are the laboratory for the experience of tomorrow's management. But if these businesses are to create more futuristic, cosmopolitan managers, they have to put their role in the larger context outlined by Drucker in his five assumptions. They require a new image of managers in order for them to become more professional in striving to fulfill their new role. To repeat Dorothy L. Harris, managers are the new creators of culture, the new educators. For managers to achieve their potential in the metaindustrial work culture, their professional development should encompass: (1) continuing education, formally and informally, in diverse subjects and in employing the latest in educational and communication technology to facilitate rapid learning, (2) management education that is both cognitive and affective, self and group, as well as comparative and cross-cultural, learning, (3) adult education that improves both thought and problem-solving processes, that draws on information and skills in business and economics, science and technology, political and behavioral sciences.

To live up to society's great expectations for corporation leaders, tomorrow's managers will be persons of exceptional competence and breadth! Managers will be superb practitioners of *synergy*—capable of promoting cooperative action among diverse and disparate peoples or groups. The objective is to increase effectiveness by sharing perceptions, insights, and knowledge in order to solve today's problems. Only then can we capitalize on people's differences by combining their talents and experience through collaborative effort. For this to happen, the professional development of managers will have to include training in synergistic skills and team building.

CAPSULE CONCLUSION—OR BEGINNING

We began this chapter with a description of a new industry involved in scientific cloning of more nutritious plants that may help the human family to satisfy its food needs in the future. It was but one illustration of the new technologies that are changing our lives, as well as the way we do business. As this is being written, Japan has announced a telecommunications innovation—remote signaling by use of fiber optics. The new system will enable users to exercise "telecontrol" at a distance from where the action is actually taking place. A twenty-first-century communication network is already under development at Nippon Telephone and Telegraph Corporation. It will enable utilities to read meters automatically, workers to turn on the ovens in their homes as they depart from the office, students to learn at home what is being taught in classrooms many miles away, travelers to make hotel and transportation arrangements, and people to order groceries for home delivery. Such advances demonstrate our thesis that change is the only constant, that technological inventions will continually alter commercial transactions. The emerging technologies will be the driving force of the metaindustrial work culture, accelerating the psychosocial evolution of the past three centuries.

In the humanization of cyberculture, and the transformation of existing enterprises, the focus of the next few decades will be on *transformational management.* As we go through the transition to metaindustrial organizations, managers will have to lead in the creation of new, more appropriate organizational structures and processes. With more diversification in products and services, and increased acquisitions and mergers, mission and goal coordination will require better strategic planning, as well as application of cross-cultural competencies. To ensure improved performance and productivity in turbulent times, managers will have to learn that workers are colleagues who want to be involved. Human energy, both psychic and physical, is a precious resource to be conserved and channeled toward achievable objectives. Only as we appreciate the interdependence of human systems will we learn to cooperate, so that in the next century we can take advantage of the wonders of the universe! Only then will we begin to actualize the upper limits of human potential!

The message in this book is simple, but readers must translate into action the information and insights shared here. To create the new world of tomorrow will demand new ways of thinking and acting. More specifically, it will require a new, more enlightened and more sophisticated management. If leaders are to inspire and energize others, they themselves need to be farsighted and to plan for future eventualities. Before we undertake space industrialization, today's managers need to comprehend the significance of the words that the President of the United States inserted into the Voyager space capsule before it was launched into outer space in 1977:

> This Voyager spacecraft was constructed by the United States of America. We are a community of 240 million human beings among the more than 4 billion who inhabit the planet Earth. We human beings are still divided into nation states, but these states are rapidly becoming a single global civilization.
> We cast this message into the cosmos. It is likely to survive a billion years into our future, when our civilization is profoundly altered and the surface of the Earth may be vastly changed. Of the 200 billion stars in the Milky Way galaxy, some—perhaps many—may have inhabited planets and spacefaring civilizations. If one such civilization intercepts Voyager and can understand these recorded contents, here is our message:
>> This is a present from a small distant world, a token of our sounds, our science, our images, our music, our thoughts and our feelings. We are attempting to survive our time so we may live into yours. We hope someday, having solved the problems we face, to join a community of galactic civilizations. This record represents our hope and our determination, and our good will in a vast and awesome universe.

THE BEGINNING, NOT THE END!

The old foundations of scientific thought are becoming unintelligible. Time, space, matter, structure, pattern, function, etc.—all require reinterpretation!

—Alfred North Whitehead

APPENDIX A Organizational Culture Survey Instrument

This questionnaire was developed by the author in his consulting practice with several corporations and government agencies. It appears in *Managing Cultural Differences,* written with Dr. Robert T. Moran, and is reprinted here with permission of Gulf Publishing Company. Permission is granted for researchers and consultants to reproduce and use this inventory as long as full credit is given to the author and the source, and as long as findings are shared with the originator: Dr. Philip R. Harris, Harris International, 2702 Costebelle Drive, La Jolla, Calif. 92037. It is my hope that others will improve on the arrangement of the questionnaire and contribute to its standardization. One doctoral student is now using it in his dissertation on a multinational corporation.

ORGANIZATIONAL CULTURE SURVEY INSTRUMENT

Instructions
This questionnaire should be as complete and authentic as possible. It provides you with an opportunity for: (a) giving feedback *anonymously* to foster your organization's development, (b) evaluating its key management, including yourself, and (c) understanding better your organizational environment, whether at home or abroad.

There are 6 major sections to this inquiry, and a total of 99 items seeking your opinion. A maximum of 50 minutes should be allowed for thoughtful completion of this inventory. Please consider your answers carefully for each point. Your first effort at responding should reflect your spontaneous reactions and thoughts on how you view your organization's culture from your position. If time permits, review your replies, and make changes if necessary.

Please check the appropriate categories that best depict your response to the inquiry. Where necessary, *fill in* the information requested.

This analysis will be for the total organization ( )
or for the subsystem of which you are a part ( )
(e.g. division, department, subsidiary)

The majority of questions are to be answered by checking one column in a 7-point scale, with the lowest evaluations on the left or low side of the continuum, average in the middle area, and higher assessments on the right side. The exceptions are questions 23, 68, 69–81, which require a checking of the appropriate category provided.

Organizational Diagnosis
On a scale of *lowest* (1) to *highest* (7), circle your rating of your organization's effectiveness or ineffectiveness on the following items. On question 23, simply mark the appropriate category for your response.

Overall Analysis   *Effectiveness*
1. The goals/objectives of this organization are clearly defined and regularly reviewed.   1 2 3 4 5 6 7
2. Managers and supervisors at all levels have the opportunity to participate in this process of setting goals/objectives.   1 2 3 4 5 6 7
3. The organization has mechanisms for periodic evaluation of its achievement of goals/objectives.   1 2 3 4 5 6 7
4. Key management devotes adequate time to advanced, dynamic planning, and involves subordinates in the process as appropriate.   1 2 3 4 5 6 7
5. Key management in this organization supports high achievers among employees.   1 2 3 4 5 6 7
6. Management regularly reviews the assignment of roles and responsibilities, as well as the delegation of authority for performance.   1 2 3 4 5 6 7
7. Key managers ensure that adequate personnel development and training are available for employees to carry out assigned tasks.   1 2 3 4 5 6 7

8. Management has an adequate system for regular and meaningful performance evaluation of employees. 1 2 3 4 5 6 7
9. The organization emphasizes cooperation as an operational norm. 1 2 3 4 5 6 7
10. The organization demonstrates commitment to providing satisfactory service to its clients/customers. 1 2 3 4 5 6 7
11. The organization utilizes well the human energies of its workforce. 1 2 3 4 5 6 7
12. The organization rewards personnel on the basis of merit and performance, encouraging competence. 1 2 3 4 5 6 7
13. The work climate encourages employees to do their best and perform well. 1 2 3 4 5 6 7
14. The atmosphere in the organization encourages people to be open and candid with management. 1 2 3 4 5 6 7
15. The organization treats employees equally, regardless of their sex or race. 1 2 3 4 5 6 7

Organizational Communication
16. Are you satisfied with the present state of organizational communications? 1 2 3 4 5 6 7
17. Do you think the communication between management and yourself is adequate? 1 2 3 4 5 6 7
18. Do you believe that organizational communications between central headquarters' staff and field personnel are satisfactory? 1 2 3 4 5 6 7
19. Do you believe that in your area of responsibility, communication is satisfactory between you and your subordinates? 1 2 3 4 5 6 7
20. Do you think there is adequate written communication in the organization? 1 2 3 4 5 6 7
21. Do you think there is adequate oral and group communication? 1 2 3 4 5 6 7
22. Are you satisfied that adequate communication is provided about organizational changes? 1 2 3 4 5 6 7
23. Your communication with various levels of management around you is *largely*
downward ( )   upward ( )   circular ( )

Management Team Evaluation
In terms of upper-level management, the emphasis as I evaluate it is:

24. Clear organizational objectives and targets. 1 2 3 4 5 6 7
25. Competency in themselves and their subordinates. 1 2 3 4 5 6 7
26. Providing a leadership model for subordinates. 1 2 3 4 5 6 7
27. Continuous, planned organizational renewal. 1 2 3 4 5 6 7
28. High productivity standards. 1 2 3 4 5 6 7
29. High service standards. 1 2 3 4 5 6 7
30. Experimenting with new ideas and approaches. 1 2 3 4 5 6 7
31. Encouragement of human resources development. 1 2 3 4 5 6 7
32. Coordination and cooperation in and among the organizational work units. 1 2 3 4 5 6 7
33. Conducting meaningful and productive meetings. 1 2 3 4 5 6 7
34. Confronting conflict directly and settling disagreements rather than avoiding or ignoring it. 1 2 3 4 5 6 7
35. Promoting creative thinkers and innovative performers. 1 2 3 4 5 6 7
36. Always *trying* to do things better. 1 2 3 4 5 6 7
37. Equal employment opportunity and affirmative action. 1 2 3 4 5 6 7
38. Creating a motivating environment for employees. 1 2 3 4 5 6 7
39. Open, authentic communications with each other and their subordinates. 1 2 3 4 5 6 7
40. Seeking suggestions and ideas from employees and the public (feedback). 1 2 3 4 5 6 7
41. Clarifying organizational roles and responsibilities so there is no confusion or overlap. 1 2 3 4 5 6 7
42. Teamwork and collaboration within and among upper-level management. 1 2 3 4 5 6 7
43. Effective concern for training subordinates to perform competently. 1 2 3 4 5 6 7
44. Willingness to consider innovations proposed to increase organizational effectiveness. 1 2 3 4 5 6 7

45. Sharing of power, authority, and decision making with lower-level management. 1 2 3 4 5 6 7
46. Policies and procedures that counteract absenteeism, slackness, and unproductivity. 1 2 3 4 5 6 7
47. Management of responsibility on the part of employees they supervise. 1 2 3 4 5 6 7
48. Problem solving and confronting issues. 1 2 3 4 5 6 7
49. Constantly improving working conditions, both physical and psychological. 1 2 3 4 5 6 7
50. Consistency in organizational policies and procedures. 1 2 3 4 5 6 7

Work Group Assessment
Please answer this section in terms of the work group you manage. That is, respond in terms of personnel who report to you or for whom you are responsible.

51. The atmosphere and interpersonal relations in my group are friendly and cooperative. 1 2 3 4 5 6 7
52. The members encourage one another's best efforts, reinforcing successful behavior. 1 2 3 4 5 6 7
53. The group organizes and problem-solves effectively. 1 2 3 4 5 6 7
54. The members maintain adequate standards of performance. 1 2 3 4 5 6 7
55. The group is open to and ready for organizational changes. 1 2 3 4 5 6 7
56. The members work effectively as a team. 1 2 3 4 5 6 7
57. The group communicates well within our work unit. 1 2 3 4 5 6 7
58. The group communicates satisfactorily with other work units. 1 2 3 4 5 6 7
59. The members provide group input and may participate in the management process as appropriate. 1 2 3 4 5 6 7
60. The group makes effective use of available equipment and resources (both material and human). 1 2 3 4 5 6 7
61. The members generally demonstrate pride in themselves and in their work. 1 2 3 4 5 6 7
62. The group actively seeks to utilize the skills and abilities of its members. 1 2 3 4 5 6 7

63. The members do not feel constrained by rules, regulations, and red tape in accomplishing their work. 1 2 3 4 5 6 7
64. The group is dynamic in its approaches and activities; that is, the work environment "turns people on." 1 2 3 4 5 6 7
65. The members of this group are not characterized by conformity and dependency. 1 2 3 4 5 6 7
66. The group has a record of consistent accomplishment in the organization. 1 2 3 4 5 6 7
67. The members in my work group generally exercise responsibility and achievement. 1 2 3 4 5 6 7

Managerial Self-Perception
68. As a leader in this organization, check the words or word combinations that best describe your management approach:

   ( ) idealistic   ( ) realistic
   ( ) innovative   ( ) pragmatic
   ( ) cooperative   ( ) individualistic
   ( ) task-oriented   ( ) sensitive
   ( ) change maker   ( ) change reactor
   ( ) hard-nosed   ( ) imaginative
   ( ) inspiring   ( ) participative
   ( ) traditional   ( ) futuristic

Managerial Self-Perception (check appropriate category)

	Rarely	Sometimes	Usually
69. Do you seek out and use improved work methods?			
70. Does your managerial performance demonstrate sufficient skill in ○ administration ○ human relations ○ obtaining results			
71. Do you reinforce and support positive behavior and performance in your subordinates?			
72. Do you actively encourage your subordinates to make the most of their potential?			

	Rarely	Sometimes	Usually

73. Are you willing to take reasonable risks in the management of your work units?
74. Do you take responsibility to ensure that the employees you manage make their best contribution toward achieving organizational goals and production targets?
75. Do your key subordinates really know where you stand on controversial organizational issues?
76. Do you demonstrate by example personal standards of competence and productivity?
77. Are you generally objective, friendly but businesslike in dealing with employees?
78. Are you doing something specific for your own personal and professional development?
79. Do you take responsibility to seek change in organizational norms, values, and standards when these are not relevant and need updating?
80. Please read back to yourself the above twelve statements. In light of the demands of modern management and employee expectations, how would you rate the above evaluations of your leadership role?

    Please check one: Inadequate ( )   Adequate ( )
81. A study by Michael Maccoby describes the new postindustrial organizational leader in this way: A gamesman, "in contrast to the jungle-fighter industrialist of the past, is driven not to build or to preside over empires, but to organize winning teams. Unlike the security-seeking organization man, he is excited by the chance to cut deals and to gamble." The author also states that such new leaders in top management are more cooperative and less hardened than the classical autocrats, as well as less dependent than the typical bureaucrats. This sociologist suggests that the new leader is more detached and emotionally inaccessible than his predecessors, yet troubled that his work develops his head but not his heart.

How does this description of the emerging executive fit you? (check one)
This is comparable to the way I am/feel ( ).
I do not identify with this new type of manager ( ).

Organizational Relations
Please check the category that best describes the present situation for you.

82. Employees generally trust top management.   1 2 3 4 5 6 7
83. Employees usually "level" in their communications with management, providing authentic feedback.   1 2 3 4 5 6 7
84. Employees usually are open and authentic in their work relations.   1 2 3 4 5 6 7
85. If employees have a conflict or disagreement with management, they usually work it out directly, or seek mediation.   1 2 3 4 5 6 7
86. When employees receive administrative directives or decisions with which they do not agree they usually conform without dissent.   1 2 3 4 5 6 7
87. Older managers are threatened by younger, competent staff members or subordinates who may have more knowledge, information, or education.   1 2 3 4 5 6 7
88. Managers are able to interact effectively with minority and female peers or subordinates.   1 2 3 4 5 6 7
89. Managers really try to be fair and just with employees, using competence only as their evaluative criterion of performance.   1 2 3 4 5 6 7
90. Many managers have generally "retired" on the job, and are indifferent to needs for organizational renewal.   1 2 3 4 5 6 7
91. Employees have opportunities to clarify changing roles and relationships.   1 2 3 4 5 6 7
92. Is organization concerned about the needs of people as well as getting the task done?   1 2 3 4 5 6 7
93. Organization encourages and assists employees in the development of community relations.   1 2 3 4 5 6 7

Organizational Changes

94. The organization is able to adapt to the dramatic shifts and changes under way in society and the larger culture. 1 2 3 4 5 6 7
95. The organization is able to handle the new demands made upon it as a result of the changes in top administration and management emphasis. 1 2 3 4 5 6 7
96. The organization does seek adequate input from employees on those changes that affect them, or that they are to implement. 1 2 3 4 5 6 7
97. The organization is able to deal effectively with the new kind of person coming into your workforce and management. 1 2 3 4 5 6 7
98. The organization has changed its management priorities and approaches with regard to scarce resources, as well as environmental and ecological concerns. 1 2 3 4 5 6 7
99. The organization is innovative in finding ways to improve the institutional environment. 1 2 3 4 5 6 7

Note: Please recognize that cultural factors influenced the way the above questions were constructed, and the way in which you responded. However, this evaluation can provide insight into your organizational culture in terms of Western perspective and future trend criteria.

APPENDIX B Management Communications Inventory

Here is a checklist for an appraisal of yourself as a communicator. Simply place a mark next to the category that best describes your present approach to the communication process.

You may wish to share your evaluation with a colleague or relative to ascertain whether your assessment is confirmed or not. When you have identified areas for improvement, develop a strategy to increase your communication skills.

In communicating, I project a positive image of myself (e.g., voice, bearing, appearance, etc.).
____ Seldom   ____ Occasionally   ____ Often   ____ Always

I try to understand and enter into the receiver's frame of reference (e.g., empathetic, restate his/her point of view, etc.).
____ Seldom   ____ Occasionally   ____ Often   ____ Always

I establish eye contact with the receiver.
____ Seldom   ____ Occasionally   ____ Often   ____ Always

I communicate respect for the receiver of my message (e.g., listening carefully, not making him/her feel inferior, etc.).
____ Seldom   ____ Occasionally   ____ Often   ____ Always

I use as many media as necessary to get my meaning across (e.g., communication symbols that appeal to several senses).
____ Seldom   ____ Occasionally   ____ Often   ____ Always

I am aware of my own inner state, which conditions my communication (e.g., feelings, needs, motives, assumptions, prejudices, etc.).
____ Seldom   ____ Occasionally   ____ Often   ____ Always

I try not to let emotionally loaded words used by the other person distort my responses.
____ Seldom   ____ Occasionally   ____ Often   ____ Always

I try to listen not only to facts and ideas (cognitive data), but to the feelings that the other reveals.
  ___ Seldom   ___ Occasionally   ___ Often   ___ Always

I try to be open to new ideas and constructive criticism regardless of the source.
  ___ Seldom   ___ Occasionally   ___ Often   ___ Always

I am willing to share the other person's views to the point of personal change if it is warranted.
  ___ Seldom   ___ Occasionally   ___ Often   ___ Always

I try to be authentic in my communication and level with others when it is appropriate.
  ___ Seldom   ___ Occasionally   ___ Often   ___ Always

I try to reduce the physical and psychological distance between me and my listeners.
  ___ Seldom   ___ Occasionally   ___ Often   ___ Always

I check to ascertain whether my real meaning is understood.
  ___ Seldom   ___ Occasionally   ___ Often   ___ Always

I allow the other person to ask questions and seek clarification regarding my message sending.
  ___ Seldom   ___ Occasionally   ___ Often   ___ Always

I ask questions and seek clarification during the communication exchange.
  ___ Seldom   ___ Occasionally   ___ Often   ___ Always

In speaking, I try
  to project my voice clearly.
    ___ Seldom   ___ Occasionally   ___ Often   ___ Always
  to vary the tone of my voice.
    ___ Seldom   ___ Occasionally   ___ Often   ___ Always
  to say what I really mean.
    ___ Seldom   ___ Occasionally   ___ Often   ___ Always
  to use a vocabulary that is understandable to the receiver.
    ___ Seldom   ___ Occasionally   ___ Often   ___ Always
  to be concise.
    ___ Seldom   ___ Occasionally   ___ Often   ___ Always

I follow up on the communication to see whether agreements or instructions are carried out.
  ___ Seldom   ___ Occasionally   ___ Often   ___ Always

Reprinted from *Improving Management Communication Skills* by D.L. and P.R. Harris. This manual and cassette system are available through EDUPAC, 231 Norfolk St., Walpole, Mass. 02081.

APPENDIX C Change Inventory for Leaders

Note: On the accompanying 5-point scale to the right of each of the 15 items below, please circle the number that best expresses your attitude or approach at this moment. For effective leadership, the choices should fall in the last two columns.

Never / Rarely / Sometimes / Usually / Always

Part I
1. **Openness**—willing to consider new ideas and people of differing opinions; tentative in communications, rather than dogmatic or closed-minded in one's approach.   1 2 3 4 5
2. **Flexibility**—adaptable to new people, situations, information and developments; able to handle the unexpected and to shift position; spontaneous in responding to the "here and now" data and experiences.   1 2 3 4 5
3. **Sensitiveness**—conscious of what is happening to oneself and others in the communications about the change and its effects; aware of the needs and feelings of others because of the proposed change; able to respond empathetically.   1 2 3 4 5
4. **Creativeness**—respond with resourcefulness to new people and situations; avoid stereotype answers and solutions; exercise initiative, imagination and innovativeness.   1 2 3 4 5
5. **Person-centered**—concerned more about people than task or mere progress; care what happens to people involved in the change; support, encourage, inform and involve people in decisions for change they will be expected to implement; respect right of dissent.   1 2 3 4 5

| | Never | Rarely | Sometimes | Usually | Always |

6. **Goal-oriented planning**—develop a case for change with others which takes into account long-range objectives, while developing a plan with different stages or targets and short-term steps to accomplish planned change; communicate these purposes and plans to all involved; state goals in terms that have positive value to those affected.   1 2 3 4 5

7. **Group understanding**—possess knowledge of the group process and skills in group dynamics; analyze the driving and resisting forces within the group relative to the proposed change; understand the character, structure, needs and wants of the group or organization to be affected by the change; involve entire group in change process.   1 2 3 4 5

8. **Communicativeness**—promote open, circular interaction; able to analyze and clarify the problem and reasons for change; motivate members to desire to change and to use the available resources; develop a helping relationship with others so they can accept and live with the change.   1 2 3 4 5

Part II
Relative to your capacity to cope more effectively with rapid change in your personal and organizational life, indicate your present typical response by checking the category in the right-hand columns which is most appropriate for each descriptive item in the paragraphs on the left. Be self-critical.

9. **Changing image**—possess the capacity to reevaluate concept of self based on new feedback, so as to expand my self-image; fluid in my self-conception, amplifying my sense of identity as a result of new encounters and experiences.   1 2 3 4 5

Change Inventory for Leaders

	Never	Rarely	Sometimes	Usually	Always

10. **Changing construct**—willing to review periodically the way I read meaning in my life; flexible in my attitudes and perceptions, so as to make "new sense" out of added inputs and insights; able to break out of "old mindsets" and to develop new rationale; able to accept, at times, inconsistencies and discontinuity in my life. 1 2 3 4 5
11. **Changing values**—able to sense new needs in myself and others, to develop new and changing life values, to abandon past, ready-made values and ideals, to revise expectations of self and others; and as a result, willing to reexamine norms or standards which I have set for myself and others and to develop new ones as appropriate. 1 2 3 4 5
12. **Changing role**—willing to have an unclear, hazy role in life or an organization—one that is dynamic and responds to current relevant needs; able to live with a role definition which is open-ended and subject to continuous clarification; accept new role definitions for women, parents and spouses, colleagues, professionals and other career people. 1 2 3 4 5
13. **Changing society**—able to be comfortable with impermanence or a lack of structure; capable of coping with constant alteration and perpetual transition; willing to live in changing times, without the traditional stability and reference groups; able to make the most of the present moment—the "here and now"—to be "existential" or to "hang loose;" ready to combat unwarranted resistance to change in myself and the communities in which I participate. 1 2 3 4 5
14. **Changing goals**—concerned about actualizing my own and others' potential, as well as increasing the levels of awareness and consciousness in both; seek improvement in my capacity for feeling, and intuitiveness, for creating and risk

	Never Rarely Sometimes Usually Always

taking; desire more knowledge and education for personal and professional development; willing to provide cultural leadership by experimenting with new lifestyles of adaptation to the demands of rapid change.   1 2 3 4 5

15. **Changing lifestyle**—willing to be more transient and mobile within and among organizations; able to change jobs and locations when appropriate; capable of abandoning old relationships when necessary, and to search for new, more meaningful ones; willing to reject past stereotypes of other people, especially various minorities or foreigners; able to participate in team efforts to solve increasingly complex problems; able to cope with stress and urban crowding, lack of privacy, noise, pollution and other modern discomforts, while seeking to improve these situations; capable of enduring discontinuities and disconnections in my life.   1 2 3 4 5

APPENDIX D Intercultural Relations Inventory

One approach to appreciating cultural differences is through a culture contrast exercise. Managers and other leaders can use this approach to study their own cultural background and compare it with that of subordinates, peers, customers, suppliers, and so on. Project members can do the same with other members of their team. However, this inventory is most advantageous when used in dealing with foreign workers, whether overseas or at home, to better understand oneself and the person(s) of a foreign culture. It is also useful in domestic operations with persons of different ethnic background or of the opposite sex.

It was first used on an Office of Naval Research project with the U.S. Marine Corps, and subsequently with managers in many human systems. It is reprinted from *Improving Leadership Effectiveness.** It is related to the cultural paradigm presented in Chapter 2 of this book. Researchers and consultants are welcome to reproduce and use it for training and study as long as full credit is given to the author and the source. The reader may wish to improve on the basic inquiry and expand the categories.

INTERCULTURAL RELATIONS INVENTORY
General Directions: Select *one* of the two situations noted below. If you engage in this exercise alone, you will have to check out your findings with another person from the target culture you choose or seek culture-specific information in a library or book. It is preferable to use this instrument in a group situation, possibly in a training session or staff meeting, and to share insights.

Should you follow the latter procedure, the process is as follows:

---

* By P.R. Harris. Available from Harris International Box 2321, La Jolla, CA 92038

1. Fill in the target culture you are studying _____.
2. Then complete the inventory on the eight categories for culture contrasting. On the left side fill out any information you now possess about the culture that is different from your own for each item.
3. Go back and do the same under each of the ten headings with reference to your own native culture.
4. Through group discussion, share your findings with other members of your group or team.
5. Compare observations and try to come to some group consensus about each of the ten items for both cultural backgrounds.
6. Select a recorder and have the summary put on a flip chart or newsprint for all to see and review.
7. If a larger audience is involved, small-group reports can be made in a cluster session.
8. Discuss inaccuracies in the report, stereotyping, and insufficient data, and encourage participants to seek out further culture specifics.

Situation One
You are a manager from the mainstream American (Canadian, or whatever) culture. Contrast your background with that of a minority employee or customer from a microculture within your country. The same approach can be used to compare the cultural backgrounds of males and females within the same macroculture. The point is to try to place yourself in the "life space" or "private world" of the other and to list the differences between their cultural perceptions and style and your own.

Situation Two
You are a manager or sales representative abroad. Contrast your macroculture with the people in the host culture. Based on information you possess or suppositions, describe the culture of the "natives" in comparison to your own. The same situation can be utilized to contrast your own home culture with a foreign worker's or visitor's culture.

Intercultural Relations Inventory

*Culture A*_____ *Culture B*_____
Foreign/Minority (*his/her* *Local/Majority* (*your back-*
background) *ground*)

I. Communication Style (nonverbal and verbal, as well as the language of the personnel)

_____ _____
_____ _____
_____
                         (additions, if necessary, on back of sheet)

II. Food and Diet

_____ _____
_____ _____
_____ _____

III. Clothing (especially off-duty dress)

_____ _____
_____ _____

IV. Appearance (hair, beard, etc.)

_____ _____
_____ _____

V. Time Sense (attention span)

_____ _____
_____ _____

VI. Values and Standards

_____ _____
_____ _____
_____ _____

VII. Work Habits and Practices

VIII. Attitudes/Practices with "Minority" Workers in the Culture—by reason of sex, class, caste, color, etc.

IX. Family and Marriage

X. Amount of Information/Education

XI. Other's Customs, Traditions, and Beliefs

XII. What Problems or Challenges Do You See in This Relationship Because of Some of the Differences That You Have Noted Above?

APPENDIX E Leadership Motivation Inventory

A. Please place an X next to the five items below which you believe are *most important* in motivating you to do better work:

(P)
1. Assurance of regular employment. ____
2. Satisfactory physical working conditions. ____
3. Suitable rest periods and coffee breaks. ____
4. Adequate vacation arrangements and holidays. ____

(S)
5. Good pay. ____
6. Having an efficient supervisor who tells me exactly what's expected. ____
7. Clear organizational objectives so that I know where I stand. ____
8. A good performance rating so I know where I stand. ____
9. Pensions and other fringe benefits (insurance, *et al.*). ____
10. A written job description which tells what's expected of me. ____
11. The avoidance of disciplining for doing an inadequate job. ____
12. Maintenance of adequate living standards for my family. ____

13. Means for knowing what is going on in the organization (inclusion). ____
14. Being told by my boss that I am doing a good job. ____
15. Getting along with others on the job by being cooperative. ____

(B) 16. Participation in management activities (e.g., attending staff meetings). ____
17. Receiving appreciation feedback when work is well performed. ____
18. Being kept informed on what's happening in the organization. ____
19. The support received from fellow workers in a work unit. ____

20. Means for promotion and advancement. ____
21. Feeling my job is important. ____
22. Respect of me as a person and/or a professional at my job. ____

(E) 23. Chance to turn out quality work. ____
24. Opportunity to gain status in the organization. ____
25. Means of achieving and proving myself. ____
26. Obtaining more freedom and independence on my job. ____

27. Opportunity to do challenging and meaningful work. ____

(A) 28. Chance for self-development and improvement. ____
29. Opportunity to experience sense of accomplishment. ____
30. Others: _____ ____

B. Place a check (√) now next to five other items which you consider to be of secondary importance in motivating you to do better work.

Note: Items 1-4 (P) refer to concerns that fit best at the first level of the Maslow hierarchy, Physiological or survival needs; 5-12 responses are seemingly in the category of Safety or security needs; 13-19 to Belonging or affection needs; 20-26 to Esteem or ego needs; and items 27-29 (A) to Self-Actualization or fulfillment needs. Refer back to Table 3 (Chapter 10) to compare your results with the motivation of other managers.

Source Notes and References

Agryris, C., in *Behavioral Science: Concepts and Management Applications*. New York: The Conference Board, 1971, pp. 28-29.

Bell, L., "Designing a Village in Space." *The Futurist*, October 1981, Vol. 15, No. 5, pp. 36-46.

Bertalanffy, L. von, *General Systems Theory: Foundations, Development, Applications*. New York: George Braziller, 1966.

Black, K., and R.O. Wilson, "The Environment of Management in the Future," in L. Benton, ed., *Management for the Future*. New York: McGraw-Hill, 1978, p. 10.

Bozzone, V., "The Management Cycle—Part I." *Northeast Training News*, December 1980, pp. 18-19.

Brancatelli, J., "Office of the Future—The People Factor." Special East/West Network Report Supplement, *United Mainliner*, October 1981.

Brevoord, C., "Effective Management in the Future," in L. Benton, ed., *Management for the Future*. New York: McGraw-Hill, 1978, pp. 31-33.

Briscoe, D.R., "HRM Comes of Age." *University of San Diego Newsletter*, Autumn 1981.

Caplin, Donald, "Corporate Culture: Training Problems and Prospects." *Northeast Training News*, August 1981, pp. 9-11.

Center for Management Research, *Strategic Planning for Human Resources: 1980 and Beyond*. (Report available from Opinion Research Corporation, 850 Boylston Street, Chestnut Hill, Mass. 02167.)

Christopher, W.F., "Too Few Results from Too Much Planning? Change the System." *Business Tomorrow*, June 1980, pp. 2-3.

Coleman, E.R., ed., *Information and Society*. Basking Ridge, N.J.: AT&T Corporate/Planning Emerging Issues Group, 1980.

Coleman, E.R., ed., *Labor Issues of the '80s*. Basking Ridge, N.J.: AT&T Corporate Planning/Emerging Issues Group, 1980.

Cornish, E., ed., *Through the '80s: Thinking Globally, Acting Locally*. Washington, D.C.: World Future Society (4916 St. Elmo Avenue), 1980.

Cribbin, J., *Leadership: Strategies for Organizational Effectiveness*. New York: AMACOM, 1981.

Devanna, M.A., C. Fombrun, and N. Tichy, "Human Resources Management: A Strategic Perspective." *Organizational Dynamics,* Vol. 9, No. 3, Winter 1981, p. 55.

Diebold, J., *Beyond Automation.* New York: McGraw-Hill, 1964.

Document No. EC42 Conference Proceedings, *Cohabitation of Centralized and Distributed Processing,* March 20-22, 1979. (Available from The Diebold Research Program—Europe, Sutherland House, 5/6 Argyll St., London, W1V 1AD, England.)

Doyle, M., "Why Your Organization Needs an Internal Collaborative Problem-Solving Group." *Training/HRD,* October 1979, pp. 74-78.

Drucker, P.F., "Managing for Tomorrow" Film Series, *BNAC Communicator.* Rockville, Md.: BNA Communications, Fall 1981, p. 104.

Engelberger, J.F., *Robotics in Practice: Management and Applications of Industrial Robots.* New York: AMACOM, 1980.

Evans, C., *The Micro Millennium.* New York: Viking Press, 1980.

Fabun, D., ed., "The Corporation as a Creative Environment." *Kaiser News,* No. 1, 1972.

Ferguson, M., *The Aquarian Conspiracy.* Los Angeles: J.P. Tarcher (9110 Sunset Blvd.), 1981.

Fournies, F.F., *Coaching for Improved Work Performance.* New York: Van Nostrand Reinhold, 1980. (Film on the subject entitled *Face-to-Face,* available from Cally Curtis Corp., Hollywood, Calif. 90038.)

Freedman, H.B., "Paper's Role in an Electronic World." *The Futurist,* October 1981, pp. 11-15.

Galbraith, J.K., *The New Industrial State.* Boston: Houghton Mifflin, 1969, p. 12

Gibson, D.V., *A Comparative Analysis of the Impact of Management on Processes of Technological Innovations with the Firm.* Unpublished doctoral dissertation, Stanford University, Stanford, Calif.; 1982.

Gibson, J.L., J.M. Ivancevich, and J.H. Donnelly, *Organization: Behavior, Structure, Processes.* Dallas: Business Publications, 1979.

Goldhirsh, B.A., *High Technology,* Vol. 1., No. 1, 1981 (Box 2531, Boulder, Colo. 80321.) See also *Science, Technology & Human Values,* MIT Press Journals (28 Carleton Street, Cambridge, Mass. 02142).

Gouran, D.S., "Unanswered Questions in Research on Communications in the Small Group." Paper presented at the Communication Association of the Pacific, Guam, July 28-31, 1980.

Greenbaum, H.H., and R.L. Falcione, eds., *Organizational Communication: Abstracts, Analysis, and Overview.* Beverly Hills, Calif.: Sage Publications, 6 vols. up to 1981, annually.

Hall, E.T., *Beyond Culture.* Garden City, N.Y.: Anchor Press/Doubleday, 1976.

Harris, P.R., and G. Malin, eds., *Innovation in Global Consultation.* Washington, D.C.: International Consultants Foundation, 1980.

Harris, P.R., and R.T. Moran, *Managing Cultural Differences.* Houston, Texas: Gulf Publishing Company, 1979.

Hofstede, G., *Culture's Consequences.* Beverly Hills, Calif.: Sage Publications, 1980.
Howe, R.J., *Building Profits Through Organizational Change.* New York: AMACOM, 1981.
Huyck, P., and N. Kremenak, *Design and Memory.* New York: McGraw-Hill, 1981.
Ingalls, J.D., *Human Energy: The Critical Factor for Individuals and Organizations.* Reading, Mass.: Addison-Wesley, 1976.
Johnson, R.A., F.E. Kast, and J.E. Rosenzweig, *The Theory of Management Systems.* New York: McGraw-Hill, 1967.
Koehn, H., "Commentary: Futurists Believe Corporate Prophets Will Increase in the Business World of Tomorrow." *San Diego Business Journal,* June 29, 1981, pp. 22-23.
Koehn, H., ed. "The Era of the Communications Link." *Trends,* February 1981. (Distributed by Futures Research Division, Security Pacific National Bank, Los Angeles, Calif. 90071.)
Koehn, H., ed., *Trends: Capitalism Goes into Orbit,* Report No. 10, 1981 (Futures Research Division, Security Pacific National Bank, Los Angeles, Calif. 90071).
Koehn, H., ed., *Trends 9: The Tin Collar Worker* (March 1981). Report available from the Future Research Division, Security Pacific Bank, Los Angeles, Calif. 90071.
Kraus, W.K., *Collaboration in Organizations: Alternatives to Hierarchy.* New York: Human Sciences Press, 1980.
Laurent, A., *Cultural Dimensions of Managerial Ideologies: National Versus Multinational Cultures.* Fontainebleau, France: INSEAD, 1979.
Laurent, A., "Matrix Organizations and Latin Cultures." Working Paper 78-28, European Institute for Advanced Studies in Management (Place Stephanie 20 B-1050, Brussels Bte 15-16, Belgium), June 1978.
Lawler, E.E., *Pay and OD.* Reading, Mass.: Addision-Wesley, 1981.
Likert, R., *The Human Organization: Its Management and Value.* New York: McGraw-Hill, 1967.
Lippitt, G.L., "Organizations of the Future: Implications for Management." *Optimum,* Vol. 5, No. 1, 1974, p. 38.
Lippitt, R., and G. Lippitt, eds., *Systems Thinking: A Resource for Organization Diagnosis and Intervention.* Washington, D.C.: International Consultants Foundation, 1981.
Lusterman, S., *Managerial Competence: The Public Affairs Aspect.* Report No. 805, 1981. (Available from The Conference Board, 845 Third Avenue, New York, N.Y. 10022.)
Luthans, F., *Organizational Behavior.* New York: McGraw-Hill, 1973.
Maccoby, M., *The Leader: A New Face for American Management.* New York: Simon and Schuster, 1981.
Mackenzie, R.A., "The Management Process in 3-D." *Harvard Business Review,* November-December, 1969.

Madden, C.H., *Clash of Culture: Management in an Age of Changing Values.* Washington, D.C.: National Planning Association, 1972, Report No. 123.

Masuda, Y., *The Information Society.* Washington, D.C.: World Future Society, 1980.

McNulty, N.G., *Management Development: International Report to Managers and Educators,* Spring 1981. (Published by the International Survey of Management Education, New York.)

Melhuish, A., and C. Cooper, "The Stresses That Make Managers Ill." *International Management* (London), April 1980, pp. 51, 55.

Middlemist, R.D., and M.A. Hitt, *Organizational Behavior: Applied Concepts.* Chicago: Science Research, 1981.

Miles, R.E., and H.F. Rosenberg, "The Human Resources Approach to Management," *Organizational Dynamics,* Winter 1982.

Miller, L.M., *Behavior Management: The New Science of Managing People at Work.* New York: John Wiley & Sons, Inc., 1978.

Mitchell, D., *Top Man: Reflections of a Chief Executive.* New York: AMACOM, 1980.

Molitor, G.T.T., "The Information Society: The Path to Post-Industrial Growth." *The Futurist,* April 1981, pp. 23–27.

Moore, B., "The Scanlon Plant-Wide Incentive Plan: A Case Study." *Training and Development Journal,* February 1976, pp. 50–53.

Moran, R.T., and P.R. Harris, *Managing Cultural Synergy.* Houston, Texas: Gulf Publishing Company, 1981.

Nadler, L., *Developing Human Resources.* San Diego, Calif.: Learning Concepts/University Associates, 1979, pp. 254, 298.

Nadler, D.A., J.R. Hackman, and E.E. Lawler, *Managing Organizational Behavior.* Boston: Little, Brown, 1979, pp. 120–133.

Naumes, W., and F.T. Paine, *Cases for Organizational Strategy and Policy.* Philadelphia, Pa.: Saunders, 1978, p. iv.

Newman, William H., "The Cultural Assumptions Underlying U.S. Management Concepts," in J.L. Massie and J. Luytjes, eds., *Management in an International Context.* New York: Harper & Row, 1972.

Oberg, J., *Red Star in Orbit.* New York: Random House, 1981.

Ohmae, K., *The Mind of the Strategist.* New York: McGraw-Hill, 1982.

Osborne, A., *Running Wild: The Next Industrial Revolution.* Berkeley, Calif.: Osborne/McGraw-Hill, 1979.

O'Toole, J., *Making America Work.* New York: Continuum Publishing, 1981.

Ouchi, W., *Theory Z: How American Business Can Meet the Japanese Challenge.* Reading, Mass.: Addison-Wesley, 1981.

Ouchi, W., and R.L. Price, "Hierarchies, Clans and Theory Z: A New Perspective on Organizational Development." *Organizational Dynamics,* Autumn 1978, pp. 41–44.

Pascale, R., and A. Athos, *The Art of Japanese Management.* New York: Simon and Schuster, 1981.

Philips, F., *45 Years with Philips: An Industrialist's Life.* Poole, Dorset, U.K.: Blandford Press, 1976, pp. 265, 267-268.

Post, J.E., *Corporate Behavior and Social Change.* Reston, Va.: Reston/Prentice-Hall, 1978, pp. 3-20.

Raymond, R.J., and S.V. Eliot, *Grow Your Roots: Anywhere, Anytime.* Richfield, Conn.: Peter H. Wyden, Inc., Publishers, 1980.

Rhinesmith, S.H., *Cultural-Organizational Analysis: The Interrelationship of Value Orientations and Managerial Behavior.* Cambridge, Mass.: McBer/Sterling Institute, 1970.

Russell, P.W., *Factors Associated with Overseas Success in Industry.* Unpublished doctoral dissertation, Colorado State University, Fort Collins, Colo., 1978. (Available from University Microfilms, Ann Arbor, Mich. 48108.)

Rymell, R.G., and R. Newsom, "Self-Directed Learning in HRD." *Training and Development Journal,* Vol. 35, No. 8, August 1981.

Sargent, A.G., *The Androgynous Manager.* New York: AMACOM, 1981.

Scobel, D.N., *Creative Worklife.* Houston: Gulf, 1981.

Servan-Schreiber, J.J., *The World Challenge.* New York: Simon and Schuster, 1981.

Seurat, S., *Technology Transfer: A Realistic Approach.* Houston: Gulf, 1976.

Shapiro, H., "I Have Seen the Future and It Works—But. . . ." *The New York Times,* cited in *Behavioral Sciences Newsletter,* August 13, 1973.

Sigel, E., ed., *Videotext: The Coming Revolution in Home/Office Retrieval.* New York: Crown/Harmony Books, 1981.

Smith, R.F., "A Communicator's Role in Business Management." *The Communicator,* June 1981, pp. 33-37.

Smith, R.F., "Matrix: A View from the Inside." *The President,* January 1979, pp. 2-5. (The Presidents Association, 135 West 50th Street, New York, N.Y. 10020.)

Society for Advancement of Management, "New Definition of Management." *ASTD National Report* (American Society for Training & Development, Washington, D.C. 20024), May 28, pp. 2-3.

Steinhart, P., "The Second Green Revolution." *New York Times Magazine,* October 25, 1981, pp. 46-53.

Terpstra, V., *The Cultural Environment of International Business.* Cincinnati, Ohio: South-Western, 1978.

Theme Packs: #1. *Learning/Education;* #2. *Networking/Organizations;* #4. *Relationships/Family/Sex Roles;* #5. *Technology and Science;* and #9. *Business/Workplace/Economics.* (Available from *Leading Edge Bulletin,* Interface Press, 231 S. Avenue 52, Los Angeles, Calif. 90042.)

Trist, E., "Between Cultures: The Current Crisis of Transition," in W. Schmidt, ed., *Organizational Frontiers and Human Values.* Belmont, Calif.: Wadsworth, 1970, p. 32.

Uris, A., and J. Benshael, "On the Job: Dissatisfaction Spreading Upward." *Los Angeles Times,* September 28, 1981, p. 2/IV.
Von Ward, P., *Dismantling the Pyramid.* Washington, D.C.: Delphi Press, 1981.
Vough, C.F., with B. Asbell, *Productivity: A Practical Program for Improving Efficiency.* New York: AMACOM, 1979.
Weinshall, T.D., *Culture & Management.* Middlesex, England: Penguin Books, 1977.
Wren, D., *The Evolution of Management Thought.* New York: Ronald Press, 1972.
Yankelovich, D., *New Rules: Searching for Self-Fulfillment in a World Turned Upside Down.* New York: Random House, 1981.
Zeitz, B., *Corporation and Two-Career Families: Directions for the Future,* 1981. (Report available from Catalyst, Department CFS, 14 East 60th Street, New York, N.Y. 10022.)

Recommended Readings

In addition to the specific references provided in the previous section, readers may find the following books and periodicals helpful to expand on the themes of *New Worlds, New Ways, New Management.*

BOOKS

Barron, I., and R.C. Curnow, *The Future with Microelectronics: Forecasting the Effects of Information Technology.* New York: Nichols Publishing, 1979.

Capra, F., *The Turning Point: Science, Society and the Rising Culture.* New York: Simon and Schuster, 1982.

Cohen, W.A., *Principles of Technical Management.* New York: AMACOM, 1980.

Cornish, E., ed., *Communications and the Future.* Bethesda, Md.: World Future Society, 1982.

Deal, T.E., and A.K. Kennedy, *Corporate Culture.* Reading, Mass.: Addison-Wesley, 1982.

DeGreen, K., *The Adaptive Organization: The Anticipation and Management of Crisis.* New York: John Wiley, 1982.

Fitch, D., *Productivity in the Microcomputer Age.* Reading, Mass.: Addison-Wesley, 1982.

Hanan, M., *Fast-Growth Management: How to Improve Profits with Entrepreneurial Strategies.* New York: AMACOM, 1980.

Katzan, H., *Office Automation: A Manager's Guide.* New York: AMACOM, 1982.

LaFleur, J., *Tax-Sheltered Financing Through R&D Limited Partnerships.* New York: John Wiley, 1982.

Lippitt, G., *Organization Renewal: A Holistic Approach to Organization Development.* Englewood Cliffs, N.J.: Prentice-Hall, 1982.

Martin, J., *Telematic Society: A Challenge for Tomorrow.* Englewood Cliffs, N.J.: Prentice-Hall, 1981.

Meltzer, M.F., *Information: The Ultimate Management Resource.* New York: AMACOM, 1981.

Norman, C., *Microelectronics at Work: Productivity and Jobs in the World Economy.* Washington, D.C.: Worldwatch Institute, 1980.

Paul, J.K., *Genetic Engineering Applications for Industry.* Park Ridge, N.J.: Noyes Publications, 1981.

Rich, R.F., *The Knowledge Cycle.* Beverly Hills, Calif.: Sage Publications, 1981.
Rowe, A.J., R.O. Mason, and K.E. Dickel, *Strategic Management and Planning.* Reading, Mass.: Addison-Wesley, 1980.
Scanlon, B.K., *Management 18: Results Management in Practice.* New York: John Wiley, 1982.
Shepherd, S., and D.C. Carroll, *Working in the Twenty-First Century.* New York: Wiley-Interscience, 1980.
Siegal, L., and I.M. Lane, *Personnel and Organizational Psychology.* Homewood, Ill.: Dow-Jones Irwin, 1982.
Starling, G., *The Changing Environment of Business: A Managerial Approach.* Belmont, Calif.: Kent/Wadsworth, 1980.
Teich, A.H., *Technology and Man's Future.* New York: St Martin's Press, 1981.

PERIODICALS

Behavioral Science Newsletter. (Whitney Industrial Park, Whitney Rd., Mahwah, NJ 07430.)
Bulletin on Training. (BNA Communications, 9401 Decolverly Rd., Rockville, MD 20850.)
Futures Survey and *The Futurist.* (World Future Society, 4916 St. Elmo Ave., Bethesda, MD 20814.)
HRD International. (Journal of Human Resource Development, Box 5542, Madison, WI 53705.)
Leadership & Organization Development Journal. (MCB Publications, Box 10812, Birmingham, AL 35201.)
Managing Tomorrow. (Global Management Bureau, Suite 1, Futures House, 26 McGill St., Toronto, Canada M5B 1H2.)
The Best of Business. (Soundview Executive Book Summaries, 100 Heights Rd., Darien, Ct 06820.)
The Tarrytown Letter. (Tarrytown House, East Sunnyside Lane, Tarrytown, NY 10591.)

Index

acquisitions, 131, 195
Advanced Genetics Science Ltd., 246
affirmative action programs, 176–177
agent of change, 24, 43–46
agricultural technology (ag tech), 4, 246, 259–260
Agrigenetics Corporation, 246, 260
air controllers, 25–26
Air Force, U.S., 110
Allied Chemical, 246
Amdahl Corporation, 66–67
American Business Council of Life Insurance, 269
American Institute of Aeronautics and Astronautics (AIAA), 252–253
American Management Associations (AMA), 156, 263–266
American Microsystems, Inc., 242
AMS (Advanced Memory Systems), 66–67
androgyny, 185–186
appearance and dress of employees, 73–74
Apple, Martin A., 256, 260, 262
Apple Computer Inc., 241, 276
Arabsat, 141
ARCO, 142
Argyris, Chris, 42
Arianespace, 141, 252
Asbell, B., 92
ASEA, 189
ASEAN, 249
Assembly of Collegiate Schools of Business, 163
AT&T, 5, 7, 9, 107, 159, 189
  communications technology used by, 141, 142
  manager training program at, 147–148
Atari, 74
at-home workers, 169, 184–185
Athos, Anthony, 83–84
Atlantic Richfield Company, 38, 246
audiographics, 103
AUGUMENT (Tymshare), 143
authority, 20, 26
  distribution of, 71
  in metaindustrial organization, 9–10
Automated Office Program (Diebold), 142
automation
  implementation of, 106–108
  integrated systems of, 142–144
  of office, 102–105
  resistance to, 105
Automax Company, 189
automobile industry
  robots in, 188–189
  technology in, 229
  unions and, 197

Baldridge, Malcolm, 92
Banc One, 54–55
banking industry, 54–55, 73–74
Bank of America, 54
Barnard, Chester A., 17
Barter, Neville, 251
Beecher, Richard, 189
behavior, organizational, 18–19, 48n–49n
  culture of organization and, 25–27
  value systems and, 61–67
Belgium, 20, 114
Bell, Larry, 252
Bendix, 240
benefits, 208, 210, 212
Bennis, Warren, 17
Benshael, Jane, 207
Bertalanffy, Ludwig von, 98
Behlehem Steel, 190
Biegler, John, 182
biochemical technology, 244–248, 259–260
Biogen, S. A., 245
Black, K., 62
Blake, Robert R., 42
board of directors
  potential of, 280
  relationships of, 200
body language, 117, 124
Boeing, 84, 100, 250
Bok, Derek, 219
Booz, Allen, and Hamilton, 102
Bosman, John, 250
Bowles, John M., 83
Bowles and Company, 83
Boyer, Herbert, 245
Bozzone, Vincent, 93, 95
brainstorming, 262
Brancatelli, Joe, 102, 105–106
Brandt, Willy, 269
Brevoord, Cornelius, 44, 45, 63n
bribery, 175

Briscoe, Dennis, 278–279
British Commonwealth, 117
Brown, David, 127
Brown, David S., 202
Bunn, Harry, 102
burnout, 183
Burns International Security Services, 62
Burroughs Corporation, 242, 247
Business Week, 15–16, 190

California, 159, 249, 272
California, University of
 at Berkeley, Center for Biotechnology Research of, 240
 at Davis, 246
CAMIS (Computer Assisted Makeup Imaging System), 103
Canada, 272
Canon USA, 250
Caplin, Donald, 147
Carlisle, Howard M., 100
Carnegie Endowment, 171–172
Carnegie-Mellon University, Robotics Institute of, 240
Casio, 101
Casmir, Fred, 137
Catalyst, Career and Family Center of, 187
CDC, 247
Center for Applied Research in the Apostolate, 205
Center for Futures Research, 144
Cetus Corp., 245, 260
Chamber of Commerce, U.S., 221
 Contact program of, 133
 Council on Trends and Perspectives of, 60
Champion International Corporation, 158–159
change, 8–9
 agent of, corporation as, 24, 43–46
 coping with, 159–160, 223–226
 in culture of organization, 26–27
 in image, 46–49
 management of, 17–18
 mechanisms of, 59
 resistance to, 105, 116
 space technology causing, 4
 in value systems, 61–67
Chase Manhattan Bank, 217
Chiles, Eddie, 78
China, 21
 Pacific Rim and, 248, 249
Christopher, William, 97
chronobiology, 76–77
Chrysler, 197
Cincinnati Milacron, Inc., 189
civil service, 176
Clarke, Arthur C., 122
coaching, 193–194
Coates, William, 83
Cohen, Stanley, 245

Coleman, Emily, 9, 70
Collaborative Genetics, 246
Commerce Dept., U.S., 248–249
Commission and Center on Transnational Corporations, U.N., 108
communication, 261
 automation affecting, 102–105
 as cross-cultural, 117–118, 122–123, 130–131
 ethics and, 131–132
 home centers for, 243–244
 images and, 128–130
 information sources and, 133
 manager and, 124–125
 MIS and, 134–138
 new directions in, 118–122
 systems orientation of, 125–128
 technology in, 139–144, 229
 transfer of technology and, 6–7
Communication Workers of America, 85
compensation, 211–212
 benefits and, 208, 210, 212
 "cafeteria" approach to, 219–220
 types of, 220–222
competence, 181–182, 273–274, 278
computer(s), 229, 258
 communications and, see telecommunications
 as compensation, 219–220
 in decision making, 110
 ethics and, 131–132
 human resources management and, 156–158, 164–166
 in MIS, 134–138
 office automation and, 102–105, 142–144
 personnel data records on, 148
 stress caused by, 224–225
 in team work stations, 110
 theft of parts of, 62–63
Condec Corporation, 189
Conference Board, The, 82, 210, 215
Connell, John, 104
Conrath, David, 145
construction industry, technology in, 229
control(s)
 lack of, dissatisfaction and, 207
 in management process, 93–95
 in metaindustrial organization, 108–110
 of multinational communications, 131–132
Control Data Corporation, 172, 217, 246
Cooper, Cary, 79
Copley, Helen, 276
counseling, personnel, 167
Cribbin, J., 284
culture(s), 6, 35–36
 adaptation to, of multinational corporations, 29, 32
 communication and, 117–118

Index

crises in, 62
 of group, 178n
 human behavior and, 18-19, 25-27
 management process affected by, 95-96, 209-210
 organization as, 15-17, 32-34, 230-233
 orientations of, 55
 relationships and, 175-177, 194-196
 reward systems and, 215-216
 synergy in, 35n
 systems approach to, 29
 training of personnel affected by, 146-148
 types of organizational, 28
cybernetics, 3n-4n, 5-6, 98-99, 127
 in metaindustrial organization, 11-12
 robotics and, see robotics
 social responsibility of corporation and, 45

Dart Industries, 195
data, 68
 automation and, 102-105
 sharing of, 181
 sources of, 133
 theft of, 62-63
Data General, 242
Davies, Derek, 248
Davis, Stanley M., 14n
Dayton-Hudson, 40, 58
decision making, 262
 in metaindustrial organizations, 110-111
 shared type of, 23-24
DEKALB AgResearch, 246
Delta Air Lines, Inc., 38, 84
Denmark, 20
De Soto, Inc., 222
Deutsch, Shea & Evans, 221
Devanna, Mary Anne, 149-150
development, personnel, 261-262
 computers affecting, 156-158
 counseling in, 167
 culture affecting, 146-148
 evaluation in, 167-168
 in future, scenario for, 149, 151-155
 reeducation for, 158-159
diagnostic human factor studies, 108-109
Dialog Information System, 104
Diebold, John, 137
Diebold Group, 60, 134-137, 142
Digital Equipment Corporation, 38, 242, 269
dissatisfaction, job, 206-209
Dodd, Alvin, 123
Donnelly, J. H., 211
Dow Chemical, 246
Doyle, Michael, 191
Drucker, Peter, v, 73, 91, 96, 109
 on employee potential, 277-278
 on relevant management, 282-283

Du Pont, 246
Duvenger, L., 137

E. F. Hutton, 70
Ean Technology, 256
Eaton Corporation, 86-87
Economist, The, 107-108, 244
education
 in business, problems with, 218-219
 computers affecting, 156-158
 in coping skills, 159-160
 culture affecting, 146-148
 in future, 198-199, 244
 obsolescence of, 169-170, 172
 of personnel, in future, 165-166
 in strategy, 161-162
 in synergy skills, 160-161
 updating of, for personnel, 158-159, 171-173
effectiveness, 14, 178n
efficiency, 14n
Ehret, Charles, 76-77
Electrolux, 189
Eli Lilly, 40, 247
Eliot, Stephen, 271
Elscint, 187
emerging-issues groups, 159
Employee Assistance Programs (EAP), 223
employees, see personnel
energy, technology and, 229
Equal Employment Opportunity legislation, 176-177
Ethernet (Xerox), 139, 142-143
ethics, 131-132
Etzioni, Amitai, 221
Eugenics, 240
Europe
 investments in and by, 272
 management in, 20-21
 pride in work in, 205
 youth in, 206
European Common Market, 6
European Economic Community (EEC), 121-122
European Space Agency (ESA), 141, 252
evaluation, performance, 214-215
Evans, Thomas Mellon, 80
Executive Committee, The (TEC), 83
executive personnel, 11, 280
expectancy theory, 221-222
extrinsic rewards, 211
Exxon, 120, 238, 242, 247

Fabun, Don, 46-48
Fairchild Camera and Instrument Corporation, 189
Fallon, Walter, 85
Fallows, James, 10
Farley, Peter, 245
FAST (Forecasting and Assessment in Sciences and Technology) Commission (EEC), 121-122

Federal Aviation Agency (FAA), 25-26
feedback
  in communication, 124, 125
  control of, 108
Feigenbaum, Edward, 173
Ferguson, Marilyn, vi, 269
fiber optics, 141, 143, 284
Fielden, John S., 282
First Global Conference on the Future, 267
fitness, physical, 78, 216-217
Florida State Senate, 142
Fombrun, Charles, 43-44, 149-150
food, 77-78
Forbes, 246
Ford, Gerald, 285
Ford Motor Co., 50, 100
forecasting, 58-60, 159, 238-240
foreign language, study of, 130-131
Fortune, 16, 79-81, 83, 123
Foundation for Management Development, 163
Fournies, Ferdinand F., 193
France, 20, 114, 240
  telecommunications industry in, 120, 142
franchising, international 7
Fraser, Douglas A., 197
Freedman, Henry B., 104-105
Fujitsu-Fanuc Co., 189
Fujitsu Ltd., 189
futures research, 58-60, 238-240
Futurist, The, 2, 159, 239

GAF, 258
Galbraith, John Kenneth, 229
Gale Research Company, 133
Gary Slaughter Corporation, 185
Geneen, Harold, 80, 83
Genentech, 245, 260
General Atomic Corporation, 70
General Dynamics Corporation, 172
General Electric, 60, 142, 155
General Foods, 217
General Mills, 212, 246
General Motors Corporation, 50, 188-189, 213-214
general systems theory (GST), *see* cybernetics
Genetic Engineering Inc., 247
genetic technology (gen tech), 2, 4, 107, 229, 244-248
Genex, 245
Germany, 20, 107, 120, 189
Gibson, David, 237
Gibson, J. L., 211
Gillespie, Harry, 82-83
Glen, Roy H., 26
goal setting, 56-58
Goldston, Eli, 220
Gouran, Dennis S., 132-133
Great Britain, 20, 79, 117
Green, Richard, 223-224
Greene, Ted, 248

Grove, Andrew, 83
group(s)
  communication within, 124-125, 132-133
  decision making by, 111
  dynamics of, 178
  quality circles as, 85-86, 190-191
  teams as, 191-193
GTI Corporation, 253
Gulf & Western Industries Inc., 239

Hackman, J. R., 66
Hall, Edward, 36, 91
Hall, Lynne, 213
Harari, Ehud, 194
Harbison, Frederick, 19
Harford, Tom, 252-253
Harris, Dorothy L., 281, 283
Harris, Louis, 221
Harris Corporation, 242
Harvard University, 247
Harvey, Jerry, 218-219
Harwood, Kenneth, 132
Hay Associates, 28
Hayes, James L., 282
Hayes-Roth, Frederick, 173
Hayward, Bert, 129
Hazard, Geoffrey, 219
health, 78-79, 215-217
Herzberg, Frederick, 203
Hewlett-Packard, 4, 40, 58, 84, 221, 241-242
Hicks, Herbert G., 17
Hiltz, R., 133
HI-NET (Holiday Inns Video Network), 142
Hitachi Ltd., 237
Hoffmann-La Roche, 247
Hofstede, Geert, 25
home communications center, 243-244
Honda Motors, 188
Horner, Matina, 274
Houston, University of, 252
Howe, Roger, 92
Hsinchu Science-Based Industrial Park, 249-250
Hudson Institute, 144
Hulett, Daniel G., 265, 267
human factor studies, diagnostic, 108-109
Hurst, Michael, 223
husband-wife relationships, 186-187, 274-275
Huyck, P., 230
Hwang, H. P., 250
Hybritech, Inc., 247-248
hydroponics, 246

IBM, 37, 70, 84, 92, 141, 189, 212, 241, 269
  executive development program of, 168
  production workers at, 180
  restructuring of, 97

image, organizational, 46
  change in, 47-49
  communication and, 128-130
  creation of, 59
Inamori, Kaxuo, 195-196
incentive plans, 221-222
India, 4, 117, 209
information sciences, 2, 5-6, 172
  at-home work in, 184-185
  global exchange of, 7-8
  home communications centers and, 243-244
  workers in, see knowledge workers
information work stations, 142-144, 229
Ingalls, John, 226
INSEAD, 20-21, 114, 173
Institute of the Future, 144
Integrated Electronic Information Network, 140n
Intel (Integrated Electronics), 4, 10-11, 27, 40, 83, 241, 242
  office productivity increased in, 97-98
intelligence, artificial, 230, 243
Intelsat, 141
Interactive Systems Corporation, 143
Interactive Television Corporation, 143
Intercontinental Hotels, 50
Interdesign, 242
International Communication Association, 133
International Management Seminar of the Pacific Basin Economic Council, 249
International Plant Research Institute (IPRI), 246, 260-262
International Resources Development, Inc., 253
intrinsic rewards, 211
invisible space, 52
Ireland, 4, 6-7
issues management, 144
Italy, 20, 21, 114, 189
ITT (International Telephone & Telegraph Corporation), 38, 83, 189, 246
IVAC, 70
Ivancevich, J. M., 211

J. C. Penney Co., 38, 142
Japan, 7, 24, 120, 141
  decision making in, 111
  lawyers in, 175
  management style in, 83-84, 196, 209
  philosophies of organizations in, 39
  pride in work in, 205
  robots used in, 189
  space technology and, 252
  suggestions from employees in, 213-214
  technology in, 228
  trade with U.S. by, 269
  worker involvement in, 16
Japan Inc., 120
Jenkins, C. David, 25

John Paul II (pope), 177
Johnson, R. A., 99
Jones, Reginald H., 43-44
Jones and Laughlin, 190
Jonishi, Arthur, 93, 196

Kahn, Herman, 249
Kalmar, 110
Karmi, Michael, 265
Kast, F. E., 99
Keyes, Gilbert, 250
Kimberly-Clark, 217
King, Richard, 249
Kingsley, James F., 263-264
kinship system, 175-176
Kintner, William, 249
knowledge workers, 2-3, 10, 11, 68
  at-home work for, 184-185
  competence of, 181-182, 273-274, 278
  expectations of, 208
  food for, 77-78
  health of, 78-79
  management of, 99-100
  profile of, 12, 71, 72, 168
  sharing among, 181
Koehn, Hank, 120, 121, 188
  on technology, 227-228, 251-252
Kollmorgan Corporation, 273
Kraft Inc., 195
Kraus, William A., 191
Kremenak, N., 230
Kyocera International, Inc., 92-93, 195-196

LaBelle, Charles D., 157
Labor Dept., U.S. 107
LaFleur, James K., 253
language, 117
  of body, 117, 124
  foreign, studies in, 130-131
Laurent, André, 20-21, 114, 116
Lawler, Edward E., 66, 220-221
Lawrence Livermore National Laboratories, 221
Likert, Rensis, 9, 42, 190, 206
Lippitt, Gordon L., 39-40, 44, 63n, 272
Lockheed, 104
Loftus, Joseph, 250
Lusterman, S., 279
Luthans, Fred, 18

Maccoby, M., 234
Mack, Raymond W., 236
Mackenzie, R. Alec, 93-94
Madden, Carl, 57, 60
Mahler, Walter, 109
Majure, Eve, 95
Making a Difference Clubs, 185
Mallinckrodt, Inc., 240
Malott, Robert, 80
management, 13
  of change, see change
  as cosmopolitan, 267, 269-272
  cross-cultural attitudes on, 19-25

management (*continued*)
  education in, 163, 171–173
  of human resources in multinational corporations, 28, 30–31
  of IPRI, 260–262
  participative type of, 16, 71, 96, 190
  philosophies of, *see* philosophy, organizational
  process of, 92–96
  of research and development, 237–238
  responsibilities and role images of, 48–49
  restructuring and, 97–98
  strategic type of, 101, 264–268
  of stress, 79, 160, 183, 223–224
  styles of, 79–85
  systems approach to, 99–101
  by teams, 111–115
  of time, 76–77
  transitions assisted by, 258–259
management information system (MIS), 118, 120, 134–138
manager(s)
  automation resisted by, 105
  as coach, 193–194
  communication by, 124–125
  cultural understanding for, 35
  dissatisfacation of, 209
  in metaindustrial organization, 180–181
  for MIS, 135–138
  needs of, 202
  professionalism of, 281–283
  as strategist, 161–162
  stress and, 79
  in transformation of work cultures, 234–236
Manufacturers Hanover Trust Company, 157
Marine Corps, U.S., 50
Markkula, Mike, 51
marriage, 186–187, 274–275
Maslow, Abraham, 190, 201–203
Massaro, Donald, 235
Masuda, Yoneji, 13, 133
matrix management, 111–115, 267–268
Matsushita Electric Co., 83
Maxwell Laboratories, 70
Mayo, Elton, 190
McBer and Company, 278
McClelland, David, 278
McCoy, John D., 54
McDonald, Thomas, 224–225
McDonnell Douglas, 251, 253
McGrath, Lorrie, 160
McGregor, Douglas, 9, 42, 82, 190, 205
McNamara, Robert S., 269
McNulty, N. G., 163
medical technology (med tech), 4, 229
Melhuish, Andrew, 79
Mellon Bank, 142
Menzies, Hugh, 81

mergers, 131, 195
merit, personnel and, 23, 181–182, 273–274, 278
Merrill Lynch Pierce Fenner & Smith, 54, 217, 271
metaindustrial organization(s)
  authority in, 9–10, 71
  control in, 108–110
  decision making in, 110–111
  defined, 2*n*
  food and health in, 77–79
  goal setting in, 57–58
  human potential utilized by, 272–281
  management style in, 81–85
  physical appearance of, 69–70
  profile of, 9–14
  prototypes of, 4–5
  psychological climate of, 70–71
  relationships in, 180–187
  systems approach used in, 99–101
  value systems in, 61–67
Metcalfe, Robert M., 139
Meyers, Charles, 19
Meyerson, Michael, 210
microelectronics, 2–3, 5–6, 227, 230
  metaindustrial organization and, 12–13
  theft and, 62–63
micrographics, 103–104
microtechnology, 45, 228, 241–242
Miles, R. E., 99–100
Miles Laboratories, 247
military, 45, 176
  rewards in, 211
  technology and, 229
Miller, James Grier, 127–128
Miller, Neill, 281–282
miniaturization, 5, 241–242
Minkin, Barry, 8
Minnesota, University of, 247
MIT, 247
Mitchel Energy & Development Co., 221
Mitchell, Don, 256–257
Mitsubishi International Corporation, 269
Molitor, Graham T. T., 2, 118, 120
Monolithic Memories, 62
Monsanto, 246, 247
Moore, Brian, 222
Moore, Gordon, 11, 83
Moran, Robert, *ix–x*, 175
Morris, William, 248–249
Mostek Corporation, 182
Motamedi, Kurt, 281
motivation, 65, 109, 261
  dissatisfaction and, 206–209
  of managers, 202–203
  needs hierarchy and, 201–203
  rewards as, *see* rewards
  theories of, 204–205
Motorola, 66–67
Mouton, Jane Srygley, 42

multinational corporations
  American management styles and, 21, 23-24, 209-210
  communications affecting, 130-132
  control in, 108
  cultural adaptation of, 29, 32
  human resources management in, 28
  management process for, 95-96
  needs considerations for, 203-204
  philosophy of organization and, 39
  relationships in, 184, 194-196
  reward systems and, 215-216
  in Third World countries, 241
  training of personnel by, 148
  transfer of technology via, 6
Murrin, Thomas, 83

N. V. Philips, 56, 281
Nadler, D. A., 66
Nadler, Leonard, 17, 149
Nakai, Hajime, 196
Nanus, Burt, 239
NASA, 110, 250, 252, 253, 269
National Academy of Science, ix, 2
National Airlines, 50
National Association of Corporate Directors, 280
National Commission on Productivity and Work Quality, 222
National Semiconductor, 4, 95, 241-242
National Steel, 190
National University (San Diego), 172
Naumes, W., 162
Navy Dept., U.S., 50
Nelson, William, 262
networks, 51
  for information, 127, 133
  as worker relationships, 185
Nevin, Joseph, 97
Newman, William H., 21
Newsom, R., 155
New York Times, The, 180, 259
Nippon Telephone and Telegraph Corporation, 284
Nomura Research Institute, 189
Northern California Research, 276
Noyce, Robert, 10-11, 83

Oberg, James, 252
obsolescence
  of conventional technology, 156
  in education, 169-170, 172
Occidental Petroleum, 246
Office and Professional Employees Union, 223
Ohio University, 247
Ohmae, Kenichi, 101
Omicron, The Center for Systems Humanics, 60, 107
Opinion Research Corporation, 65, 208-209
organization(s)
  behavior within, 18-19

  as energy exchange system, 47-49
  future-oriented type of, profile of, 59-61
  as microculture, 17
  redesign of, 97-98
  social responsibility of, 44-45, 67-68
  space of, 49-52
  traditional type of, change and, 8-9
  value systems in, 61-67
Organization for Economic Cooperation and Development, 132
Ortho Pharmaceuticals, 251
Osborne, Adam, 4, 170, 188
O'Toole, James, 218
Ouchi, William, 190, 205
  on metaindustrial objectives, 58
  on organizational philosophy, 38-40
  Theory Z of, vi, 24, 27
Oxford Strategy Unit, 173

Pacific Rim ventures, 248-250
PACTEL, 102
Paine, F. T., 162
Pan American Airways, 50, 97
paper micrographics replacing, 104-105
Parks, Michael, 1
participative management, 16, 71, 96, 190
Pascale, Richard, 83-84
PATCO, 197
Peace Corps, U.S., 149
Pearson, Andrall, 81
Peccei, Aurelio, 254
Penney, James Cash, 38
PepsiCo, 38
performance evaluation, 214-215
personnel
  cross-cultural management of, 30-31
  culture of organization and, 25-28
  data from, 28n
  dissatisfaction of, 206-208
  honesty of, 62
  invisible space and, 52
  merit-based selection of, 23
  potential of, actualization of, 272-281
  psychological space and, 51
  quality of worklife for, 85-88
  recruitment and selection of, 163-165, 260
  relocation of, 195, 225-226, 271-272
  in teams, 191-193
  value systems of corporation and, 61-67
  working at home, 169, 184-185
Philips, Frederik, 56
Phillips Petroleum, 247
Phillips-Ramsey, Inc., 112, 114
philosophy, organizational, 37-38
  change as part of, 43-45
  functions of, 38-39
  social responsibility in, 44-45
  synergy as basis for, 41-43
  trends in, 39-40

physical fitness, 78
Pioneer Hi-Bred International, 246
planning
  in management process, 93-95
  strategic type of, 101
PLATO Model (Control Data), 172
Polaroid, 142
Portillo, Lopez, 269
Post, James E., 57
Price, Raymond L., 38-39
pride in work, 205
Prime Systems, 217
Procter & Gamble, 84
profit-sharing plans, 221
Prudential Insurance Company, 253
psychological space, 50-52, 70-71, 177n

quality circles, 85-86, 190-191
quality of worklife (QWL), 85-88
QUEST (quick environmental scanning technique), 239

R&D (research and development), 236-240
Randall, Philip, 217
Rand Corporation, 173
Rasmussen, Wallace, 80
Raymond, Ronald, 271
RCA, 141
Red Cross, American, 147
reinforcement, positive, 48n-49n, 214
relationships, organizational
  coaching type of, 193-194
  culture affecting, 175-177
  education and, 198-199
  importance of, 178-180
  intercultural type of, 194-196
  in metaindustrial organization, 180-187
  as synergistic, 190-191
  in teams, 191-193
  types of, 177-178
  unions and, 197-198
relocation of personnel, 195, 225-226, 271-272
research
  automation affecting, 103
  on future, 58-60, 238
  on small-group communication, 132-133
  SRI model of, 172
respect, from management, 207
retirement, 275-276
rewards
  benefits as, 208, 210, 212
  in metaindustrial organization, 212-213
  in multinational corporations, 215-216
  suggestion systems and, 213-214
  trends in, 214-219
  types of, 211-212
  wellness programs as, 216-217

Reynolds Electrical and Engineering Co., Inc., 223
Rhinesmith, Stephen H., v-vii, 17, 195
  on cultural orientations, 55, 95, 215
  on relocation, 271-272
  on Theory Z, 205
Rickover, Hyman, 124
robotics, 7, 12, 229, 231
  relationships and, 187-189
  work space affected by, 52
Rockefeller, David, 67-68
Rockwell, 40
Rosenberg, H. F., 99-100
Rosenzweig, J. E., 99
Rothman, Howard, 107
Rubinyl, Paul, 53
Russell, Paul, 225
Rymell, R. G., 155

Salk, Jonas, 9, 36, 98
Salk Institute, Biotechnology Industrial Associates of, 247
Salter, Malcolm, 131
San Jose University, School of Business of, 278
Sara Lee Bakery, 188
Sargent, Alice, 185-186
Satellite Data Corporation, 169
satellites, 7, 107, 169
  automation and, 102-103
  new technology in, 141
  teleconferencing through, 102n
Saudi Arabia, 209
Scanlon Incentive Plan, 222
Science Applications, 70
Scobel, Don, 86-87
Scripps Clinic and Research Foundation, 247
Scripps Memorial Hospital, 160
Sears, Roebuck and Co., 60, 239
Secunda, David J., 81-82
Security Pacific National Bank, 60
  Futures Research Division of, 159, 208, 251
selection, personnel, 164-165, 260
self-fulfillment, 257-258
self-regulation, 108-110
Servan-Schreiber, Jean-Jacques, 6, 13
Seurat, Silvère, 234
Shaklee Corporation, 194
Shapiro, Harvey, 180
Shea, Gordon, 217
SIBIA, 247
Signal Companies, 70
Signetics Corporation, 4, 182
Sinetar, Marsha, 280
Skinner, B. F., 48n, 214
Smith, Robert F., 112, 114, 129
social responsibility, 67-68
  in corporate philosophy, 44-45
  expectations for, 182
Sony Corporation, 105, 156
South Africa, University of, 172-173

Index

Southern California, University of, 159
    network information services study at, 172
Soviet Union, 1, 92, 236, 252
space, corporate
    invisible type of, 52
    physical components of, 49-50, 69-70
    psychological components of, 50-52, 70-71
Spacelab, 252
space shuttle, 250-253
space technology, 7-8, 229, 285
    change caused by, 4
    industrialization due to, 250-253
Space Transportation Company, 269
Spatial Data Management Systems (SDMS), 143-144
Sporck, Charles, 242
SRI International, 172, 237
Stanford University, 172, 173, 240, 245
    Center for Integrated Circuits of, 247
status
    automation and, 105, 106
    communication and, 118
    dining situation and, 77-78
    lack of, dissatisfaction and, 207
Steinhart, P., 259
Stone, Robert, 80
strategic management, 101, 264-268
stress
    computer causing, 224-225
    management of, 79, 160, 183, 223-224
    relocation causing, 225-226
Submicron Structures, 241
suggestions, employee, 213-214
Sun Yat-Sen, 265
Supreme Court, U.S., 244-245
Sutherland, Joy, 276
Sweden, 20, 21, 107, 189
synergy, 35
    as management principle, 41-43
    quality circles and, 85-86
    skills in, 160-161
    in teamwork, 191-193
    in work relationships, 190-191
systems, 98-99
    in communication, 125-128
    in management, 99-101
Systems, Science and Software, 70
systems humanics, 107

Tarrytown Group, The, 239
TDF (transborder data flow), 7
Teague, Burton, 215
team management, 111-115
technology
    biochemical and genetic types of, 244-248
    in communications, 139-144
    conventional, obsolescence of, 156
    directions of, 227-230, 240-242
    innovations in, 5-6, 284
    leadership and, 234-236
    Pacific Rim ventures and, 248-250
    research and, 236-240
    social responsibility and, 45
    transfer of, 6-7, 234
    transitions caused by, 258-259, 270-271
Technology Assessment, Office of, U.S., 245
Teknowledge model, 173
telecommunications, 5, 7, 107
    in automated office, 102-105
    future of, 120-122
    satellites for, see satellites
    work space affected by, 51
    see also communication
teleconferencing, 102, 142, 158
telematics, 157
teletuition, 172-173
Televideo Systems, Inc., 250
television, private networks of, 102n
Terpstra, Vern, 29, 148, 227
Texas Instruments, 4, 84, 110, 182, 189
    redevelopment at, 235-236
    strategic management system of, 111
theft
    of information, 62-63
    of time, 75
Theory X (McGregor), 204-206
Theory Y (McGregor), 9, 42, 82, 205-206
Theory Z (Ouchi), 27, 205
Theory Z corporate culture, 24, 182
Third World countries, 4
    aid to, 269
    needs in, 203-204
    multinational corporations in, 241
    technology affecting, 6, 25
Thornton, Charles B., 277
3Com, 139
3M, 247
Tichy, Noel, 149-150
time
    away from work, 220, 279-280
    in metaindustrial organization, 74-77
Time (magazine), 218-219, 244
Toffler, Alvin, 122, 262
Townsend, Robert, 282
Toyota Motor Company, 188, 213-214
transnational corporations, see multinational corporations
Transnational Corporations, Commission and Center on, U.N., 108
transportation technology, 229
Trends (newsletter), 159, 208
TrendTRACK, 144
Trist, Eric, 63n
TRW Systems, 110, 156, 251
Turoff, M., 133
Tymshare, 143

ultrastability, 67, 124, 139
Unimation (Condec), 189
Union Carbide, 70, 246
unions, 222
    displacement of employees and, 223

unions (*continued*)
  food and feeding of personnel and, 77–78
  future of, 197–198
  QWL programs and, 85, 86
United Auto Workers, 189
United Nations
  Commission and Center on Transnational Corporations of, 108
  Conference on Trade and Development of, 269
United States
  communications businesses in, 120
  cultural changes in, 218
  education level of worker in, 212–213
  foreign investment and, 272
  language abilities in, 130–131
  management in, 20–21, 23–24
  Pacific Rim and, 248–250
  pride in work in, 205
  service industries in, 67
  suggestions from employees in, 213–214
  technology in, 228
  trade with Japan by, 269
  work week in, 75
  youth in, 207
United Steel Workers, 85, 190
United Way, 213
universities
  business collaborations with, 240
  new directions for, 198
  research at, 239–240
Uris, Auren, 207

value systems, corporate, 61–67
Vernon, Raymond, 272
video
  automation by, 102–103
  projection of, technology in, 141–142
videotext, 243
Viking space crafts, 188
VISTA, 149
Voich, Dan, Jr., 99
Volvo, 110
Von Ward, Paul, 231, 234
Vough, C. F., 92
Voyager space capsule, 285

Wada, Sadami, 218
Walker, Alfred J., 148
Wang Laboratories, Inc., 143, 198, 242
Washington University, School of Medicine of, 240
Watson, Thomas J., 37
Webber, James, 107
Weinhold, Wolf, 131
Weinshall, Theodore, 19
wellness programs, 215–217
Wesolowski, Jerzy, 189
Western Behavioral Science Institute, 173

School of Management and Strategic Studies of, 161
Western Company of North America, 78
Western Union, 141
Western Union International, 143
Westinghouse, 16, 83, 231, 240
Westinghouse Electric, 155
Westinghouse Learning Corporation, 149
Wharton, Keith, 106–107
White, Gene, 67
Whitehead, Alfred North, 285
White House Conference on the Aging, 275
Whittaker Corporation, 245–246
Whyte, W. H., 123
Wiener, Norbert, 3n, 9, 98–99
Wilson, R. O., 62
Wineapple, Maxine, 275
Wisconsin, University of, 207, 244
Wolf, Edward, 241
women, 176–177, 257
  androgyny and, 185–186
  images of, 129, 130
  potential of, 274–275
  relationships with, 184
Woodsworth, George, 196
word processors, 103
work ethic, 205, 209
Work Institute of America, 75
work space, 51, 69–70
work stations, information, 142–144, 229
work week, 75
World Business Council, 269
World Future Society, 60, 159
  on communications, 122
Wren, D., 99
Wriston, Walter, 68

Xerox, 189, 217, 241
  Ethernet of, 139, 142–143
  Massaro of, 235
  Office Information Systems Group of, 142
  Reprographics Technology Group of, 190–191

Y. S. Gypsum, 214
Yager, Ed, 85–86
Yankelovich, Daniel, 257
Ylvisaker, William, 80
Young, John, 83
youth
  dissatisfaction of, 206–207
  expectations of, 208

Zager, Robert, 75
Zeira, Yorham, 194
Zilog, 4